Well-Versed
Exploring Modern Japanese Haiku

OZAWA Minoru

Translated by
Janine Beichman

Photographed by
MAEDA Shinzō and Akira

Japan Publishing Industry Foundation for Culture

Well-Versed: Exploring Modern Japanese Haiku
Ozawa Minoru. Translated by Janine Beichman.

Published by
Japan Publishing Industry Foundation for Culture (JPIC)
2-2-30 Kanda-Jinbocho, Chiyoda-ku, Tokyo 101-0051, Japan

First English edition: March 2021

This book is a translation of *Meiku no yuen: Kingendai haiku o jikkuri yomu*, which was originally published by Mainichi Shimbun Publishing Inc., in 2018. English publishing rights arranged with Mainichi Shimbun Publishing Inc., Tokyo.

Book design: alema Co., Ltd.
Photographs: Maeda Shinzō and Akira (TANKEI)

Printed in Japan
ISBN 978-4-86658-179-8
https://japanlibrary.jpic.or.jp/

JAPAN LIBRARY

Contents

Guide to This Book ⋯⋯ 4

Preface to the English Edition ⋯⋯ 6

New Year ⋯⋯ 9

Spring ⋯⋯ 35

Summer ⋯⋯ 133

Autumn ⋯⋯ 207

Winter ⋯⋯ 289

Seasonless ⋯⋯ 351

Twenty Haiku by Ozawa Minoru ⋯⋯ 355

Afterword ⋯⋯ 359

Supplementary Notes ⋯⋯ 361

Index of Seasonal Images ⋯⋯ 368

Index of Poets ⋯⋯ 371

Photo Credits ⋯⋯ 374

Biography ⋯⋯ 375

Guide to This Book

The main section of the book contains three hundred poems by three hundred poets. These are divided into five chapters: New Year, Spring, Summer, Autumn, Winter, and Seasonless. Each page features one poem and has three basic components: the poem, the author's commentary on the poem, and a profile of the poet.

- Twenty poems by the author are presented without commentary on pp. 355–358.

18

At the wall clock's last stroke
the old year closes
and the new one opens ————— ❶

Saitō Miki

The old wall clock mounted on a pillar of the poet's house has loudly struck twelve. Now all is still, the only sound the tick of the pendulum, which almost seems to be beating out the passage of time as the old year changes to the new. *Kozo kotoshi*, "old year new year," is a New Year's seasonal image that expresses the sense of time's passing.

These days the boundary between the old year and the new one is marked and measured to the precise second in radio and television broadcasts. It would have been vaguer in the days before television, more similar to the way this haiku locates the boundary between the old and new as the moment when the wall clock finishes striking midnight.

In his note to the poem, the poet reveals that his home had a large octagonal wall clock. Here, its familiar and well-loved chime rings out twelve times, as time flows pleasantly on. ————— ❷

Uchiowari / hashiradokei no / kozokotoshi ————— ❸
It finishes striking / wall clock's / old year new year ————— ❹

Saitō Miki (1923–2012) studied haiku with Katō Shūson and was a contributor to Shūson's *Kanrai*. He later founded and led *Fumoto*. This poem is from *Saitō Miki jikai hyakunijukkusen* (2005). ————— ❺

- Term and names with * are further explained in the Supplementary Notes on pp. 361–367.

- Japanese terms are in principle romanized according to the Hepburn system. Long vowels are indicated by macrons except for well-known place names. Chinese terms are romanized according to the pinyin system. The custom of placing the family name first has been followed for Japanese and Chinese names.

. . . .

Main Section

❶ Poem in English translation

❷ Commentary

❸ Romanized Japanese of the original haiku
  • The word in gray is the seasonal image. All seasonal images are indexed on pp. 368–370.

❹ Word-for-word translation of the poem

❺ Profile of the poet
  • Italicized words such as *Hototogisu* and *Ashibi* are the names of a haiku group and/or the group's magazine. Most Japanese haiku poets belong to a poetry group whose members meet regularly to share each other's poems. These groups publish their poems in a magazine whose name is typically the same as that of the group.

  • The book or magazine in which the featured poem appears is given at the end of the poet's profile.

  • All featured poets are indexed on pp. 371–373.

Preface to the English Edition

In my travels to America, Canada, Russia, and Poland I have met many people interested in haiku, including those who write haiku in their own languages. As we chatted, the conversation would often turn to the seventeenth-century haiku master Matsuo Bashō,[*1] and I was gratified to see that he held a special place in their hearts, for he does in mine too. But it always struck me that modern haiku and haiku poets were almost never mentioned. I frequently wanted to remind my new friends that haiku is still being written today and tell them about the many superlative modern haiku poems and poets. The translation of this book gives me that chance.

One of the salient features of modern haiku is its great variety. Haiku with seasonal images (*yūki haiku*) is still the mainstream, but haiku without seasonal images (*muki haiku*) also has many practitioners. Likewise, the orthodox 5-7-5 syllable haiku is the norm but experimental, free form haiku (*jiyūritsu haiku*),[*2] sometimes shorter and sometimes longer, also has a strong presence. I hope you will enjoy this variety.

In the commentaries I often remark on the pleasure of sound in a haiku. A large part of poetry's charm lies in the resonance of sound as well as in meaning and images. It may be difficult for readers to appreciate this in English, but I hope they can turn to the romanized versions of the originals to get a taste of the soundscape.

I am grateful for permission to use photographs by Maeda Shinzō and Akira for the book's cover and the inside pages. Seasonal images are an important element in haiku—especially the snow, the moon, and flowers—and the Maeda's photographs convey their beauty vividly. At the same time they quietly and eloquently communicate the charms of

Japan's natural world. I am confident that they will help foreign readers understand haiku.

Some years ago I asked myself, "Why are haiku always written vertically, whereas most modern Japanese can be written either vertically or horizontally?" At present almost all haiku magazines and books in Japan are printed vertically. It seemed to me that this was not just a matter of custom or tradition, but rather was related to the essence of the haiku form. As I pondered the question, I came to think that the single vertical line of a haiku might well function as something similar to the ancient *yorishiro*, vertical natural forms believed to be sacred conduits channeling the power of the gods.

One of the earliest, if not the earliest, *yorishiro* is a six-pillared monument from the Jōmon period (ca. 10,000–ca. 300 BCE), constructed with the trunks of giant chestnut trees at the Sannai Maruyama Site in Aomori Prefecture. It is thought that Jōmon people saw this as a link between heaven and earth and a way to pray for peace in this world. The vertical haiku, too, may be only a very small poetic form, but I think of it as in some way being a prayer for harmony between heaven and earth. I feel that this is the true significance of sending this little book out into a world increasingly divided by the great powers and full of ceaseless conflict.

In English, the haiku can not be written vertically, of course, but I am very happy that the progressive indentation from left to right, a form the translator made up for this book, suggests a movement between heaven and earth.

I would like to express my deep gratitude to Janine Beichman for undertaking the labor of translation in the midst of the coronavirus pandemic, as well as Yuiko Kimura-Tilford, Meredith McKinney, Lisa Wilcut, and the staff of Japan Library.

Ozawa Minoru
Tokyo
Febrary 2021

New Year

At the wall clock's last stroke
the old year closes
and the new one opens

Saitō Miki

The old wall clock mounted on a pillar of the poet's house has loudly struck twelve. Now all is still, the only sound the tick of the pendulum, which almost seems to be beating out the passage of time as the old year changes to the new. *Kozo kotoshi*, "old year new year," is a New Year's seasonal image that expresses the sense of time's passing.

These days the boundary between the old year and the new one is marked and measured to the precise second in radio and television broadcasts. It would have been vaguer in the days before television, more similar to the way this haiku locates the boundary between the old and new as the moment when the wall clock finishes striking midnight.

In his note to the poem, the poet reveals that his home had a large octagonal wall clock. Here, its familiar and well-loved chime rings out twelve times, as time flows pleasantly on.

> *Uchiowari / hashiradokei no / kozokotoshi*
> It finishes striking / wall clock's / old year new year

Saitō Miki (1923–2012) studied haiku with Katō Shūson and was a contributor to Shūson's *Kanrai*. He later founded and led *Fumoto*. This poem is from *Saitō Miki jikai hyakunijukkusen* (2005).

Ocean trench—
an eyeless creature glides through
the old year into the new

Ōishi Etsuko

Ocean trenches are elongated, steep-walled depressions in the deepest parts of the ocean, formed at depths of roughly 6,000 to 10,000 meters. This is the midnight zone, where the sun's light does not penetrate, yet even here there is life.

I imagine this eyeless creature as a long, eel-like, deep-sea creature. Perhaps its eyes have atrophied from living in darkness, and it locates its prey by other senses. Even in a midnight world like this, one year turns into the next and the flow of time is unimpeded.

The combination of darkness with the seasonal image "old year new year" (*kozo kotoshi*) is not unusual in haiku. But in this poem the darkness is absolute. No world could be more alien than this.

> *Kaikō o / me naki mono yuku / kozokotoshi*
> Ocean trench / eyeless creature goes / old year new year

Ōishi Etsuko (b. 1938) is a longstanding member of *Tsuru*. She studied with its founder Ishida Hakyō as well as Ishizuka Tomoji,*[1] and Hoshino Bakukyūjin,*[2] the successive leaders of the group. She also contributes to Shibuya Michi's magazine *Shibi*. This poem is from her prizewinning collection *Yaya* (2004).

With fire and water
bursting forth
the newly born year begins

Ono Emiko

How many households today still cook on a wood-burning stove? The season word "first kindling of the stove," *hatsukamado,* has died a natural death. It's hard to use it (not to mention the season word "first kindling," *takizome*) now, when almost everyone cooks with gas and electricity. The season word "first water," *wakamizu,* describes water drawn from a well, but it would sound odd to use it for water gushing from a faucet.

Changes in the way we live have turned some traditional seasonal images into anachronisms. This haiku, it seems to me, is trying to bring them back to life in a new form. By masterfully distilling and simplifying, the poet has evoked the essence of the New Year's kitchen, whose life is (and was) in fire and in water.

Fire and water are necessary for us to live. They must have been as vital for people in ancient times as they are to us now. Through the fire and water of the new year, this poem reminds us of our beginnings.

> *Hi mo mizu mo / hotobashiri toshi / arata nari*
> Fire and water both / surging forth, the year / begins anew

Ono Emiko (b. 1942) studied with Mizuhara Shūōshi and contributes to *Ashibi,* the magazine founded by Shūōshi. This poem is from *Kyōho* (2008).

On New Year's
I look out at the mountains
but all is snow

Murō Saisei

When the Japanese government adopted the Gregorian calendar in 1873, the start of the new year and the first day of spring, which coincided under the traditional lunar calendar, became separated by more than thirty days. The poet feels something lacking when he looks out at the nearby mountains on New Year's Day and sees no sign of spring. Yet despite his discontent, the immaculate snow makes him feel the purity and auspiciousness of the new year. Plain and simple though its expression is, this nuanced shift lends the poem added richness. There are two seasonal images, "New Year" and "snow," both of them weighty; but in this case, "New Year" dominates.

In the original collection where it appears, this poem is followed by: "New Year/mountains behind mountains/and all is snow." To me, the first poem's shift of feeling from mountain to snow makes it the more interesting of the two.

> *Shinnen no / yama mite aredo / yuki bakari*
> New year's / mountains I look but / snow only

Murō Saisei (1889–1962) was a well-known poet of modern verse and a writer of fiction, but his first literary efforts were in haiku and his interest in the form never waned. The famed novelist Akutagawa Ryūnosuke, who was also a haiku enthusiast, was his good friend. This poem is from *Saisei hokkushū* (1943).

Waves roll in on the shore
of the land of poetry—
New Year's morning

Ōtani Hiroshi

With the sweeping phrase "the land of poetry," this haiku declares its subject to be the country of Japan and Japanese culture. In this land where the waves are always rolling in from the four corners of the earth, the poet welcomes the first morning of the new year.

Japan is celebrated as "a land blessed by the spirit of words" in the eighth-century *Man'yōshū*,[*1] and the preface to the tenth-century *Kokin wakashū*[*2] declares that "every living being has its song." Down through the ages, emperors of every generation have composed *waka*, and everyone, including commoners, has been familiar with the various forms of poetry. When the waves roll in to this land of poetry, their sounds, like everything in this land, become poetry. You can also read the waves as a metaphor for the "waves" of cultural influence from China and the West. Without those waves, especially the importation of writing, there would not have been any Japanese poetry.

I read this poem as a record of the poet's joy at living in a land of poetry and being able to compose haiku, and also as a record of his resolution to continue his dedication to his art.

> *Nami yosete / shiika no kuni ya / ōashita*
> Waves rolling in / poetry's land / New Year's morning

Ōtani Hiroshi (b. 1980) is a follower of Hasegawa Kai and a member of Kai's *Koshi*. In 2011, Kai named the 30-year-old Hiroshi as the group's leader, which made him the youngest leader of a modern haiku group at the time. This poem is from *Ōashita* (2010).

On a golden kerria's
withered leaf white frost and the first
dawnlight

Masuda Ryū-u

Frost on the withered leaf of a golden kerria is lit up at dawn by the first sunrays of the new year.

This haiku is almost entirely made up of seasonal images. To be precise, it consists of four season words separated by three instances of the possessive particle *no*. That being the case, you would think that it could not hold together as a poem; and yet it presents a telling picture of the branch of a bush in a garden. The first image, "golden kerria," effortlessly evokes the bright yellow of that flower. This then changes to the brown of a "withered leaf" and then, moving on, to the pure white of "frost." Finally, shining down over those layered colors comes the celestial light of the first dawn of the year. "First dawnlight" (*hatsuakari*) is the main seasonal image.

This poem depicts a considerable stretch of time, including both the present first dawnlight of the new year and the past when the flower bloomed and then withered. It has a kind of hidden splendor that is unique in modern haiku.

> *Yamabuki no* / *kareha no shimo no* / *hatsuakari*
> A golden kerria's / withered leaf's frost's / first dawnlight

Masuda Ryū-u (1874–1934) began to write *haikai* linked verse[*1] at a young age under the influence of his adoptive father. Later, while working as a clerk in the Yoshiwara pleasure quarters of Tokyo, he studied haiku under Kubota Mantarō. In 1930, he became Setchūan the Twelfth,[*2] inheriting the title from his adoptive father. This poem is from *Ryū-u haikushū* (1933).

First dawnlight shines
on a little village in
the Milky Way—Earth!

Arima Akito

The first dawnlight of the year shines in from the window as people busily exchange their New Year's greetings. At such times, we humans may feel we are the center of the universe, but in truth the Earth is no more than a little village in the hinterlands of the Milky Way Galaxy.

Aza, "a little village," is the smallest administrative unit of a municipality. To superimpose this tiny artificial division on the boundless universe has the wit of haiku adapted to our modern age. The poem has a kind of vast and capacious feeling, one that rejects both an earth-centered and a human-centered viewpoint.

Akito was a scientist whose specialty was nuclear physics. Haiku poets write about the "Galaxy" and "Milky Way," which are seasonal images, but for most, gazing is about as far as they go. They tend not to think of Earth's place within that vastness. This poem was born from a deep recognition of the universe.

> *Hatsuakari / gingakei aza / chikyū kana*
> First dawnlight / Galaxy small village / Earth!

Arima Akito (1930–2020) had a triple career as poet, nuclear physicist, and educator, and was also active in the internationalization of haiku. He began composing haiku in college and studied with Yamaguchi Seison. After Seison's death, he founded and led *Ten'i*. This poem is from *Bunkō* (2007).

Under the year's first sky
Ōmi, land of water
lies unwavering

Akezumi Reiko

New Year's Day has arrived. Lake Biwa, a large lake in the region near Kyoto formerly called Ōmi, lies spread beneath the sky, so vast and calm that the poet speaks of the land that holds it as "Ōmi, land of water."

The tone is lofty in its juxtaposition of earth and sky on the year's first day. I thought at first that the expression "Ōmi, land of water" must be borrowed from classical waka, but it seems to be the poet's own coinage. It is a direct and apposite phrase to describe Ōmi and the broad expanse of Lake Biwa at its center. Lake Biwa sometimes has waves but the province of Ōmi itself is stable and solid. To describe it as "unwavering" emphasizes the stillness and silence of Lake Biwa. This is a sacred landscape in which heaven and the lake's surface reflect one another.

Akezumi Reiko's birthplace is Ōmi and the faith she feels in it, renewed at the new year, is here given poetic shape. I somehow feel that she is also expressing her sense of trust in the self that came into being in her place of birth.

Hatsumisora / mizu no Ōmi no / yuruginashi
First sky / water of Ōmi / is unwavering

Akezumi Reiko (b. 1972) studied haiku with Arima Akito and is a contributor to *Ten'i*. This poem is from her prizewinning *Seisa* (2006).

The sky where once
bales of rice went flying—
the year's first landscape

Ibaraki Kazuo

The scene that lies spread before the poet on the first day of the year is the sky over sacred Mount Shigi, where rice bales are said to have flown through the air. The note to the poem says, "Mount Shigi is in Heguri, where I live."

Mount Shigi, site of the famous twelfth-century illustrated scroll called *Miraculous Origins of Mount Shigi,* is located in the area of Heguri in Nara Prefecture. One legend from the scroll is "The Flying Granary," which tells how the monk Myōren used to send his begging bowl flying to the granary of a rich man at the foot of the mountain, where it scooped out rice and brought it back for Myōren to eat. One day the rich man got fed up and locked the begging bowl in the granary, so Myōren made the begging bowl fly the whole granary back to the mountain, complete with all its bales of rice. The rich man asked Myōren to return his rice, whereupon Myōren made the begging bowl fly back again, with the bales of rice in its wake. However, he kept the granary. This legend suggests how fertile this area has been for rice cultivation.

The poem depicts a majestic illusion in the sky on New Year's Day. It may also embody a prayer for a good harvest.

Komedawara / tobikemu sora o / hatsugeshiki
Bales of rice / went flying sky / the year's first landscape

Ibaraki Kazuo (b. 1939) studied haiku with Ushiro Boseki[*1] and inherited *Unga* from him. He also contributes to Shibuya Michi's *Shibi* as well as *Shin*, the magazine founded by Ōmine Akira.[*2] This poem is from *Sanshōuo* (2010).

Nipponia nippon soars
above the year's
first mountains and rivers

Suhara Kazuo

Nipponia nippon is the scientific name of the crested ibis, as the poet's note tells us. The image of this bird soaring upwards fits perfectly with a New Year's landscape of mountains and rivers. Its scientific name comes from the fact that it was once so common, especially on the main island of Honshū, that it was a symbol of Japan. However, there was so much overhunting that it is now extinct in Japan, except for a few that have been artificially reared on the island of Sado. We have destroyed the wild *Nipponia nippon*, the bird that was once so intimately tied to this land. I daresay the poet uses the scientific name to express his sorrow all the more strongly.

The poem describes the beauty of the crested ibis as it flies over a landscape of mountains and rivers at New Year, but in fact, this can only be an imaginary scene. The beauty magnifies the emptiness left by the loss of the crested ibis.

It may be the New Year, but reality has a bitter taste.

> *Nipponia / nippon no tatsu / hatsusanga*
> *Nipponia / nippon* rises / first mountains and rivers

Suhara Kazuo (b. 1938), a professor of English literature, studied haiku with Kawasaki Tenkō and is a contributor to *Ten*. This poem is from *Kunihara* (2010).

Mother's house—there
is the year's first wind
in the pines

Yamamoto Yōko

At the house of the poet's mother there is a pine that sounds when the wind blows through it. Now she can hear, perhaps in memory, the wind blowing there for the first time in the new year.

The pine is a noble tree where a deity dwells, and the wind in the pines and the sound it makes feel like a heavenly welcome. This spiritual quality intensifies on New Year's Day. One of the pleasures of the visit to her mother's home is gazing at the pine and listening to its song, for the tree itself is identified with her mother.

The possessive particle used in the Japanese for "mother's house" (*haha ga ya*) is the classical *ga* rather than the usual *no*. Using *ga* evokes the history and gravitas of the house as home and suggests that this is the house where her mother lived in the past, and that her mother is no longer alive. The use of the simple verb "is" (*aru*) to describe "the first wind in the pines" (*hatsushōrai*) is another subtle effect. To describe the wind with a sound, like "sings" or "echoes," would destroy the effect. The simple "is" brings the first wind in the pines to life.

In the Japanese, the first vowel sound of all three segments is "a" (pronounced like the English "ah"). In addition, the first two segments begin with the vowel-consonant combination *ha*. This creates a light, graceful tone, which goes well with the poet's quiet yet intense longing for her mother.

> *Haha ga ya wa* / *hatsushōrai no* / *aru tokoro*
> Mother's house / first pine wind / is place

Yamamoto Yōko (b. 1934) studied haiku with Katsura Nobuko and Ōmine Akira,* and currently contributes to and is the editor in chief of *Shin*. This poem is from her prize-winning *Ki no hana* (1987).

A mirror mochi sits
on a rock on the path to
Kifune Shrine

Igarashi Bansui

The poet is making his first visit of the year to Kifune Shrine in the north of Kyoto. Atop a rock by the roadside he notices a round mirror mochi (a glutinous rice cake), a particular kind of flat, round mochi only made for New Year as an offering to the gods.

There is nothing special-looking about the rock but it must have sacred associations for the people who live around there. There is an unexpected freshness about this mirror mochi found apart from a stone Buddhist image or a wayside shrine. There is something auspicious about it as well. It is as if we are seeing the shape of earlier beliefs, from before the time when beliefs took shape in statues and shrines.

The sacred path to Kifune Shrine remains in its original place. This New Year's mochi that "sits / on a rock" speaks of the long history of belief that it has witnessed. The plain and simple words are objective yet evocative, well suited to a sketch from life,[1] which is what this poem is.

Kagamimochi / iwa ni nose ari / Kibunemichi
Mirror mochi / placed atop a rock / Kifune Shrine path

Igarashi Bansui (1899–2000) began to study haiku with Takahama Kyoshi while a medical student at Kyoto University. He was already an active member of *Hototogisu* before the ascendancy of the Four S's,[2] but rather than aspiring to their new style, he remained committed to the earlier style of poems from nature. He later became leader of *Kunenbo*. This poem is from *Bansui kushū* (1931).

Shuttlecock atop,
the racket is handed to
the next player

Hara Gesshū

This is a poem about battledore (a kind of badminton), a traditional game played by girls at New Year. There are many haiku about hitting the shuttlecock, but very few about handing it to the next person. He says "shuttlecock atop," so it is not being held there by a human hand. It is being handed over perfectly balanced on the racket.

There are two kinds of battledore. In one kind, the shuttlecock is batted back and forth between two players, and in the other, a single player bats it up and down while singing a counting song. In this case, it may be the latter. It is even more auspicious to hand over the shuttlecock in this way if one has managed to keep it in the air without it once falling during one's own turn. Since battledore is a girls' game, "the next person" is of course also a girl. Both would be wearing brightly colored New Year kimono.

Gesshū has been criticized for describing trivial things, but his close observation of reality is worth reappraisal.

> *Hane noseshi / mama hagoita o / tsugi no hito e*
> Shuttlecock atop / still racket / to the next person

Hara Gesshū (1889–1920) was a follower of Takahama Kyoshi and an influential member of *Hototogisu*. He rose to become a judge for the group's magazine at a young age. This poem is from *Gesshū haikushū* (1922), edited by Hasegawa Reiyoshi.

Playing poem cards—
Team West nothing but
eyeglasses!

Ra Sosanjin

At New Year, a group of friends has gotten together to play the traditional game of matching poem cards, *utagaruta,* dividing themselves up into Team East and Team West. When the speaker looks across at Team West, he sees that all of them wear eyeglasses.

In this card game, there are two kinds of cards: those with the entire poem on them and those with only the finishing phrase. The reader begins reading a poem and players compete to see who can anticipate the finishing phrase of the poem most quickly. Most often the poems are from the canonical *Ogura hyakunin isshu* (*100 Poems by 100 Poets*).[*1] The game can be played by two individuals or in a group, but in this case, it is a group, and the speaker must be on Team East.

At the same time as this poem, Sosanjin published another: "Being in love/I lose at cards/on purpose!" (*Katsubundan,* February 1901). When this poem was first published, Ozaki Kōyō's[*2] famous novel *Konjiki yasha* (*The Golden Demon*) was being serialized in a newspaper. Its opening scene depicts a game of poem cards at which all three members of the love triangle that dominates the novel are present. I wonder if the poet had that scene in mind.

> *Utagaruta / megane bakari ya / nishi no kumi*
> Poem card game / eyeglasses only / west group

Ra Sosanjin (1881–1902), born to a Chinese father and a Japanese mother, first wrote poems in Chinese but then began to write haiku. After participating in a group associated with the Shūseikai,[*3] he left and became a follower of Masaoka Shiki. This poem is from *Sosanjin haikushū* (1982), edited by Murayama Kokyō.

For the daimyo's house
ten carp—
first purchase of the year

Kaneko Senjo

At the beginning of the year, business is good for merchants. This poem gives voice to a happy fishmonger who has just sold a lot of auspicious fish on the first shopping day of the year. The buyer is a servant from one of their best customers—the wealthy daimyo's family. We can imagine that this is the fishmonger's cheerful thought shortly before wrapping and delivering the purchase.

Senjo's husband, Kaneko Naokichi, was the head of Suzuki Shōten, one of the new merchant houses of the late nineteenth and early twentieth centuries. Senjo's hope for the continued success of the family business lurks in the background of the poem, but when she wrote it, both the daimyo and the Edo residences they used when they had to pay attendance on the shogun[*1] were no more. The poem's subject is taken from history, specifically the traditions of New Year in the early modern period.

This poem was first published in the February 1917 issue of *Hototogisu*. When republished in Senjo's collection *Natsukusa* in 1933, the carp's number was increased to twenty: "For the daimyo's house/twenty carp—/first purchase of the year." As the poet and critic Matsuoka Hidetaka (b. 1949) pointed out, the original version was best. Twenty fish is too many to imagine in a single image.

> *Hantei ni / tai juppiki ya / okaizome*
> Daimyo's mansion to / carp ten / first purchase of year

Kaneko Senjo (1889–1944) studied haiku with Hasegawa Reiyoshi[*2]and was a contributor to Reiyoshi's *Kareno* (later renamed *Nukago*). She eventually joined *Suimei*, which was founded and led by Reiyoshi's widow, Hasegawa Kanajo.

Such a splendid-looking kanji—
"treasure" on
the treasure ship's sail

Gotō Hinao

In order to have a good dream on the first night of the year, many people put under their pillows a picture of the legendary treasure ship bearing the Seven Lucky Gods and their wonderful treasures. The poet is looking at such a picture and admiring the character for "treasure" (*takara*) which is traditionally written on the sail of the ship. If you know the character, the poem creates the impression of seeing the well-known picture printed on traditional *washi* paper before your very eyes.

There are two characters for *takara*; their meaning and pronunciation are identical, but which one is used depends on the occasion. When used as a season word the *takara* of *takarabune* ("treasure ship") is written with 宝, the simplified version for common use, while in most pictures of the treasure ship, the traditional form of this character, 寶, is used on the ship's sail. In the traditional character, jewels 玉 and shells 貝 nestle beneath the element for roof 宀. Its origin is thought to lie in the custom of presenting offerings of jewels and shells (an early form of money) at places where members of the nobility were enshrined after death. The power of the traditional character for *takara* may very well bring good dreams.

In the Japanese, both the second segment and the third begin with the same word, *takara*, and all three parts begin with a "t" sound: *tsukuzuku*, *takara*, *takarabune*. The sound of the poem is rhythmical and chimes with its promise of good things to come.

> *Tsukuzuku to / takara wa yoki ji / takarabune*
> Truly / *takara* splendid *kanji* / treasure ship

Gotō Hinao (1917–2020) studied haiku with his father Gotō Yahan and inherited the editorship of *Fūei* from him. In 2012, he handed over his position to his son and became the group's leader emeritus. This poem is from *Kindei* (1973).

The year begins with
snow dropping
into transparent water

Hirose Naoto

The time here is *shōgatsu*, which can mean the whole month of January or the period of time at the beginning of that month. The former is an ordinary measure of time, but what is meant here is the beginning of the month, probably only the first seven days, when the traditional New Year's pine decorations are displayed and other traditional observances are carried out.

The snow is not falling into the water from the sky. It is a clump of snow that plops off a branch, hits the surface of the clear waters of a bubbling spring, and then sinks. The first segment of the poem runs over into the second, so that the phrase "The year begins with/snow" (*Shōgatsu no/yuki*), straddles two lines. The enjambment makes you feel the weight and size of the lump of snow.

This is a sanctified place where clear water bubbles up all year round. When the weather is hot, the water feels cool, and when the weather is cold, the water feels warm. Imagining the lumps of snow melting and disappearing in the warmth of the clear water reminds me that snow is a guarantee of a bountiful crop of rice. This is an auspicious poem, looking ahead to good things in the coming year.

Shōgatsu no / yuki mashimizu no / naka ni otsu
Year's beginning / snow clear spring water / into drops

Hirose Naoto (1929–2018) studied haiku with Iida Dakotsu and Dakotsu's son Ryūta, and helped edit *Unmo*. After *Unmo* ceased publication in 1992, he founded and led *Hakuro*, which ceased publication in 2012. This poem is from *Hi no tori* (1977).

Spring

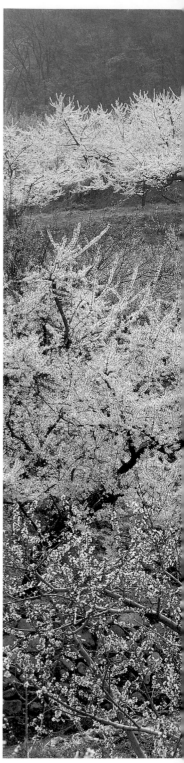

In spring I idle the days away
while birds and insects
live in pain

Takahashi Mutsuo

While spring is a difficult season for birds and insects to survive, the poet passes the time in complete idleness.

Traditionally, spring and autumn are seasons one praises. We wait for them impatiently and miss them when they are over. But for the insects and birds down there in the middle of the food chain, spring is a hard season. As predators, they are continually on the move; and they are continually fleeing to avoid becoming prey themselves. Even a human being, who is not part of the food chain, may feel for the insects and birds and rather than dance about delighting in the season, remain idle.

I hear an echo of "April is the cruelest month," the opening line of T. S. Eliot's poem *The Waste Land*, in this haiku. The author placed it next to: "Auschwitz:/Spring grief—/a hundred or so/eyeglass earpieces," as if to suggest that this haiku is also about our post-Auschwitz age.

> *Mushi tori no / kurushiki haru o / nani mo sezu*
> Insects' birds' / painful spring in / doing nothing

Takahashi Mutsuo (b. 1937) is best known for his free verse poems and his essays, but has written haiku and tanka since his middle school days. In haiku, he was mentored by Andō Tsuguo. This poem is from *Tamamono* (1998).

Is everything well
with the birds and beasts today
as spring begins?

Kitahara Shimako

Today is the beginning of spring. Were the birds and beasts who live nearby able to live through the winter safely? Though the harsh winter was difficult even for the poet, she somehow survived it. But she wonders about the birds and beasts who live around her; were they able to get through it safe and sound?

The phrase "is everything well" must be quoted from the popular children's song "My Old Hometown" ("Furusato," lyrics by Takano Tatsuyuki): "How are my mother and father? Is everything well with my old friends? Whenever it rains or blows I think of my old hometown." Since the poem begins with "is everything well" it naturally evokes "my old friends," the words that follow in the song. That is, the birds and beasts of the poem are among the poet's "old friends."

It is not only human beings with whom she wants to live together as friends, but the birds and beasts as well.

Tsutsuganashi ya / kyō risshun no / tori kemono
Is everything well? / Today spring's beginning's / birds beasts

Kitahara Shimako (1917–2015) was a follower of Katō Shūson and a contributor to *Kanrai*. Later she also became a follower of Kaneko Tōta and contributed to *Kaitei*. This poem is from *Tsukushino shō* (2004).

Proofreading
with a vermilion brush I felt
the spring begin

Shibata Shōkyoku

Shōkyoku was a book editor for his entire career. He was involved in the compilation and editing of a tremendous number of books about poetry, including the complete works of the haiku and *tanka* poet Masaoka Shiki and Shiki's multi-volume compendium of haiku through the ages, both published by the famed ARS Publishing Company. Sometimes he worked on the same project for months. In this poem, he's been working on the same book month after month and suddenly feels renewed at the beginning of spring.

These days proofreading is done with a red pencil or a red ballpoint pen, but Shōkyoku must have used a brush dipped in vermilion sumi ink. This was the instrument of his labor, so this is also a poem about work.

Sho wo kōsu / shuhitsu haru tatsu / omoi ari
Proofreading / vermilion writing brush spring begins / feeling had

Shibata Shōkyoku (1897–1966) began submitting his haiku to magazines when in grade school and began to study haiku in earnest while working as an editor at the magazine *Hototogisu*. After leaving the magazine, he edited many books about haiku. As a haiku poet, he founded and led *Kodama*. This poem is from *Shōkyoku kushū* (1969).

Of light, the beating heart
knows nothing—
snow melting in the river

Yamaguchi Yūmu

The heart resides within the body and beats steadily on without ever knowing of the existence of light. The river, its volume increased by melting snow, flows tumultuously along.

The phrase "Of light …/knows nothing" (*hikari o shirazu*) in reference to the heart—that organ essential to life that lies deep within the chest—leaped out at me when I first read the poem. Our very lives depend on the heart, and its motion is what allows us to perceive light; yet it's true that the heart knows nothing of what we see and keeps beating on in solitude. I find this unaccustomed way of thinking about it refreshing.

There is a definite pause between the second and third segments of the poem, because of the emphatic cutting word[*1] *zu*, replicated in the translation by "nothing." The sharpness of the cut between the two parts of the poem is extremely effective. "Snow melting in the river," the seasonal image juxtaposed to that of the heart, is also bold and vivid. With spring, the deep snowdrifts in the mountains begin to melt, so that the volume of water in the river increases, becoming cloudy and sometimes causing floods. The image evokes the possibility of a life-threatening emergency and thus creates a taut balance with the life-giving heart. The implicit association of the river with a blood vessel adds to the effect.

Shinzō wa / hikari wo shirazu / yukigegawa
The heart / light does not know / snow melting river

Yamaguchi Yūmu (b. 1985) won the grand prize at the National High School Haiku Championship (Haiku Kōshien) in 2003. He later studied haiku with Nakahara Michio[*2] and now contributes to *Ginka*. This poem is from *Shinsen 21* (2009), an anthology of twenty-one promising young poets.

One sheet of thin ice and
another, wind-blown—
layered at the edges

Fukami Kenji

Blown by the wind, one sheet of thin ice slides a little over another, so that the edges are layered.

"Ice" is a winter seasonal image, but "thin ice" is an early spring one. The first days of spring are past but in the morning the temperature sometimes drops to freezing again and then an entire pond can be iced over. In the afternoon, the temperature rises and then the ice melts and breaks apart, usually into several separate fragments. Ordinarily these shrink as they melt, and then disappear. Here, however, the wind has blown two sheets of the thin ice together in such a way that one slightly overlaps the other and they remain layered for a while, perhaps because as the wind blew the temperature dropped a little.

There is something intriguing about a sheet of thin ice breaking up and one edge sliding over another, almost as if on purpose. As a single sheet, the thin ice would be almost transparent, but the barely overlapping part must look a little whiter.

> *Usurai no / fukarete hashi no / kasanareru*
> Thin ice / being blown edges / are layered

Fukami Kenji (b. 1922) was mentored from his high school days by Takahama Kyoshi. He later studied with Yamaguchi Seison and contributed to Seison's *Natsukusa*. In 1989, he cofounded *San* and two years later founded and became the leader of *Kachōrai*. This poem is from *Yokō* (1999).

Thin ice, swept
away
sparkles in sunshine

Fujimatsu Yūshi

Here the poet's focus is sunshine and sparkling ice, but in the background, unspoken, is shade.

We can fill the scene in like this: Since the fragments were "swept away," there must be a puddle of water nearby, which froze over when the temperature dropped late at night. The seasonal image "thin ice" tells us that this is early spring, so by morning a broom can break the ice up and sweep it away. The puddle is in the shade but the ice has been swept into the nearby sunshine.

Even though it is still cold, the rays of the spring sun will make quick work of the thin ice, so it must have been swept away just now. There is someone there, not observed but present, who is attentively caring for this space. The poem invites us into a beautifully described world with secret depths.

Usurai o / fukidashite aru / hinata kana
Thin ice / swept aside / sunshine!

Fujimatsu Yūshi (1924–1999) was a follower of Takahama Kyoshi and a contributor to *Hototogisu*. Together with Fukami Kenji and Imai Chizuko, he founded the magazine *San*. This poem is from *Fugaku*, a posthumous collection (2004).

The cold spring's
eraser shaved off
the entire line of words

Washisu Shigeo

In this poem, the first segment runs over into the second. You read "The cold spring's/eraser" in one breath, followed by a slight pause, or caesura. Then the rest of the poem comes in another single breath: "shaved off the entire line of words."

Those first two segments set the season and the subject: cold spring and eraser. Also, even though the characters for "cold spring" 春寒 are usually pronounced *harusamu*, a rather soft sound, here they are pronounced as the alternative *shunkan,* whose strong consonants give a forbidding impression. Holding a cold eraser in the chill of early spring would feel like holding a solid chunk of coldness.

The single line referred to must be a haiku he has jotted down in his notebook and thinks is no good. He can't bear to just leave it there. That is why he says "shave off." He doesn't just "erase" it. He goes farther, he cuts it out, deletes it, excises it. He is unsparing with himself.

The action of deleting his own poem shows, paradoxically, his feeling for poetry. As I read the poem over, it also makes me think of war, when an entire human life can be made to disappear as easily as that single line.

In the Japanese, the middle seven-syllable segment has an extra syllable, making it rather awkward. Perhaps this is because when Shigeo wrote this poem he had been studying how to write haiku for less than a month.

Shunkan no / keshigomu ichigyō no / ji o sogeri
Spring cold's / eraser one line's / characters shaved off

Washisu Shigeo (1915–1982) began writing haiku during World War II while hospitalized for wounds suffered during war. Attracted to the New Rising Haiku* poets, he studied haiku with Tomizawa Kakio and contributed to Hino Sōjō's *Kikan.* After writing haiku for ten years, he shifted to the free verse for which he is best known today. This poem is from *Sekitai: Washisu Shigeo kyūkuchō* (1981).

A cat in love
suddenly grows
something like a mane

Inoue Katsuko

Suddenly something for all the world like a horse's mane rises from the back of an amorous male cat. He is off to see his lady love.

When a horse gallops, its mane streams in the wind, setting off the horse's beauty. The poem points to something similar that happens when a cat is aroused, though it usually goes unnoticed.

The cat here must be a male about to set off for the home of a female cat. Isn't this exactly the sort of handsome suitor the female cat dreams of? What makes this poem interesting is that the author imagines how the male cat would look through the eyes of his lady love. Otherwise, the thing that is "something like a mane" would go forever unnoticed.

Koineko ni / sa to tategami no / yō na mono
Cat in love on / suddenly mane / like thing

Inoue Katsuko (1943–2015) studied haiku with Ueda Gosengoku and also founded and led *Kanran*. This poem is from *Maoroshi* (2004).

A cat in love—

yearning as one-sided

as an abalone shell

Naitō Meisetsu

Here we have another cat in love, but its yearning is unrequited. This poem is no more than the seasonal image "a cat in love" followed by the familiar saying, "the one-sided yearning of an abalone shell," but it has a strange charm. The abalone has been used as an image for unrequited love from ancient times because it is a one-sided shell. The usage is thought to have originated in the *Man'yōshū*[1] poem, "Like the abalone shells/the fisher-girls of Ise/dive for day and night/my love/is one-sided."

In Meisetsu's poem the part about the abalone shell is strictly unnecessary in terms of meaning, but the iridescence of the abalone shell's lining seems to reflect the inner feeling of the cat yearning for love. Abalone is supposed to be poisonous for cats so there might also be a slight suggestion that such abalone-like love could sicken the cat.

This is not a realistic poem in the sketch from life[2] style of Masaoka Shiki, who was Meisetsu's first haiku teacher, but comes from an older, playful tradition which depends on wordplay.

> *Koineko ya / awabi no kai no / kata omoi*
> Trysting cat / abalone shell's / one-sided yearning

Naitō Meisetsu (1847–1926), was educated in the Chinese classics from childhood. As housemaster of the Matsuyama domain's Tokiwakai Dormitory, where Masaoka Shiki lodged as a student, he came to know Shiki and was mentored by him in haiku. He served as a selector for several haiku publications, and founded and led *Nanka*. This poem is from *Meisetsu haikushū* (1926).

Live whitebait:
failing to slurp them down
never made anyone die

Saitō Gen

Certain seafoods are eaten live—the style is called *odorigui*, "eating as they dance," and whitebait, any of several varieties of young fish 1 or 2 inches long, is one of them.

It is easy to imagine that the poet, who had terminal colon cancer, was encouraged to swallow live whitebait in the hope that their young life would prolong his. Gen himself may well have projected his strong wish for recovery onto the live fish. However, he was too ill to swallow them, or perhaps felt too sorry for them to do it. Whatever the reason, he regretted his failure. And yet he could not help noticing with surprise that despite this failure he did not die.

Life is frail, and death is certain. The whitebait's life and Gen's are layered in my mind.

> *Shirauo o / susuri sokonete / shinu koto nashi*
> Whitebait / slurping failing / dying is not

Saitō Gen (1914–1980) first studied haiku with Saitō Sanki. He founded *Tsubo*, but it was forced to suspend publication after four years due to the war. In 1943 he joined Ishida Hakyō's group and contributed to Hakyō's *Tsuru*. Postwar, he revived and led *Tsubo*. This poem is from the posthumous *Muhan* (1983).

On my mountain
I plant trees from seed—
of other things, I know not

Nishiyama Haku-un

On my own mountain, says the poet, I am planting trees from seed. All my attention is focused on that, and I know nothing of other things, nor do I have any interest in them.

In the foreword that Tokutomi Sohō, one of the most influential journalists of the time, contributed to *The Haiku of Haku-un* (*Haku-un kushū*), he used the words "your eventful life." Haku-un, dreaming of venturing abroad, embarked on a sailing ship from Yokohama when he was 17 but was shipwrecked in a violent storm. Falling ill, he returned to his hometown deep in the mountains of Hyōgo Prefecture. Then, after his father died, he inherited the family saké business. For someone who led a life like this, "of other things I know not" are not words said lightly. He has turned his back on his youthful dreams, and now on his mountain he cultivates trees. The essential ingredient for brewing saké is good water, and trees are vital to this, for they keep the spring water from drying up and preserve water quality. Looking after the mountain's water means everything to him.

> *Wagayama ni / ware konomi u-u / ta o shirazu*
> My mountain on / I trees from seed plant / other do not know

Nishiyama Haku-un (1877–1944) began his study of haiku in 1903, under Takahama Kyoshi. Together with his younger brother, Nomura Hakugetsu, he became one of the leading poets of the *Hototogisu* group in the early twentieth century and was devoted to sketch from life* haiku. This poem, composed in 1913, is from *Haku-un kushū* (1934).

To the dogtooth violet
I offered my greetings
kneeling in respect

Ishida Kyōko

The word used for "dogtooth violet" in this poem is the archaic *kataka-go*. The poet went for a forest hike in early spring to search for dogtooth violets, and when she found one she knelt down as though looking it in the eye and examined it closely. The use of the humble "offered my greetings/... in respect" shows that she feels as one would when meeting an aristocrat or noblewoman. For her, this spring flower, its blooming long awaited, is a precious being.

The eighth-century poet Ōtomo no Yakamochi has a poem about the dogtooth violet in the *Man'yōshū*:[1] "Many girls/boisterously draw water—/dogtooth violets/cluster around/the temple well." Another way to read Kyōko's poem is as a description of one of the ancient maidens in Yakamochi's poem kneeling down before the flower.

> *Katakago ni / mamiemu hiza o / tsukinikeri*
> Dogtooth violet to / offer greetings knee / to the ground

Ishida Kyōko (b. 1958) is the daughter of Ishida Katsuhiko and his wife Izumi, both followers of Ishida Hakyō. She studied haiku with Yamada Mizue,[2] who was also a follower of Hakyō. In 2004, after Mizue's group was dissolved, Kyōko founded and now directs *Muku*. She is also a cofounder of the four-woman haiku group *Hoshi no ki*. This poem is from *Ki no namae* (2004).

Such a strong wind—
spinach
on the ground

Chiba Kōshi

A strong wind is blowing, and when the poet steps outside he sees a bunch of fresh green spinach lying in the middle of the road. There are no fields nearby. Even in a wind like this, it's unlikely that a bunch of spinach would be blown all the way here. Who might have dropped it? What is going to happen to this spinach? The situation has something vaguely humorous about it.

Spinach appears on our tables all year round but as a seasonal image it belongs to spring, especially early spring, when it is the most common green vegetable. A bundle of spinach lying in the road is almost like an announcement of the arrival of spring. In that sense, this seemingly simple and naive poem is born from the poet's strong feeling for the traditional seasonal image of spinach.

In the Japanese, the poem has a relaxed, easygoing feeling because of the repeated "o" sounds—the three doubled "o's" of the first and second segments (*ōkaze, hōrensō*) and the single "o" at the beginning of the third (*ochite*). This creates an impression of a strong wind continuously blowing in the sky.

> *Ōkaze ya / hōrensō ga / ochite iru*
> Strong wind / spinach / fallen

Chiba Kōshi (b. 1947) is a renowned seal-carving artist as well as a haiku poet. He studied haiku with Ishida Katsuhiko and Ayabe Jinki,* but at present he is not affiliated with any haiku group. This poem is from *Kōgai* (1991), his prizewinning first collection.

A hint of
the fragrance of stars
mixed in with the butterbur

Watanabe Chieko

The poet is savoring a dish of butterbur, a fragrant but bitter shoot that is a traditional spring food. Its bitter taste, strangely enough, carries a whiff of the fragrance of distant stars.

"The fragrance of stars" is an arresting image. Stars are usually apprehended with the eyes, but here they are sensed through smell. The juxtaposition of the earthy butterbur with the fragrance of far-off stars is very odd. It's like something you might find in one of the avant-garde short short stories of Inagaki Taruho.* And yet, the light green butterbur that pops up among the dry grasses remaining from winter does have something about it that resembles a star in the dark cosmos. Perhaps the idea for this poem comes from that.

With age, we sometimes come to love the bitter foods that we hated as children. Butterbur would be at the head of that list for many. The way likes and dislikes change with the passage of time is really strange, almost as strange as the idea that butterbur's taste carries hints of the fragrance of stars.

Hoshi no ka no / sukoshiku majiri / fukinotō
Star's fragrance / a little mixed in / butterbur

Watanabe Chieko (b. 1925) was a follower of Mizuhara Shūōshi and is a senior contributor to *Ashibi*. This poem is from *Seishin* (2005).

With the plum trees in bloom
blue sharks visit every nook
of my garden

Kaneko Tōta

A surreal, fantastic scene. When republishing this poem, the poet described it as "a poem about the great joy of spring's arrival,"* and on first reading it does seem to be quite cheerful in tone.

However, when originally published in "Blue Sharks" ("Aozame no shō," a section of *Yūbokushū*), this poem was placed between two others which add deep shadows to the image of the shark in spring. Those two poems are: "The spirit/of a blue shark in the mist/stabs me," in which the spirit of a shark attacks him; and "The blue shark/turns over, shows its stomach/at the house where I was born," in which a shark turns over on its back, as sharks do before snatching their prey.

I can't help thinking that the blue shark showing its stomach might be about to devour the flesh of fallen soldiers. Tōta was a soldier during World War II and wrote about his experience in the fighting at Truk Atoll (Chuuk Lagoon). You can read the blue sharks who visit his garden in spring as the souls of his comrades who died there and never returned.

> *Ume saite / niwajū ni / aozame ga kite iru*
> Plum trees in flower / in the garden / sharks have come

Kaneko Tōta (1919–2018), who studied haiku with Katō Shūson, became one of the most influential haiku poets in postwar Japan and helped bring avant-garde haiku into the mainstream. In 1962 he cofounded *Kaitei,* and then led it from 1985 until his death. In 2008 he received the Masaoka Shiki International Haiku Grand Prize for lifetime achievement. This poem is from *Yūbokushū* (1981).

The grass is pushing up
fresh shoots—human beings
follow in its wake

Hoshino Tatsuko

Now that spring is here, new grass is pushing up from beneath the withered grass. Human beings, acting in conformity with it, are beginning their activities.

The first surprise in this poem is the presence of the word *ningen*, "human beings," in a haiku. The expression includes the author Tatsuko, but she is speaking not only of herself but of all human beings. The scale is different from the usual scale of haiku. Demonstrative pronouns like *sore*, meaning "it" or "that," are rare in haiku, too. In the world of this poem, human beings become active because the grass does and they live humbly, like the grass. Naturally, romantic love is included among the activities of the human beings who follow the lead of the freshly burgeoning grass.

> *Shitamoenu / ningen sore ni / shitagainu*
> Grass pushing up / human beings to it / follow

Hoshino Tatsuko (1903–1984), the second daughter of Takahama Kyoshi, began writing haiku under his guidance. In 1930 she founded *Tamamo*, the first haiku magazine to be run by a woman. She is known as one of the Four T's,* the four most significant female haiku poets of the modern period. This poem is from *Sasame* (1950).

When the eyes are put in
how it must hurt—
the doll's face

Hasegawa Kai

The first two lines, "When the eyes are put in/how it must hurt" are read together, but at first their meaning is far from clear. The meaning of "When the eyes are put in" is obscure, and this is suddenly followed by pain. But all is solved with the last line: It is "the doll's face" into which the eyes have been "put." The gradual unfolding of meaning intensifies the pleasure. Now we see—it must be painful for the doll when the doll maker paints in her eyes with his delicate brush.

"Doll" refers to one of the female dolls in the Girls' Day festive display. On her white face, the eyes are added in with a very thin brush specifically designed to draw human features. "How it must hurt" is a brilliant touch. Who felt this pain? The doll first, then the doll maker who wielded the brush, and finally we the readers. At the moment of pain, the doll comes to life under the doll-maker's brush, as a second self that the doll maker has brought into the world. And at that moment, for the reader, the poem itself acquires life.

Me o iruru / toki itakaran / hina no kao
Eyes put in / when must hurt / doll's face

Hasegawa Kai (b. 1954) began writing haiku in middle school and was later mentored by Ameyama Minoru. He founded and led *Koshi* from 1993 to 2009, then handed it over to Ōtani Hiroshi and began a group to explore seasonal images and their compendiums. In addition to composing haiku, he is a prolific critic and essayist. This poem is from *Tenkyū* (1992).

No flute in the hand
that humbly offers a tune—
the old doll

Matsumoto Takashi

The doll is one of the five musicians in the set of dolls in ancient court costumes traditionally displayed for Girls' Day on March 3. This is an old set, perhaps an heirloom, and the flute player's flute was lost some time ago. There is something touching about those empty fingers.

For "to play," the poet uses a verb that means "to humbly offer." Even without his flute, the doll continues to display a reverence for the imperial dolls on the top tier of the display.

In terms of form, "the old doll," which is the subject, is kept back until the last line. When you read the first two lines on their own, they could be describing someone who wants to play the flute but does not have one. Takashi was born into a family of professional Noh actors attached to the Hōshō school, which was patronized by the Tokugawa shogunate in earlier times, and began to study Noh performance at the age of 5. However, lung disease forced him to give up the idea of performing. This poem could almost be a self-portrait.

> *Tsukamatsuru / te ni fue mo nashi / furuhiina*
> Humbly offering / hand in flute not there / old doll

Matsumoto Takashi (1906–1956) was a follower of Takahama Kyoshi and one of the leading members of *Hototogisu* in the 1930s. Postwar, he founded and led *Fue*. This poem is from *Matsumoto Takashi kushū* (1935).

The evening clouds
are edged with gold—time
to put the dolls away

Kagiwada Yūko

As she is putting the dolls of the Girls' Day festival away, the sun sets beyond the distant clouds, lighting their edges with gold. It is the evening of a beautiful clear day. If the dolls are packed away for the year on a rainy day, the box might be damp and the dolls would get a little moldy, so it's important that the weather is fine.

The description of the clouds as "edged with gold" (*fuchi no kin'iro*) is a lovely touch. The light of the setting sun, seen through the clouds, has a whitish glow, but the cloud edges are banded in gold. In the original Japanese, the words for "edge" (*fuchi*) and "gold" (*kiniro*) are written out in the expansive hiragana syllabary, as ふちのきんいろ instead of using the more compact and elaborate kanji, which would be 縁 and 金色. The graceful shapes of the hiragana subtly echo the shapes of the clouds.

Perhaps the poet also perceives the light edging the clouds as a farewell to the glittering costumes and accessories being wrapped up and put back in their boxes until next year's festival.

> *Yūgumo no / fuchi no kin'iro / hinaosame*
> Evening clouds' / edge's gold / dolls putting away

Kagiwada Yūko (1932–2020) studied haiku with Nakamura Kusatao and contributed to his haiku magazine *Banryoku*. After Kusatao's death, she founded and led *Miraizu*. This poem is from *Asuka* (1986).

The mountains smile—
now and then the fetus moves
behind my navel

Senda Yōko

Spring has come and the poet feels the mountains are smiling. "Behind my navel" evokes the sensation of the fetus' movement within her pregnant body with a striking concreteness.

After the baby is born and the umbilical cord is cut, a tiny stump will be left and when it falls off in a few weeks, what remains will become the baby's navel. Before that, at her own birth, her mother's umbilical cord had become her navel too. A woman's navel evokes the memory of that cycle and the continuity of life.

It is daring to choose the seasonal image "the mountains smile," but the tiny fetus and the large mountains resonate with each other. It is said that for the people of Japan's early Jōmon period (ca. 10,000–ca. 300 BCE) mountains were an object of worship imbued with a life force, which was at its peak in the spring. I feel that this poem is suffused with the wisdom of the people of Jōmon times.

> *Yama warau* / *taido toki ni* / *heso no ura*
> Mountains smile / fetal movement at times / navel's back

Senda Yōko (b. 1962) joined the haiku group led by Ishihara Yatsuka* as a college student and is a contributor to its magazine *Aki*. She also contributes to *Ten'i*, the magazine founded by Arima Akito. This poem is from *Senda Yōko shū* (2004).

Lives lived apart turn in the end
to deaths met apart—
spring water

Yamamoto Shikō

The strength of this poem lies in the way it uses the seasonal image of "spring water" (*haru no mizu*). As something which is vital to human life, water naturally figures in the compendiums of seasonal images called *saijiki*. You will not find "summer water" there, but you will find "autumn water" (*aki no mizu*) and "winter water" (*fuyu no mizu*). Winter, however, is the season of death for plants and small creatures, and autumn is the season in which they are approaching death. So both of those seasonal images evoke death too strongly to be used with the first part of the poem. "Spring water," on the other hand, suggests the birth of new life, though it does not go so far as to suggest the expectation of meeting again in another life.

And so the poem comes together like this: In the warm and cheerful season of spring, the poet came to hear of the death of someone he had once known well. The radiance of "spring water" highlights by contrast the death of the distant person. This poem makes you feel the gravity and weight of parting.

> *Seibetsu mo / izure shibetsu ya / haru no mizu*
> Living apart / after all dying apart / spring water

Yamamoto Shikō (1921–2007) contributed to *Suimei*, a magazine founded by Hasegawa Kanajo. He was also associated with the New Tendency Haiku movement* through *Haiku hyōron* and *Men*. This poem is from his last collection, *Hyōtan'ike* (2007).

Laid on the fire, it gives off
a grassy fragrance—
the first gudgeon

Mori Sumio

As it starts to cook over a charcoal fire, the gudgeon (a freshwater fish found in Lake Biwa) gives off a grassy fragrance. Gudgeons are about 10 centimeters long and best when grilled with salt. This is the first time the poet is eating gudgeon this spring. While savoring the taste, he is also affirming that this spring he has arrived safely at Lake Biwa once again.

The word order is very effective. What has been laid on the fire is not revealed until the last line, leaving space to wonder what might be giving off the grassy fragrance. When the first gudgeon does appear, there is a moment of surprise—oh, so that's what it is? At the same time, you sense a fragrance, and the poem as a whole leaves you with an unusual aftertaste.

This fish's shape resembles a willow leaf, so another name for it is "willow gudgeon." There may be a faint echo of this in the phrase "grassy fragrance."

> *Hi ni nosete / kusa no nioi su / hatsumoroko*
> Fire on laid / grassy fragrance makes / first gudgeon

Mori Sumio (1919–2010) was a follower of Katō Shūson and was a longtime contributor to and editor of Shūson's *Kanrai*. In 1970, he founded and led *Sugi*. This poem is from *Yūhō* (1980).

Emperor Sutoku
lies at peace in Sanuki—
Saigyō's Death Day

Uesaki Bochō

In Sanuki (now Kagawa Prefecture on the island of Shikoku), where Retired Emperor Sutoku (1119–1164) lies buried, they are today observing the anniversary of Saigyō's passing (the fifteenth day of the second lunar month).

Saigyō was a twelfth-century waka poet whom Bashō[*1] revered. Saigyō and Sutoku, who lived in the same period, were drawn together by their mutual love for waka poetry. Because of his role in the Hōgen Rebellion of 1156, Sutoku was exiled to Sanuki and it was rumored that he became a vengeful spirit after death. It was believed that when Saigyō went to pay his respects at Sutoku's grave at Mount Shiramine in Sanuki, Sutoku's soul was pacified. Thus, the poem conjoins Sutoku who "lies at peace" with Saigyō's death anniversary.

Having three proper nouns one after another is unconventional but because all three begin with an "s" sound—Sutoku, Sanuki, Saigyō— there is a musical unity to the poem. On the anniversary of Saigyō's death, the poet remembers that there was a time when Sanuki was a focus of interest throughout Japan. In this sense, the poem is also a hymn of praise to his own birthplace, Sanuki.

> *Sutokuin / shizumoru Sanuki / Saigyō ki*
> Retired emperor Sutoku / lies peacefully Sanuki / Saigyō's Death Day

Uesaki Bochō (1922–2013) studied haiku with Takahama Kyoshi, Takahama Toshio,[*2] and Inahata Teiko, and contributed to *Hototogisu* under their successive leadership. In 1946 he helped found *Iya,* a haiku group and magazine based in his hometown of Tokushima, and from 1987 became its leader. This poem is from *Bizan* (2006).

He is not crucified—
the Buddha naps
on his way to Nirvana

Oikawa Tei

Looking at an image of the Reclining Buddha, which depicts the historical Buddha lying peacefully in his last illness and about to enter Nirvana, the poet thinks of the Crucifixion. When Christ was executed, his hands and feet were nailed to the cross and as he hung there his side was pierced with a spear. The contrast with that terrible death brings home to her the ease of the Buddha's death.

The poet draws a contrast between Christianity and Buddhism through the manner of their founders' deaths. You can also feel her smile a little at the idea that the Buddha on his way to Nirvana looks like he is just taking a nap.

But there may be a little more to this poem. Tei married a naval officer and brought her son up to follow in his footsteps. Her son died in World War II in the South Pacific. Tei's postwar life was lived in the shadow of that loss. Poems such as the following describe the mourning that never ended: "Deep rainy season—/my son died in war/having never been in love" and "Pouring a beer—/the child in my heart/is fifty years old." I cannot help reading this poem as in its own way a prayer to the Reclining Buddha for the peace of her child's soul in death.

Haritsuke ni / arazu Neshaka wa / netamaeri
Crucifixion / it is not the Sleeping Buddha / sleeps

Oikawa Tei (1899–1993) was a follower of Mizuhara Shūōshi and a contributor to Shūōshi's *Ashibi*. She began the women's haiku group within *Ashibi* and nurtured many gifted women poets there. In addition to the son she lost in the war, she had two daughters, who also predeceased her. This poem is from her prizewinning collection *Yūyake* (1967).

In the Nirvana painting
I made out the words
"Mother Maya"

Gotō Yahan

Nirvana paintings show the Buddha lying on his side under a pair of sal trees as he enters Nirvana at death. Surrounding him, weeping, are his disciples, heavenly dragons, and demons of various sorts. It is rare to see writing on such paintings. Among those I have seen, there are some in which the human and supernatural beings are identified by name. Many animals are also often depicted, though none are named.

"Mother Maya" (Mayabunin, more commonly read as Maya fujin) is the Buddha's mother. She died seven days after giving birth to the Buddha and was reincarnated in the Heaven of the Thirty-Three Gods (Tōriten). In the painting, she must be coming to welcome her son. The poet's focus on Mother Maya may have something to do with his feelings for his own mother.

> *Nehanzu ni / Mayabunin to zo / yomarekeru*
> Nirvana painting in / Mother Maya as / I could read

Gotō Yahan (1895–1976) was a follower of Takahama Kyoshi. He founded and led *Kachōshū* (later named *Fūei*). This poem is from *Suitai* (1940).

When I lie on my stomach
my breasts overflow—
the warmth of them

Doi Akiko

The poet is lying in bed on her stomach, and the flesh of her own breasts seems to overflow beneath her, giving her a warm sensation.

This is the moment she suddenly becomes aware of her breasts in a new way. The warmth of spring and the warmth of her own breasts are superimposed on each other.

An earlier poem by a woman about her breasts, by Katsura Nobuko, describes the gloom of the long, drawn-out rainy season together with her annoyance at having breasts: "The sorrow of breasts/filling my clothes—rainy season/drags on" (*Nyoshin*, 1955). Nobuko does not seem to be happy about being a woman. In contrast, for the contemporary Akiko, being a woman and having breasts is perceived positively. Her pleasure has nothing to do with nursing an infant or making love. She is simply experiencing the sensation of her own womanly body as a source of quiet joy.

> *Harabaeba / chibusa afurete / atatakashi*
> Lying on stomach / breasts overflowing / warm

Doi Akiko (b. 1964) is a contributor to *Esora*. Her publications include *Achikochi sōshi*, a collection of haiku, drawings, and essays. This poem is from *Kujira ga umi o eranda hi* (2002).

It's so warm —
those long Kyoto greetings
go on forever

Tabata Michijo

It is spring and the weather has grown warm. When people meet in Kyoto the greetings tend to be long and flowery, but at this time of year they seem to go on and on.

I imagine the Kyoto residents exchanging news when they meet about where the cherry blossoms are coming into bloom or are already blooming. Michijo was 12 and an apprentice geisha (*maiko*) in 1907 when she first met poet and novelist Takahama Kyoshi, and she became the model for the heroine of his novel *Fūryū senpō*, set in Kyoto. While she was aware of and proud of the uniqueness of the Kyoto dialect, she wrote him a letter criticizing his clumsy reproduction of it in his novel: "You make Kyoto speech sound weird, just like gobbledygook!" She was very conscious of spoken language.

Kyoshi himself has a good haiku about the Kyoto dialect: "Battledore and shuttlecock!/Kyoto words are/smooth as oil" (*Gohyakku,* 1937). With its striking simile for the fluidity of Kyoto speech, Kyoshi's haiku is quite poetic. Michijo's haiku, in contrast, situates Kyoto dialect within the everyday, and has a refreshing plainness.

> *Atataka ya / aisatsu nagaki / Kyō kotoba*
> It's warm / greetings long / Kyoto dialect

Tabata Michijo (1895–1958) was a follower of Takahama Kyoshi and a contributor to *Hototogisu,* as was her husband Tabata Hiko, with whom she ran a restaurant in Kyoto. This poem is from the posthumous collection edited by her husband, *Michi Michio ikushū* (1986).

A house in spring—
pushed from behind, it toppled
over

Wada Gorō

What a flimsy house, you might think, but then one must not put too much trust in human-made things like houses. And it's not only the physical house that is fragile; the ties between the family members that live there are easily broken as well.

Read in the light of our own time, it is tempting to take this poem as a prophecy of the recent violations of safety laws in new buildings and the disintegration of the family system. It could be a parable of the contemporary age. It makes me wonder if the poet described things as yet unwitnessed but that he sensed would come.

The expression "a house in spring" (*haru no ie*) is not a traditional seasonal image and does not appear, so far as I know, in any *saijiki* compendium of haiku seasonal images. That lack of verbal stability contributes to the effect of the poem. However, this poem would not work for any other season. It grasps the essence of spring's floating, restless feeling.

Haru no ie / *ura kara oseba* / *taorekeri*
Spring house / behind from pushed / toppled over

Wada Gorō (1923–2015) was a follower of Hashi Kanseki. While contributing to Kanseki's magazine *Byakuen*, he also contributed to *Uzu*, the magazine led by Akao Tōshi. After Kanseki's death in 1992, he became editor in chief of *Byakuen*. This poem is from *Sankaishi* (1980).

The sound we call
spring rain is here
is now

Washitani Nanako

This poem has nothing visual in it. It is all sound—a soft, gentle sound. "The sound we call/spring rain" does not mean only the sound the rain makes as it falls. It is also the sound of the words "spring rain" (*ha-ru-sa-me*) when you say them aloud, which very sound, the poem tells us, is close to the sound the rain itself makes as it quietly falls.

In haiku, "spring rain" (*harusame*) is different from "the rain of spring" (*haru no ame*). "Spring rain falls on and on without pause," the eighteenth-century haiku textbook *Sanzōshi* tells us. This poem says only that the poet is listening to the sound of the spring rain. Yet although its seventeen syllables convey no more meaning than that, something about it draws us in. If you say it aloud to yourself, you have the feeling that the words themselves, the sound of the poem, become the very sound of the rain.

In one sense, the poem has no content, yet in another sense it is brimful. It could stand as a fine contemporary example in haiku of what the novelist and poet Orikuchi Shinobu termed the "contentless tanka."[*1]

> *Harusame to / iu oto no shite / kitaru kana*
> Spring rain / called sound has / come

Washitani Nanako (1923–2018) was a follower of Yamaguchi Sōdō[*2] and inherited the leadership of *Nanpū* from him in 1984. In 2004, she handed it over it to a younger poet, and three years later stopped writing haiku entirely. This poem is from the award-winning *Shinshō* (2004).

The wreath
carried there so carefully
stands propped in muddy slush

Settsu Yoshiko

This must be a funeral wreath. Out of respect for the dead, it feels important to keep it pristine, but the ground where it is displayed is covered with muddy melted spring snow. It disturbs us to think of the man who carried the wreath there so carefully and then had to set it up in the slushy snow, knowing that the wreath would get filthy.

Life is a series of unavoidable moments of frustration and regret. The poet tastes just such a moment at the funeral that is the setting for this poem. The recently deceased person, on the other hand, has at long last been liberated from life's suffering.

> *Katsugikoshi / hanawa no ashi o / shundei ni*
> Carried on shoulders / wreath's legs / spring mud in

Settsu Yoshiko (b. 1920) studied haiku with Katsura Nobuko. She was a founding contributor to Nobuko's *Sōen* and also contributes to *Sōju*, the magazine founded by Nobuko's followers after her death. She is the mother of the haiku poet Settsu Yukihiko, who died tragically young. This poem is from *Kōhīkan* (1998).

Spread your thighs to split-
ting they seem to tell themselves—
that's tilling soil!

Sakurai Do'on

This poem describes the process of turning the soil of a field over and over, to break it up and prepare it for planting rice. These days it is an easy job because of machines such as the mechanical tiller, but back in the days when the poem was composed it was extremely heavy labor, as this poem demonstrates. Standing braced with legs spread wide, field workers brought the hoe down with all their might.

The phrase "spread your thighs to splitting" (*mata mo hari/sake yo*) vividly evokes the spirit with which they worked and the way they moved. The phrase is enjambed, straddling the first five syllables and the second seven, so the form itself echoes the image of the thighs forced far apart.

Murakami Kijō's famous poem "Dying and being/reborn again and again/to till the soil" was published the year before this one, as the first poem in the "Miscellaneous" (Zatsuei) section of the June 1915 issue of *Hototogisu*. This poem, which appeared in the same place in August 1916, seems to have been produced as a response to Kijō's.

> *Mata mo hari / sake yo to bakari / utsuta kana*
> Thighs spread / split! saying to extent that / tilling soil!

Sakurai Do'on (1887–1964), a contributor to *Hototogisu* and a farmer, often wrote about his daily work and was known as "the poet of the soil" (*tsuchi no haijin*).

The flower words
seem to shine—
seed-planting

Igusa Keiko

The seasonal image, "planting flower seeds" (*hana tane maku*), is divided between the beginning and the end of the poem. While planting flower seeds, the poet is imagining them gradually growing and coming into bloom. And going beyond that, she is thinking about the meaning they have in the language of flowers, "the flower words" in which each flower is given a symbolic significance. For example, in the language of flowers the morning glory (*ipomoea nil*) signifies deep affection, calmness, and fleeting love, while garden balsam (*Impatiens balsamina*) means cheerfulness, "don't touch me," and impatience.

The language of flowers includes many references to feelings and human relationships, some of which a young person would probably not yet have experienced. Perhaps this is why she says "seem to." It is surprising to find such lyric romanticism reaped from mundane garden work.

Through the language of flowers, the flowers that will bloom are skillfully linked to her own future.

> *Hana kotoba / kagayaku bakari / tane o maku*
> Flower words / shine extent that / seed plant

Igusa Keiko (b. 1959) studied haiku with Yamaguchi Seison and Kuroda Momoko and is a contributor to *Shū*, the magazine founded by one of Seison's followers. She also co-founded and contributes to *Hoshi no ki*. This poem is from *Tōki ki* (2003).

Eating Spanish mackerel—
after a pub crawl
around five temples

Nishimura Kirin

The poet is eating Spanish mackerel (*sawara*), a popular fish in Japan, after having made the rounds of five Buddhist temples in one day. Instead of using a word that means visited, though, he uses a word that means "pub crawling" (*hashigo*). For him, visiting a number of temples is as much fun as drinking his way from pub to pub. Indeed, someone who visits five temples in one day must be a real aficionado of temples.

Is this Kyoto or Nara, which both boast many famous temples? Probably not. If he is eating fresh Spanish mackerel, it is more likely that he is near the sea. Perhaps it is even somewhere near his hometown of Onomichi, a port town on the Seto Inland Sea known for its Temple Walk, a network of paths connecting dozens of temples. Visiting five large temples in one day is usually quite difficult, but it would not be hard to do in this little seaside town with its many small temples.

Thus the poem: in the evening, he leisurely enjoys delicious seafood together with good saké, after spending the day soaking up the sun and visiting temples.

> *Sawara kuu / itsutsu no tera o / hashigo shite*
> *Sawara* eat / five temples / pub crawl doing

Nishimura Kirin (b. 1983) is a follower of Hasegawa Kai and a contributor to *Koshi*. He is one of the new generation of haiku poets with a strong Internet presence. This poem is from the prizewinning *Uzura* (2013), his first haiku collection.

Reflected in
the horse's eye—
red camellias!

Yoshida Tōyō

Leading a horse along, the poet comes upon a camellia bush with red flowers in bloom, and notices that the flowers are reflected in the horse's eye. Where is he positioned in order to see the horse's eye? He might be standing near the horse, but in that case the camellias would be close by so the element of surprise would be lacking. We might also imagine the poet as mounted on the horse and arriving at a spot close to the camellias—but from horseback it would surely be difficult to see the horse's eye. So I read it as him walking along leading the horse.

Tōyō must have had in mind Bashō's* haiku: "The wayside mallow/ was gobbled up/by my horse" (in *Nozarashi kikō*, 1685*).* Unlike Bashō, however, Tōyō did not compose his poem while on horseback, and his horse did not eat flowers.

The flowers reflected in the horse's eye suggest a kind of dark passion.

> *Uma no me ni / utsurite akaki / tsubaki kana*
> Horse's eye in / reflected red / camellias!

Yoshida Tōyō (1892–1956) studied haiku with Ōsuga Otsuji. After Otsuji's death, he founded and led *Dassai*. This poem is from *Tōyō daiichi kushū* (1922), edited by Itō Gessō.

Eating mountain asparagus—
I'm one hundred fathoms
behind the times

Enomoto Yoshihiro

Eating the wild spring vegetable known as mountain asparagus (*udo*), hardly considered a gourmet food today, the poet feels he has been left behind by the world. And that's fine with him. He expresses exactly how far he has been left behind by the phrase "one hundred fathoms" (*hyakuhiro*),* itself a word with an archaic flavor, especially when, as here, it is used to express distance rather than depth.

Reading this poem, an image suddenly floats into my mind: one hundred fathoms deep, way below the surface of the surging ocean, someone is kneeling at a low table set up on the white sand, with a porcelain carafe of saké, about to partake of a bowl of mountain asparagus. It has to be this fragrant, crunchy, fresh spring vegetable. Merely tasting such a word in the mouth provokes a feeling of bliss.

It occurs to me that perhaps while he takes pleasure in being left behind by the world, he may actually be far ahead of it.

> *Udo kuute / yo ni hyakuhiro mo / okurekeri*
> Mountain asparagus eating / world one hundred fathoms / behind

Enomoto Yoshihiro (b. 1937) studied with Mori Sumio and was a founding contributor to Sumio's magazine *Sugi*. He founded *Kō* in 2014 and still leads it, while also contributing to *Kudan*. This poem is from his prizewinning *Saishi* (2008).

On the hill behind
there lives a woman—
look, she's herding heat haze!

Mamura Shun'ichi

According to the haiku scholar Yamamoto Kenkichi,[*1] the basic meaning of *kagerō* is a wavy, shimmering phenomenon of some kind. Besides its present meaning of spring heat haze, the word was earlier used to describe water vapor, the light of dawn, or even insects like mayflies and dragonflies whose thin wings shimmer as they fly. But the older meanings don't come into play here. This woman is a herder of heat haze.

When water vapor evaporates and rises it stirs the air and creates a heat haze that distorts distant objects. This strange, distorting phenomenon is what the woman keeps and "herds," as though it were a living creature. The daring image has *hai-i*, the down-to-earth yet sophisticated and witty way of changing perspective that is integral to haiku. It perfectly captures the magic of *kagerō*, the Japanese word for "heat haze."

At the same time, the poem creates the image of a woman of almost shamanic power. She can stir a man's heart wildly, but when he reaches out to touch her, nothing is there. The worship of the feminine and the sense of otherworldliness bring to mind the world of the novels of Izumi Kyōka.[*2]

> *Urayama ni* / *kagerō o kau* / *onna kana*
> Hill behind on / heat haze herds / woman!

Mamura Shun'ichi (b. 1954) is a book designer whose specialty is poetry books. He writes tanka as well as haiku. Influenced by the tanka poet Tsukamoto Kunio,[*3] he has a tendency toward fantasy and the supernatural. This poem is from his first haiku collection, *Tsuru no utsu* (2007).

What's that shimmering heat haze?
I look again—
the dustpan!

Ikenouchi Takeshi

I thought at first that the seasonal image "heat haze" (*kagerō*) referred to the distant shimmer of water vapor above a steaming road, but it seems that it may be used in a broader meaning, too. In this poem, "heat haze" describes an illusion created by a dustpan that someone has just used when cleaning up their garden. Whether made of metal or wood, it's unlikely that it would give off water vapor. What must be happening is that the earth's surface is warmed by the sunlight and the warmth passes into the layer of air close to the earth's surface so that between it and the layer of cooler air above, the light refracts irregularly.

An object that someone was holding until just a moment ago suddenly appears distant and ungraspable. That is the sort of strangeness this poem celebrates. Closing the poem with the sentence-ending particle *ka,* which in this case expresses surprise, adds to the effect.

> *Kagiroeru / mono wa to mireba / chiritori ka*
> Heat haze shimmer / thing wondering looked / a dustpan?

Ikenouchi Takeshi (1889–1974) was the son of the prominent scholar of the Noh theater Ikenouchi Nobuyoshi, who was Takahama Kyoshi's older brother. Takeshi studied haiku with Kyoshi and became a loyal follower of his style. He later founded and led *Keyaki*, through which he mentored many poets. This poem is from *Takeshi kushū* (1933).

From battleship *Yamato*:
"ON PATH TO LAND OF DEAD
VIOLETS IN BLOOM"

Kawasaki Tenkō

The note to this poem is "The battleship *Yamato*, sunk on April 7, 1945." The last two lines of the poem are a telegram that has arrived from the *Yamato*. Written in the katakana script customarily used in telegrams, it announces that violets are blooming on the path to the land of the dead.

At the end of World War II, the battleship *Yamato* was dispatched to Okinawa to try to slow the Allied advance but was attacked by American bombers. When it sank off Cape Bōno in Kagoshima Prefecture, 2,740 soldiers lost their lives. Telegrams have played an important role in the history of modern warfare. For example, there was the encoded telegram sent from Japan's Imperial Forces headquarters to seaborn mobile troops on December 8, 1941, which conveyed the order for war to begin. But the telegram in this poem is fictional. The poet imagines it being sent from the sunken battleship *Yamato* on the ocean floor.

In Japanese mythology, *yomotsu hirasaka* is a slope that straddles the boundary between the land of the living and the land of the dead, and this is where the telegram was sent from. The lovely violets embody the poet's wish to console the dead and pray for the repose of their souls. It reminds us that *Yamato*, the name of this powerful and imposing battleship, was originally a lyrical place name for Japan.

Yamato yori / yomotsu hirasaka / sumire saku
Yamato from / path to land of dead / violets bloom

Kawasaki Tenkō (1927–2009) met Katō Shūson when Shūson was a teacher in his high school. Later he joined Shūson's group and contributed to *Kanrai*. In 1980, he became a founding contributor to Mori Sumio's magazine *Sugi* and ten years later, founded *Ten* and became its leader. This poem is from *Yoshinaka* (1978).

Sakura mochi
for another blind one, not me—
my generous husband

Tamaki Aiko

Aiko developed leprosy at the age of 5 in 1902. When she was 30, she entered the Kaishun Leprosarium in Kumamoto, where she became familiar with the Bible and was baptized. Later her right leg required amputation and she became unable to walk. She subsequently lost her sight after moving to the Nagashima Aiseien National Sanatorium near the Seto Inland Sea. What sustained her through these trials was her religious belief, her practice of haiku, and her husband, Maki Shisui, who had the same disease.

This poem is about jealousy. She is lamenting her husband's kindness to another blind woman. Did her husband perhaps give off a whiff of sakura mochi[*1] when he came back to their room? Or did he tell her that he received a gift of a sakura mochi and gave it to another blind woman? The scent of this traditional sweet heralds the arrival of spring and can stir the imagination in many ways.

I'm thankful that my husband is always kind and generous towards me, she says, but when he's the same towards others too, it makes me uneasy. This is a poem about a great love.

Sakuramochi / yoso no meshii ni / tsuma yasashi
Sakura cake / another blind one for / husband generous

Tamaki Aiko (1887–1969) was a follower of Takahama Kyoshi and Abe Midorijo.[*2] She became interested in haiku in her 40s and began submitting poems to *Hototogisu*. She then organized a haiku group with other sanatorium residents and nurses. Her husband, Maki Shisui, was also a haiku poet. This poem is from *Ama no kizahashi* (1973).

She who trains me in koto
is another man's wife—
daphne in bloom

Nakamura Rakuten

As the poet is receiving a koto lesson from a married woman, he suddenly notices the sweet smell of daphne blossoms drifting into the room. During the Meiji period (1868–1912) when this poem was written, taking lessons on the koto may have been one of the few times a man could converse with a married woman. "She who trains me" has an old-fashioned formality, while the contrast with the wistful tenderness of "another man's wife" may be the highlight of the poem.

There is a theory that the origin of *jinchōge*, the Japanese name for daphne, lies in the fact that it combines the scents of agarwood (*jinkō*) and cloves (*chōji*). With their beguiling fragrance, the daphne blossoms lend a distinct sensuality to the poem. Who could think that the man is focused solely on the training he is receiving from this woman married to another man?

Unspoken desire pervades the poem. This is the power that resides in juxtaposing images.

> *Hito no tsuma no / koto no shinan ya / jinchōge*
> Someone's wife's / koto instruction / daphne blossoms

Nakamura Rakuten (1865–1939) was a follower of Masaoka Shiki and later of Takahama Kyoshi. He was one of the earliest members of *Hototogisu*. When this poem appeared in *Hototogisu* in May 1899, Masaoka Shiki chose it as the best on the assigned topic of "wife."

Paperbush flowers—three
times three is nine
three times three is nine

Inahata Teiko

The Oriental paperbush, used for making Japanese *washi* paper, is in bloom. At the tip of each of the tripartite stalks sits a cluster of small flowers. Next year each stalk will again divide into three and flowers will again bloom on each stalk tip—for all the world like the "three times three is nine" multiplication chant.

Before the Oriental paperbush sets leaves in spring it blooms with bright yellow tubular flowers clustered like the cells of a honeycomb. Its Japanese name, *mitsumata*, literally means "three again" or "three divisions," and its distinguishing feature is that its stalks always divide into three. This poem highlights that characteristic perfectly.

When a plant is described in a "one thing haiku" (*ichimotsu haiku,* haiku that do not rely on the juxtaposition of two images to create their effect), it is difficult to keep a steady focus on the plant. However, this poem manages to do so, perhaps because of the strong rhythm that repeating a verse from the elementary school multiplication table creates. As the flowers bloom, the shrub itself also seems to grow bigger and bigger and the words brighten our mood.

> *Mitsumata no / hana sazan ga ku / sazan ga ku*
> Paperbush / flowers three threes are nine / three threes are nine

Inahata Teiko (b. 1931) is the granddaughter of Takahama Kyoshi. She studied haiku with her father Takahama Toshio* and inherited the leadership of *Hototogisu* from him. At present, she is its director emeritus. This poem is from *Sayuragi* (2001).

With the fresh white gleam
of the magnolias
here comes my morning

Usuda Arō

Every single white magnolia flower is vivid and bright. With the sight of these flowers, the poet's morning arrives.

"Fresh white gleam" is a good phrase to describe the large white magnolia flowers, while "my morning" is his own bright, vivid and expansive morning. The outward gleam of the white magnolias and the inner feeling of excitement have a pleasing resonance that gives a strong sense of life.

According to the poet Murayama Kokyō, Arō disliked the nasal sound of the final *n* of *hakuren* (white magnolia) so he had a habit of borrowing a classical variation and writing it as *hakuremu*. Here is another poem in which he used this word: "On the white magnolia/the gold of the setting sun/drips down."

> *Hakuremu no / tekireki to waga / asa wa kinu*
> Magnolias' / fresh white gleam with my / morning comes

Usuda Arō (1879–1951) studied haiku with Takahama Kyoshi but later distanced himself from *Hototogisu*'s traditional approach, and was also critical of the New Tendency Haiku movement.* With the help of Ōsuga Otsuji, he founded and led *Shakunage*, from which emerged such talented poets as Ōno Rinka and Shinohara Bon. This poem is from *Teihon Arō kushū* (1949).

In spring, the dawns—
do me a favor and
go home soon

Kai Michiko

"In spring, the dawns" (*Haru wa akebono*) is the famous opening phrase of Sei Shōnagon's eleventh-century classic *The Pillow Book* (*Makura no sōshi*).*¹ It says that dawn is the most beautiful time of day in spring. Here, the words also imply that someone has been with the poet overnight. Despite the romantic connotations, however, she hopes that this person will leave very soon.

The drop from the classical register to the down-to-earth colloquial gives a pleasant jolt. Who might she be addressing? It could be a friend with whom she stayed up all night talking, but it's more interesting to read it as being a lover who came to spend the night, as was the custom in the Heian period (794–1185). Even a woman with a heart full of love might prefer to enjoy the beauty of dawn on her own. Come to think of it, some of the women in those famous classical poems about lingering partings at dawn might have felt exactly like this.

Haru wa akebono / sorosoro kaette / kurenai ka
Spring, dawn / pretty soon go home / could you please?

Kai Michiko (b. 1960) started writing haiku in the group of Ōmaki Hiroshi*² and later moved to *Ginka*, the group led by Nakahara Michio.*³ She also co-directs *Gunjō*. This poem is from *Mōkohan* (2000).

I put my body into
a spring afternoon
and stand it up straight

Aza Yōko

Rather than depicting the real world in a haiku, the poet manipulates language to construct a strange new space. The seasonal image of a leisurely spring afternoon denotes a particular time, but she uses the word "spring afternoon" exactly as if it meant a particular space. This bold transposition of time to space allows the word to evoke the image of a large fishtank-like place with room for something (perhaps even a human being) to step inside.

The poem's speaker is somewhere separate from the spring afternoon but still connected to it. Her rational consciousness has absented itself. What enables her to move is will, pulsing through her body. What an unusual, almost uncanny sensation this is.

In a single poem the poet conveys all the languid, listless sense of a spring afternoon. This poem exemplifies one of the fresh haiku styles of our time.

> *Shunchū ni / karada o irete / tatete ori*
> Spring afternoon in / body put / make it stand

Aza Yōko (b. 1947) was at one time a prominent member of *Tenrai tsūshin*, the long-standing haiku magazine in her home region of Kyushu. She later joined Tsubouchi Nenten's* *Sendan*, and after *Sendan*'s dissolution, founded her own group *Hanagumi*. This poem is from *Sarugaku* (2000).

Twilight in spring—I meet
an old man and what do you know
it's my dad

Nomura Kenzō

In haiku there are poems in the first person where knowing the author's name is unnecessary, but with some poems, knowing the author's name adds another layer of meaning. This poem is an excellent example of the latter. Without knowing that the author (and speaker) is anyone other than Nomura Kenzō, son of the well-known haiku poet Nomura Toshirō, it would be difficult to fully appreciate it.

The setting is a sweetly languorous evening in spring, when faces are difficult to make out in the twilight. Among several kanji that mean "to meet" the poet chose 逢う, which means a sudden and unexpected meeting and also suggests deep feeling. The swift move from darkness to illumination as he recognizes his father is expressed in the casual "it's my dad."

A boy grows up by opposing his father. However, the moment when he sees his father as an old man, he also realizes that his father is no longer someone to oppose. This is the drama of fathers and sons.

Haru no kure / *rōjin to au* / *sore ga chichi*
Spring of twilight / old person with meet / it's dad

Nomura Kenzō (b. 1949) inherited the leadership of *Oki* from his father, Nomura Toshirō. This poem comes from his prizewinning *Taka no ki* (1992).

Spring evening—
her hand sliding the door open
Mother comes to me

Ishida Hakyō

The concrete specificity of "her hand sliding the door open" is powerful. It allows us to experience vicariously the tactile sensation of his mother's hand on the door as she slides it open, and to sense in that gesture the joy she feels on seeing her beloved son after a long time apart.

As an army draftee during World War II, Hakyō contracted tuberculosis and never fully regained his health. When bedridden, the sliding paper door to his sickroom was the boundary between the exterior and interior worlds. It is easy to imagine how he gazed at it intently, knowing his mother would arrive soon and anticipating the joy of her arrival.

"Sliding paper door" is a winter seasonal image, but in this poem it does not set the season. Rather, the poem's center is the spring evening, whose image enfolds the entire poem in gentleness. The soft "h" sounds that begin each of the three syllabic segments: *haru*, *fusuma*, *haha* (*fu* is considered an "h" sound in Japanese), reinforce this.

> *Haruyūbe* / *fusuma ni te kake* / *haha kitamau*
> Spring evening / sliding paper door on hand placing / mother comes

Ishida Hakyō (1913–1969) began writing haiku in his teens, mentored by Ikazaki Kokyō. By his mid-twenties, he was a member of Mizuhara Shūōshi's *Ashibi* and had begun his own group and magazine *Tsuru*. He was labeled a "humanist" poet,* treating personal themes in a traditional style. In 1954, he received the Yomiuri Prize for Literature for his complete works, which includes this poem from *Shakumyō* (1950).

The clock store's clocks
on a night in spring—which one is
telling the truth?

Kubota Mantarō

A variety of gleaming wall clocks and table clocks are displayed in the window of a clock store. Quartz clocks had not yet been invented when this poem was written, so these are all mechanical windup clocks and the clock hands point to different times. Usually people feel pressed for time, but this variety of times produces the happy feeling of being liberated for once from time's constraints. One of the clock faces might even hide the secret entrance to a timeless world.

The poem pauses after "The clock store's clocks" and again after "on a night in spring." Then, after setting up that objective scene, comes the sudden question "which one is telling the truth?," the words spilling out as if he were whispering to himself in the spring night.

> *Tokeiya no / tokei haru no yo / dore ga honto*
> Clock store's / clocks spring's night / which is real

Kubota Mantarō (1889–1957) was primarily a novelist and playwright but he also wrote haiku with such friends as Matsune Tōyōjō and Okamoto Shōhin. Although he always called haiku his "hobby," he founded and led *Shuntō*. This poem is from *Kubota Mantarō kūshū* (1942).

The pleasures of truth
pale next to those of lies
under spring lamplight

Yoshiya Nobuko

In daily life we avoid people who pepper their talk with lies. Convention dictates that a good person be truthful and instructs us to reject lies and affirm facts. But this poem turns that idea on its head.

The prefatory note is "One night while writing at my desk." Nobuko must be writing a novel, which was what she did for a living. The world of fiction is impossible to create from nothing but facts. Softly lighted by the "spring lamplight," lies come alive at night as she creates the love scenes in her novel.

In haiku, too, it is the same. There is a space between word and thing, and lies step in to bridge the gap. Poetry without lies is no poetry at all.

Makoto yori / uso ga tanoshi ya / harutomoshi
Truth more than / lies is fun / spring lamplight

Yoshiya Nobuko (1896–1973) is best known for her pioneering feminist and lesbian fiction but she also contributed to Ishida Hakyō's *Tsuru*, and was later a follower of Takahama Kyoshi. This poem is from her posthumous *Yoshiya Nobuko kushū* (1974), edited by Yoshiya Chiyo.

The mole at the nape of
her neck spells danger
under the hazy moon

Takehisa Yumeji

In Japan, a mole that is visible on the hairline of a woman with her hair up is considered alluring and attractive. Here the sharply defined mole, startlingly dark against the pale skin, contrasts with the vague light of the hazy moon.

Yumeji was a painter famous for his portraits of beautiful women and one feels the painter's eye at work in the composition of this poem. The word "danger" is arresting. What is behind it? Only this perhaps: Noticing the mole, he finds himself intensely attracted to her, and this makes him anxious. Yet the fact that the mole is clearly visible on a hazy moonlit night also suggests that this pair is already rather close to each other.

Not many poets in the history of haiku have written about love. Among those who have, Yumeji is one of the very best.

Eriashi no / hokuro ayaushi / oborozuki
Nape of neck / mole dangerous / hazy moon

Takehisa Yumeji (1884–1934) is best known as a painter and a free verse poet, but he wrote haiku on his own and with fellow artists and writers. He also traveled to Europe and the United States and even lectured on Japanese painting at the Itten-Schule of the Bauhaus-related artist and educator Johannes Itten in Berlin. This poem is from *Yumeji kushū* (1994), edited by Kogure Susumu.

I'll think myself
        a tortoise caught on its back—
                who moaned in longing

Ishikawa Keirō

The poet decides to think of himself as an overturned tortoise that can only flounder about on its back. No matter how it struggles to right itself, it will never be able to get back on its legs and walk again. The tortoise is a symbol of long life, but in these circumstances it will not be alive much longer.

Then the imaginary tortoise cries out. The cry of the tortoise is a seasonal image, used in haiku to describe a male tortoise crying out in longing for a mate.

Keirō was dying of tuberculosis when he wrote this poem. To cry out while fatally ill is not only an expression of grief about dying; even then, like the tortoise, you can long for love. Playing at comedy while on the verge of death, the poet shows us what it means to be human and alive.

Uragaeru / *kame omoubeshi* / *nakeru nari*
Overturned / tortoise I will think of / it cried out

Ishikawa Keirō (1909–1975) studied haiku with Sugita Hisajo and contributed to Ishida Hakyō's *Tsuru*, Saitō Gen's *Tsubo*, and Mizuhara Shūōshi's *Ashibi*. Later he became editor in chief of Kadokawa Shoten's influential magazine *Haiku* and then editor in chief of *Fūdo*, through which he eventually formed his own group. This poem is from his posthumous collection *Shion* (1976).

Feasting on
its friend—
the tadpole's jaws!

Shimamura Hajime

The softly moving jaws of the tadpole devouring its onetime friend!

When I was a boy I once raised tadpoles, and I have witnessed scenes like the one this poem describes. Tadpoles can morph into cannibals in an instant if they don't get enough animal protein. I remember how frightened I was when I saw the scraps of cannibalized tadpoles floating about. It's terrifying the way these small animals with their cute name can calmly devour their own. Yet if shut up in a confined space with nothing to eat, human beings have been known to behave the same way. This poem records a living organism in the most extreme phase of its existence.

The tadpole presses down on the corpse with its jaws as it swallows, and the closure of the final "jaws" provides an effective focal image for the poem.

Tomo o hamu / otamajakushi no / agito kana
Friend eat / tadpole's / jaws!

Shimamura Hajime (1893–1923) was born in the United States, where his father was stationed as a diplomat, and returned to Japan as a young child. He was mentored in haiku by Takahama Kyoshi, and helped edit *Hototogisu*, but was sickly and died young. This poem is from his collection *Shimamura Hajime kushū* (1924).

Dawn—for my rendezvous
with the blossoms
I put on new underwear

Ōno Rinka

The poet has gotten up early to go cherry blossom viewing. However, he doesn't use the word "see" or "view." He has chosen the word *au* (literally "meet"), a word ordinarily used for people, making this a kind of personification. The blossoms are not mere plants; it is almost as if he is going to meet with a living spirit.

"I put on new underwear" can be read as suggesting the kind of reverence one might feel for a god at whose holy site one is preparing to worship. It could also be read as expressing a certain sensuality, as if looking forward to making love after a long separation. I take it as both—reverential and sensuous at once.

He has yet to see the blossoms when he writes down this poem, but hints of their holy presence are already making themselves felt from beyond the dawn.

> *Akebono ya / hana ni awamu to / hadagi kae*
> Dawn / flowers to meet with / underwear change

Ōno Rinka (1904–1982) was a follower of Usuda Arō and a contributor to *Shakunage.* Postwar, he founded and led *Hama.* He was also editor in chief of Kadokawa Shoten's influential magazine *Haiku* and an esteemed haiku critic who mentored many younger poets. This poem is from *Hōenshū* (1979).

In the spring chill
I'm off to meet
a different set of breasts

Manabe Kureo

A sudden chill has struck when the cherry blossoms are flowering. I'm off for a rendezvous with a woman whose breasts are not those I usually touch.

In haiku, to say "I'm off for a rendezvous with a different lover than usual" would not necessarily be uninteresting, but reducing the woman to the specific physical image of her breasts is startling and makes the poem hard to forget. The "spring chill" (*hanabie*), a seasonal image, enwraps the atmosphere of the poem, even to breasts, and the color of the cherry blossom petals sets off the paleness of skin. You experience vicariously the coldness of the breasts touched by the spring chill.

This is a poem about sexual desire, but it says nothing about inward emotion. Because of that, the woman he is describing so partially feels as transient as the very spirit of the flowers. Even if he keeps the rendezvous you wonder if there will be anyone there to meet.

> *Hanabie no / chigau chibusa ni / ai ni yuku*
> Spring chill's / different breast to / meet I go

Manabe Kureo (1934–2012) was a novelist. He began to compose haiku under his father's influence, and as a New Rising Haiku* poet he participated in *Shibabi* and *Shintairiku*. This poem is from his prizewinning collection *Yukionna* (1992).

No demon doings
spoiled the sutra chanting—
a noon of blossoms

Nawa Sankanchiku

"Demon doings" (*maji*) is a Buddhist term for the actions of demons that hinder us on the path to salvation. Having deposited the ashes of a friend or relative at the Higashi Ōtani Cemetery in Kyoto, where he worked as a priest, the poet holds a memorial service of sutra chanting for the repose of the person's soul.

As a friend, he must feel sad that someone with whom he has been close is no longer alive to enjoy the beauty of the cherry blossoms. At the same time, as a priest, he feels a sense of satisfaction for having done all he could for this person on their way to the next life.

It is sometimes said that when cherry blossoms are in bloom evil spirits run wild in them, and the mention of demons suggests that the poet shares this feeling. In fact, the cherry blossom festivals that occur all around Japan under various names originally arose to quell such demons. Being a priest, this poet was well qualified to sense these obstacles to Buddhist salvation.

Maji nakute / nōkyō sumishi / hana no hiru
Demon things without / sutra chanting completed / cherry blossom's noon

Nawa Sankanchiku (1892–1975) was a follower of Ōsuga Otsuji and also editor of *Kakeaoi*, one of the magazines founded in western Japan by Masaoka Shiki's followers. This poem is from *Sankanchiku kushū* (1967).

In Kamakura
even after night has come
rain wets the flowers

Hoshino Takashi

Even though sad that the rain will shorten the flowers' lives, he enjoys the beauty of the rain-soaked blossoms.

Takashi also wrote this haiku: "At Kamakura/Yoritomo and Kyoshi heard/cicadas sing." For him, Kamakura is associated with both Minamoto no Yoritomo, the great warlord who established the Kamakura shogunate there in 1185, and the haiku poet Takahama Kyoshi, who lived there for most of his life.

Kyoshi himself wrote many well-known haiku about the sights and scenery of Kamakura, including: "Winter's chill/lingers on, astonishing/Kamakura." This poem has given Kamakura the status of a *haimakura*, a special place name that inspires other haiku poets, and from some point it acquired a certain luster and gravitas. As a great-grandchild of Kyoshi, Takashi is particularly aware of this aspect of Kamakura, and this poem embodies it.

> *Kamakura no / yoru ni irite mo / hana no ame*
> Kamakura's / night at entered even / flowers' rain

Hoshino Takashi (b. 1952) studied haiku with his grandmother Hoshino Tatsuko, the daughter of Takahama Kyoshi. He leads and is editor in chief of *Tamamo*, which was founded by his grandmother. This poem is from *Yato* (1997).

Flying through the sky
in a cluster—
a flurry of cherry blossoms

Takano Sujū

This poem unfolds almost like a riddle. What might follow, after the clustered mass that flies through the sky of the first two lines? Personally, I would be at a loss to reply. It cannot be birds—they can fly close together, but not close enough to appear as a solid clump. What about butterflies? If they were clustered in such a tight mass they would be unable to move.

Reading on, the unexpected answer comes: this is a dense mass of cherry blossom petals blown by a strong wind across the sky. Such flurries of petals are usually thought of as light swirls lifted on a gust, but here they seem to be a single mass flying across the sky, as if they had a will of their own, making a strange spectacle. Seen through the swirling petals all around him, this flying cluster seems almost like the spirit of the blossoms in concentrated form.

This poem was composed at Yoshino, famous for its cherry blossom trees.

Sora o yuku / hito katamari no / hanafubuki
Sky moving through / a cluster of / flower flurry

Takano Sujū (1893–1973) was a follower of Takahama Kyoshi and became one of the four most esteemed poets of *Hototogisu* in the 1920s (Four S's*). He stopped writing haiku for some time in order to pursue his career as a doctor of forensic medicine. After his retirement, he founded and led *Seri*. This poem is from *Yakashū* (1953).

Want to quit quit quit
this office job—falling
flowers flying flowers

Matsumoto Tefuko

I want to quit working in an office, want to quit it more than anything. Spring is at its peak, the earth is filled with falling cherry blossoms, and the sky is filled with scattering petals flying everywhere.

The threefold repetition of "quit," odd though it is, well conveys the strength of her longing to resign from her job. However, we can imagine that she's very unlikely to really quit, no matter how much she wants to. If she allows herself to act on this momentary impulse, she will not be able to get another job. The stagnant employment situation in Japan known as the "Employment Ice Age," a part of our contemporary reality, lies behind this poem.

"Falling flowers flying flowers" (*rakka hika*) is a variation on "flying flowers falling flowers" (*hika rakka*), a phrase that was coined by Mizuhara Shūōshi. The poets of *Ashibi* took up Shūōshi's original "flying flowers falling flowers" and so over-used it that ultimately Shūōshi forbade its use altogether. In spite of that, it continued to be used and is still widespread in the world of haiku. Tefuko here uses it in reverse order, as "falling flowers flying flowers." This must be because she wanted to make all three segments of the poem begin with a syllable that contains the vowel sound *a* (pronounced *ah* in Japanese): *kaisha, yametashi, rakka*. The effect is also to intensify the sense of desperation.

The more I look at this poem, the more the repeated word *yametashi* itself begins to look like scattering blossoms.

> *Kaisha yametashi / yametashi yametashi / rakka hika*
> Company want to quit / want to quit want to quit / falling flowers flying flowers

Matsumoto Tefuko (b. 1981) studied haiku with Tsuji Momoko* and is a contributor to Momoko's *Dōji*. She was selected as one of twenty-two emerging haiku poets in the haiku anthology *Haikore* (2011), where this poem appears.

"You can stop working now"
whisper the flowering
cherry blossoms

Imase Gōichi

The poet was for many years a high school teacher and this was written on the eve of his retirement. As he feasts his eyes on the beautiful cherry blossoms, they seem to be inviting him to rest after his long labors. Such inner voices transferred to natural things often appear in Gōichi's poems. Here, as he mulls over the long years of effort, he must be experiencing the joy of liberation but at the same time, a sense of regret as a long career comes to an end.

In Tokyo, the cherry blossoms usually bloom at the beginning of April, although in recent years they tend to be earlier. The Japanese school year also begins in April, so the blossoms naturally suggest the new students, excited as they begin a fresh stage of their lives. Their happy faces contrast with the clouds shadowing the heart of the retiring teacher.

"So many different things/come to mind when I see/the cherry blossoms," wrote Bashō.* The cherry blossoms have always affected peoples' hearts in many ways.

> *Mō tsutome / nakute mo ii to / sakura saku*
> Enough work / no more okay say / cherry blossoms in flower

Imase Gōichi (b. 1936) studied haiku as a member of Yamaguchi Seison's *Natsukusa*, and was a founding contributor to Nomura Toshirō's *Oki*. Later he founded *Taigan*, and he still leads it. This poem is from *Shinsen* (2002).

In the unpeopled
Forest of the Night—
see, the cherry blossoms!

Komakine Junko

Close to the poet's hometown of Iwaki is a place called the Forest of the Night (Yonomori), which has long been famous for its cherry blossoms. In spring the blossoms used to be illuminated at night, and there is even a train station that bears the place's name.

However, the Forest of the Night is in Fukushima Prefecture and was heavily contaminated by radioactivity from the Fukushima Daiichi nuclear power plant accident that followed the Great East Japan Earthquake and tsunami on March 11, 2011. When this poem was written, no one was allowed to set foot there, and the train station was also closed, wrapped in a silence as thick as a sorcerer's spell. After being rebuilt, the station was reopened in March 2020, but the local residents were still not allowed to return to their homes.

When spring comes, the cherry blossoms still flower in the darkness of the Forest of the Night, even now when no one is there to see them. The image of the blossoms enfolds the poet's prayer to return to her home, take up her life where it broke off, and enjoy the natural beauty of her hometown again.

Miru hito mo / naki Yonomori no / sakura kana
To see people even / none Night's Forest's / cherry blossoms!

Komakine Junko (b. 1952) is a native of Fukushima Prefecture. After a decade of membership in *Seizan*, in 2005 she joined Yamashita Chizuko in founding the magazine *Rin*, which focuses on women haiku poets, and currently serves as its editor. This poem is from the prizewinning *Yoru no mori* (2016).

To quiet the heart of
the mountain god
the cherry blossoms opened

Takada Chōi

These cherry trees are flowering deep among the mountains, not down at the foot where people live. Humans almost never see them, but when the deity who presides over the mountain gazes on them, they do his heart good.

At one time the flowering of the mountain cherry blossoms was the time of an advance celebration of a good rice harvest. This was based on the traditional poetic comparison of the cherry blossoms to snow. When snow lay deep in the mountains, the farmers could be sure of an abundant supply of snow meltwater in the coming months, which was necessary for the young rice plants to grow. The blossoms, because of their visual resemblance to snow, thus became prophets. With its slightly formal ceremonial quality, this poem reminds us of the old belief.

Chōi made a deep study of the history of the Shinto prayers called *norito*, and at one time served as the head priest of Minatogawa Shrine in Kobe.

> *Yamazumi o / suzushimu sakura / sakinikeri*
> Mountain god / quiet the heart cherry trees / bloomed

Takada Chōi (1886–1930) began writing haiku under the influence of his high school teacher Ōtani Jōseki. After graduation, he joined *Hototogisu* and became a follower of Takahama Kyoshi, but after Kyoshi's withdrawal from the haiku world, Chōi distanced himself from *Hototogisu* and contributed to *Kakeaoi*. He also helped found Usuda Arō's *Shakunage*. This poem is from *Chōi haiku zenshū* (1941), edited by Takagi Sōgo.

He strips the pelt off at noon
under the cherry trees
in full bloom

Satō Onifusa

Fur used to be necessary for humans to endure and survive through extreme cold. Having skinned the animal, the man must be looking up at the cherry blossoms with a feeling of relief at having made it alive through another winter.

The flowering of the cherry blossoms marks the beginning of the agricultural season, and for over a thousand years the beauty of their blossoms has been celebrated in Japanese poetry. There is something almost grotesque in the juxtaposition of this flower with stripping the pelt off a dead animal. He has left the corpse of the dead and skinned animal on the ground and the smell of blood is in the air.

This is a poem that feels born out of the poet's actual experience. At the same time, it can also be read as describing a man in prehistoric times living in close confrontation with nature. This must be because Onifusa has shown something at the basis of human life.

Kegawa hagu / nitchū sakura / mankai ni
Pelt strip / noon cherry trees / full bloom in

Satō Onifusa (1919–2002) studied haiku with Saitō Sanki and was one of the postwar poets who stressed social awareness in haiku. After contributing to Yamaguchi Seishi's *Tenrō* and other magazines, in 1980 he founded and led *Kogumaza*. This poem is from *Na mo naki nichiya* (1951).

In full flower
the cherry blossoms
look so wan and pale

Nozawa Setsuko

These are cherry blossoms at their height, fully open. However, the joy of the opening is over. Already they are beginning to look a little pallid. "Wan and pale" (*aozame*) can refer to the flowers at dawn or evening, but I prefer to read it as descriptive of the flowers at noon, the brightness of the hour contrasting with the washed-out color of the flowers.

The medieval Japanese sense of beauty is best expressed in the famous lines from Yoshida Kenkō's *Essays in Idleness* (*Tsurezuregusa*, fourteenth century): "Should we look at the spring blossoms only in full flower, or the moon only when cloudless and clear?"* The cherry blossoms at their zenith and the moon when full were both shunned as over-perfect. This aesthetic is reflected in the pale cherry blossoms in full bloom. You almost feel that the cherry blossoms themselves share it, and grow pale and wan with shame.

Setsuko contracted spinal tuberculosis as a teenager and was an invalid for many years. Having lived with illness so long, she may have seen herself reflected in the pallor of the cherry blossoms.

Sakimichite / sakura aozame / itaru kana
In full flower / cherry blossoms pale / are!

Nozawa Setsuko (1920–1995) contributed to Usuda Arō's *Shakunage* before the war and to Ōno Rinka's *Hama* after it. After recovering from her years of illness, she became a teacher of ikebana, wrote essays and manuals on haiku, and in 1971 founded *Ran*, through which she mentored a number of younger poets. This poem is from *Hisen* (1974).

Back and forth, back and forth
the big branch sways—
cherry blossoms open wide

Murakami Kijō

Among the multitude of excellent modern haiku on the topic of cherry blossoms, this poem is arguably the pinnacle. It is also an exemplary model of a "one thing haiku," that is, a haiku that focuses on a single thing (*ichimotsu haiku*) rather than being a juxtaposition of two. The meaning is clear as day: his gaze zeroes in on a single large bough of a cherry tree in full bloom.

The first two lines, "Back and forth, back and forth/the big branch sways," describe the branch, but do not name the tree. Reading on to the third line, we discover it is a cherry tree. Cherry trees are most themselves when in full flower. It almost seems as though the blossoms on this tree suddenly open all at once, like a magical tree in a fairytale.

The onomatopoeic *yusayusa to* ("back and forth, back and forth") is perfect here. There is a bit of overlap with the swaying described by *yururu*, but together the words give a vivid sense of motion.

Yusayusa to / *ōeda yururu* / *sakura kana*
Back and forth / big branch sways / cherry blossoms

Murakami Kijō (1865–1938) studied haiku with Masaoka Shiki and Takahama Kyoshi and became one of the leading poets of the early *Hototogisu*. His deafness forced him to become a judicial scrivener instead of the judge he had dreamed of being, and due to illness and poverty he struggled to support his wife and ten children. This poem, composed in 1919, is from *Kijō kushū* (1940).

Plied that boy with saké
'til he was drunk as a lord—
oh, the blossoms!

Sakamoto Shihōda

Wakashu is an Edo period (1603–1867) word for a young man who has not yet come of age. It can also mean a young man in a same-sex relationship, as it does here. The speaker came with the young man in tow to drink under the blossoms. The fully open flowers and the handsome, drunken youth emanate the same voluptuous beauty.

Shihōda, who lived in the Meiji era (1868–1912), is not describing something from his own experience. There is a scene of drinking under the blossoms in *The Great Mirror of Male Love* (*Nanshoku ōkagami*), Ihara Saikaku's seventeenth-century collection of stories of gay male love. Shihōda entered the world of that time in his imagination and wrote about what he found there. This is a historical poem. In the same vein, he also wrote: "In a palanquin/I enter the pleasure quarters—/oh, the blossoms!" (*Shin haiku*).

It seems that for Shihōda the cherry blossoms were associated with the Edo period's spirit of playfulness. This lighthearted feeling has been mostly lost in contemporary haiku.

> *Sake shiite / wakashu o yowasu / sakura kana*
> Saké plied / young man made drunk / cherry blossoms!

Sakamoto Shihōda (1873–1917) was a professor of literature and a librarian at Tokyo Imperial University. He was mentored in haiku by Masaoka Shiki and contributed to the extension of the sketch from life* into prose, publishing often in *Hototogisu*. This poem is from *Shunkashūtō: Haru no bu* (1901), compiled by Masaoka Shiki.

In the water of the pond
a cresset collapses—
oh, the blossoms!

Ōtani Jōseki

It's night, and the cherry trees in the garden are in full flower, illuminated by cressets (iron baskets holding burning wood, used as lights). Blossoms and cressets are both reflected in the garden pond, but as he is thinking this beautiful sight might last forever, suddenly the wood in one of the cressets collapses with a hiss. As the reflection breaks up, perhaps he returns to himself from the thoughts inspired by the night cherry blossoms.

The first two lines, "In the water of the pond/a cresset collapses" are the scene as it is reflected in the water, while the last line, "oh, the blossoms!" must be the blossoms as they are reflected in the water and also as they are seen on the shore of the pond.

There have been so many haiku about scenes reflected in water that to a contemporary reader this poem may not seem original. But in fact, this poem itself may be the ur-poem, the mother of them all. Remarkably enough, it does not even use the word "reflected." What we see is the reflected scene as it changes. This brilliant stroke makes the poem fresh even today.

Sensui ni / kagari kuzururu / sakura kana
In pond water / cresset collapses / cherry blossoms!

Ōtani Jōseki (1875–1933) was introduced to haiku as a high school student through his classmates Takahama Kyoshi and Kawahigashi Hekigotō. After coming to Tokyo, he became a follower of Masaoka Shiki and contributed to *Hototogisu*. This poem is from *Ochitsubaki* (1918).

Felled by the wind—
a cluster of
Yang Guifei cherry blossoms

Sugita Hisajo

The wind has blown off a cluster of Yang Guifei cherry blossoms all at once, instead of scattering the petals separately.

According to the headnote, this is the first of six haiku on the Yang Guifei cherry blossoms that the poet composed on the same day. This variety has a double-blooming pink blossom about 5 centimeters in diameter. It takes its name from the favorite consort of Emperor Xuanzong of the Tang dynasty, whose guards forced him to have her murdered during the An Lushan Rebellion (755–763). There is a story that this variety of Japanese cherry tree was named after the Emperor's famous consort because it resembles the flowering crab apple, to which he once compared his beloved's sleepy face. Another story has it that it acquired its name because Priest Gensō of Kōfukuji Temple in Nara, whose name is written with the same characters as Emperor Xuanzong, had a special fondness for it. No one knows for sure, but the association of this flower with Yang Guifei is put to excellent use in this poem.

The tragic fate of Yang Guifei is echoed in the cherry blossoms that fell whole in a single cluster rather than scattering in the normal way. It also recalls Hisajo herself, who was treated cruelly by her teacher Takahama Kyoshi in spite of her extraordinary talent.

> *Kaze ni otsu / Yōkihizakura / fusa no mama*
> Wind in fall / Yang Guifei cherry blossoms / cluster unbroken

Sugita Hisajo (1890–1946) is arguably the greatest woman haiku poet of modern Japan. She began submitting her haiku to *Hototogisu* in the 1910s and with the support of Takahama Kyoshi became a member of the group in 1934. Two years later, however, Kyoshi expelled her from the group for reasons that have never been fully explained. This poem is from *Sugita Hisajo kushū* (1952).

The pale gray blossoms
are
not an illusion—they scatter

Tabata Mihojo

The pale gray cherry blossoms without a doubt exist, and are not an illusion. And like all that exists, they end, they scatter.

These are the blossoms of The Pale Gray Cherry Tree (Usuzumizakura) in the city of Motosu in Gifu Prefecture, a double weeping cherry that is over 1,500 years old. As the flowering progresses, the blossoms magically change color. The buds are light peach, the blossoms when fully open are white and then, just before scattering, the petals turn a pale gray like thin sumi ink. It is from this last stage that the tree takes its name.

This poem is about the poet's deep emotion upon encountering this famous tree. Its name is not just a figure of speech, nor is the tree itself "an illusion." As the name says, its petals really are pale gray. Like all things its beauty is fleeting, and the petals have begun to scatter. The poet cannot turn away from this reality. The run-on second line, spilling over into the third, "are/not an illusion," expresses the force of her encounter with this ancient tree.

Usuzumi no / *sakura* **maboroshi** / **narazu chiru**
Pale gray / cherry blossoms illusion / not being scatter

Tabata Mihojo (1909–2001) studied haiku with Takahama Kyoshi and other *Hototogisu* leaders and was a lifelong contributor to the magazine. This poem is from *Mihojo shō* (1982).

In the women divers' hut
the electric meter
revolves

Sugihara Yūshi

Even in the women divers' hut—not a proper house but a place for the divers to rest—there is an electric meter. The dial with gradations marked on it is revolving.

The poet was startled to see that the divers, who follow the age-old occupation of free diving for seafood and seaweed, use electric appliances when they return to their hut. Maybe it is a refrigerator to store their catch. Or a washing machine to wash their clothes. Or an electric range for preparing meals. The image of the revolving meter makes the reader wonder what it is measuring.

The expression "the meter revolves," though common in everyday speech, is not really accurate. Strictly speaking, you ought to say "the electric meter's dial revolves." However, that would run over the haiku's syllabic limit. I interpret the use of the abbreviation as due to the poet's respect for form. The description may be a little imprecise but it draws you in.

Amagoya no / denki mētā / mawari ori
Woman diver hut's / electric meter / revolves

Sugihara Yūshi (b. 1979) studies haiku with Motoi Ei* and Mimura Jun'ya. He is on the steering committee of Ei's *Natsushio* and is a contributor to Jun'ya's *Sazanka*. This poem is from *Sakippo e* (2010).

Digging down
the razor clam
stands up straight in water

Enomoto Yumi

The razor clam's body was at a slant when it started burrowing down into the sand, but now it is completely upright in the shallow tidepool. That strong verticality is what the poem captures. It evokes a sense of the strong will of the clam, and has an almost otherworldly air.

This poem is the second of a three-poem sequence. The first poem in the sequence is "Digging in the sand/the razor clam flops/over and up" and the third poem is "At full tide/still visible—/the razor clam's hole."

In the first poem, the location of the razor clam when it starts digging in the sand is probably a tidepool at low tide. The razor clam is trying to burrow down under the sand. In the third poem, the clam has already disappeared into the sand leaving a hole behind, which is now filled with sea water. Several hours must have passed between the first and third poems, so the poet must have been observing this razor clam for quite some time. This bespeaks a deep respect for nature.

Kuguri yuku / mategai sutto / mizu ni tatsu
Burrows down / razor clam straight / water in stands

Enomoto Yumi (b. 1974) was a follower of Nishino Fumiyo* and contributed to Fumiyo's *Fumi* until it was discontinued. She now publishes *Nandja* (its name is taken from André Breton's novel *Nadja*), a small magazine begun in 2008 by herself and seven other poets including Ishida Kyōko. This poem is from *Menkoiko* (2007).

One, two, three, four
five, six, seven, eight—
cherry blossom shells

Kakuta Chikurei

A list poem, one to eight, with the shells of cherry blossom clams (*Nitidotellina hokkaidoensis*) at the end. In terms of form, this is an extremely daring poem. Is he counting a lot of these tiny pink shells that washed up on the beach in early spring, pointing them out one by one? Or has he already picked up the shells and is counting them now, as he holds them in his hand? Whichever it is, you can feel his heart dancing at the sight of their beauty.

This poem may have influenced Kubota Mantarō's "One haiku, two haiku/three, four, five haiku/a withered field haiku." As a middle school student, Mantarō participated in the haiku reform group called the Shūseikai*[1] that Chikurei formed with Ozaki Kōyō*[2] and Iwaya Sazanami at the turn of the twentieth century.

> *Hī fū mī yō / itsu mu nana ya / sakuragai*
> One two three four / five six seven eight / cherry blossom clams

Kakuta Chikurei (1857–1919) was a poet, a lawyer, and a member of the Diet. This poem is from *Chikurei kushō* (1920).

If there were
>beauty unchanging it would be
>>this cherry blossom shell

Ueda Hizashi

In this world, everything is transient and fleeting, but if there were any unchanging beauty, it could only be what I hold in my hand, this fragile shell of the cherry blossom clam.

Iro usually means "color" but in this poem its meaning is the broader one of the beauty of things. The shell of the cherry blossom clam epitomizes this beauty. The poet despairs as she confronts this world in all its mutability and constant change. Out of this despair comes the phrase "if there were unchanging beauty." Not "when" or "because" but *if*. The absence of unchanging, immutable beauty is the premise.

The deeper her despair about the mutable world, the brighter shines the beauty of the shell of the cherry blossom clam.

>*Kari no yo ni / iro araba kono / sakuragai*
>In fleeting world / color if there were this / cherry blossom shell

Ueda Hizashi (b. 1961) began composing haiku in her teens under the guidance of her father Ueda Gosengoku, and contributed to his *Aze*. After her father died, she founded *Ranburu* and is its leader. This poem is from her prizewinning collection *Waon* (2010).

The tulip
is about to lose
its petals

Hatano Sōha

There is a children's song about the tulip that goes "it's bloomed, it's bloomed!" The little children project their future hopes onto the flower. This flower, in contrast, has already reached its end. The petals have not yet fallen, but they will very soon. The description of its in-between state draws you in.

The tulip was an important flower for Sōha because his teacher Takahama Kyoshi used it in a poem he composed for the first issue of Sōha's magazine *Ao* (*Blue*) in May 1954: "The magazine/called *Blue,*/spring tulips, and hyacinths." Here, three fresh and beautiful things—the magazine, a tulip, and a hyacinth—are equated, like a series of three fresh and beautiful things in a row, expressing Kyoshi's wish for the success of Sōha's new endeavor. That tulip in turn becomes a kind of second self for Sōha. Perhaps by saying the tulip is about to lose its petals, Sōha is hinting at his own imminent death? Or it may be that his poem suggests that a distance had grown up between Sōha and Kyoshi and that the relations between *Ao* and Kyoshi's *Hototogisu* had become strained. In any case, things have changed from the way they were at the beginning.

A new uncertainty has crept into the poet's feeling about his own life.

Chūrippu / *hanabira hazure* / *kakete ori*
Tulip / petal come off / about to

Hatano Sōha (1923–1991) was an avid reader of *Hototogisu* in his teens, and after college became a follower of Takahama Kyoshi. He later founded and led *Ao*, which nurtured many young poets. This poem, composed in 1989, is from his complete works, *Hatano Sōha zenshū*, vol. 2 (1992).

At the Lost and Found's
little window
a hyacinth blooms

Natsui Itsuki

On the counter in front of the window of the Lost and Found—it might be at a police station or a train station—sits a potted hyacinth. Its small, curly blue flowers could be read as an image of the anxiety that fills the people who visit in search of their lost belongings. For the workers behind the counter, on the other hand, the flowers could be a screen or a bulwark against the anxious feelings of their visitors.

In Japanese, the first and last words of the poem (*ishitsubutsu* and *hiyanshinsu*) both have "i" for their first vowel and "u" for their last and include the syllable "shi." (The translation repeats "a" and "s.") Losing and blooming form a circle of sound. The resonance makes me feel a strange sense of peace.

The structure of this haiku is very simple—it focuses on only one thing rather than juxtaposing two, and is made up of three nouns connected by the possessive particle *no*—but it is very thoughtfully made. There is room to imagine a variety of dramatic scenes taking place under its wings.

Ishitsubutsu / kakari no mado no / hiyashinsu
Lost and Found / Department's window's / hyacinth

Natsui Itsuki (b. 1957) is a follower of Kuroda Momoko and a member of Momoko's *Aoi*, as well as the leader of the haiku group *Itsukigumi*. Through numerous introductory books on haiku and media appearances, she makes haiku accessible to a wide audience. This poem is from *Itsuki shū* (1999).

The birds have mated and
the puddle left by the rain
is dazzling bright

Kabata Yoshio

Under what conditions do birds mate? A certain degree of warmth is surely required, but what about light? Mating would hardly take place in the dark, but the light would not need to be "dazzling bright" either. In that sense, "birds mating" and "dazzling bright" are not directly related. And that lack of relation is what makes this poem work.

The "puddle" is "dazzling bright" for the two birds in the trees. The image seems to capture the ecstatic feeling of the birds who have fulfilled their instinctual longing to procreate. The enjambment, or running over, of *sakari-tari* ("have/mated") from the first segment to the second suggests the brevity and fleeting nature of their act.

This is a poem of youth.

Tori sakari / *tari niwatazumi* / *mabushikute*
Birds mat- / ed puddle / dazzling bright

Kabata Yoshio (1926–1971) was a follower of Tomiyasu Fūsei and a contributor to *Wakaba*. This poem is from *Jiritsu* (1957).

Even when I'm alone
the waves come to call—
flowering sweet peas

Tomooka Shikyō

Even when he is all alone on the beach, the waves still lap at the shore, and nearby there is a bright field of sweet peas in flower.

This poem was composed in spring, 1995, not long after the January 17 Great Hanshin-Awaji Earthquake. Shikyō, who experienced the earthquake, wrote fifty-nine haiku about it, including some excellent ones that are also precious records of the disaster, like these: "Fallen. Split. Smashed./Collapsed. A town of rubble—/winter sparrow," and "Glittering clouds/of winter dust rise—/transporting the dead."

The poem here comes immediately after those fifty-nine, and the note to it is "Cape Anori," which overlooks Matoya Bay on the Shima Peninsula, not far from his disaster-stricken town.

The earthquake brought home to the poet the tremendous power of nature and its danger, but now on the quiet shore with the gentle lapping of the waves and the flowering sweet peas tossed in the breeze, he feels at peace. In this too he feels the power of nature, how it can solace and encourage a human being, a survivor.

Human beings have no choice but to live within nature and together with it. That insight, perhaps won from his own suffering, is the basis of this poem.

Tada hitori / ni mo nami wa kuru / hana endo
All alone / even waves come / flowering sweet peas

Tomooka Shikyō (b. 1934) first studied haiku with Hatano Sōha and contributed to *Ao*, then moved to Iida Ryūta's *Unmo*. Later he founded and led *Yashi* until 2012. This poem is from *Akuruhi* (1996).

A butterfly
in whose eyes I am a giant monster
wings on by

Sōda Yasumasa

Butterflies are often described in haiku as small and pretty harbingers of spring. But the butterfly in this poem is different—the poem is a record of how a butterfly looks at the speaker as it passes by, and decides he must be a monster or goblin. The point is that to a small creature like a butterfly, that is how a human being looks. Seen through the eyes of a butterfly, a human being is perceived anew.

What is strange is that the speaker experiences a direct glimpse of the butterfly's bizarre compound eye image of himself. Perhaps the "I" of this poem is divided into two: himself and the butterfly. This is a kind of variation on Zhuangzi's dream of the butterfly, in which he could not tell if he was a man dreaming he was a butterfly or a butterfly dreaming it was a man.* But there is no sense of fleeting beauty in this poem. In fact, you might even call it grotesque.

Yasumasa also composed other butterfly haiku that are rather unusual: "Of the human body and/the butterfly, which is/the heavier?" and "In autumn's depths/I mix most deeply/with the butterfly."

> *Chō ware o / bakemono to mite / sugiyukeri*
> Butterfly me / monster as seeing / passes by

Sōda Yasumasa (b. 1930) was a follower of Yamaguchi Seishi. As a professional book editor, he was involved in several publications on haiku, including *Gendai haiku zenshū* (1977–1978), a six-volume compilation of modern haiku. This poem is from *Hyakutō* (2000).

The wind of spring
is blowing all over
my whole face today!

Narita Senkū

In *Sanzōshi*, a poetic treatise based on Bashō's* teachings, a distinction is drawn between "spring rain" (*harusame*) and "the rain of spring" (*haru no ame*). The former is characteristic of late spring and falls continuously and gently, while the latter is a general term for rain that falls anytime in spring. By the same token, the "spring wind" (*harukaze*), and "the wind of spring" (*haru no kaze*) also differ. The former blows softly in late spring, while the latter is a general term for any wind or breeze in spring.

In this poem, the wind of spring (*haru no kaze*) can hardly be a gentle breeze, since it is described as "blowing all over my whole face." It must be blowing rather strongly. And yet it does not have the coldness of the north wind. It includes warmth. The poem conveys the joy of spring felt after having come through the harsh winter.

Senkū's hometown was in Aomori, the cold, northernmost prefecture of Japan's main island, in the area known as Tsugaru, and this is what the winds of spring are like there. The oddness of sensing the spring all over his face, but nowhere else, gives rise to the wry humor of the poem. This poem evokes the carefree personality of Senkū himself.

> *Haru no kaze* / *kao ippai ni* / *fuku hi kana*
> Spring's wind / face full in / blows day

Narita Senkū (1921–2007) was a member of Nakamura Kusatao's *Banryoku* from its inception, and after Kusatao's death was eventually prevailed upon to become editor of its magazine and then its leader. He spent most of his life in Aomori and was a central figure in haiku activities there. This poem is from *Jippōgin* (2007).

Spring breezes—
the ship calls in at Iyo for
Dōgo Hot Springs

Yanagihara Kyokudō

When the ship that goes around the Seto Inland Sea nears Matsuyama in Iyo (the earlier name for Ehime Prefecture), it calls in at the port of Takahama. There the passengers debark and head for the healing waters of Dōgo Hot Springs. They are not there to go sightseeing in Matsuyama. They are mostly merchants traveling on business, who may be stopping off at several towns as they circuit the Inland Sea and make a point of going to the hot springs, reputed to be the oldest in Japan, when their ship stops there. The medical efficacy of the water was long believed to be miraculous, so not to take advantage of the chance to visit it was almost unthinkable.

This early twentieth-century poem gives a sense of the leisurely quality of life then compared to now. "Spring breezes" (*harukaze*) goes well with this, adding a feeling of peace and calm. The second line, "the ship calls in at Iyo for" is one syllable over the usual seven, and that too goes with the leisurely feeling of making a detour.

Later, in 1928, Takahama Kyoshi wrote this haiku: "My hometown lit up/by the moon as I cross the harbor—/only that." Kyoshi must have been thinking of his old friend Kyokudō's haiku, which had been highly praised by their good friend and haiku mentor Masaoka Shiki.

Harukaze ya / fune Iyo ni yorite / Dōgo no Yu
Spring breeze / ship Iyo at makes a stop / Dōgo Hot Springs

Yanagihara Kyokudō (1867–1957), a haiku protégé of Masaoka Shiki, launched *Hototogisu* in 1897 but handed it over to Takahama Kyoshi the following year. Later he founded and led *Keitō*. This poem is from *Shunkashūtō: Haru no bu* (1901), compiled by Masaoka Shiki.

So many duplicates of myself
born —
soap bubbles

Tsugawa Eriko

As the poet blows soap bubbles for fun, she notices that she is reflected in each bubble. But the word "reflected" is omitted, and instead she exclaims without explanation that myriad duplicates of herself have been born. This way of perceiving expands her world and conveys her delight in a more immediate way than an explanatory "reflected" would. It also creates a slightly off-center and uncanny feeling. At the root of this poem is the idea that at any moment oneself, human beings, and life itself can change shape.

In 2007, Tsugawa Eriko received the Kadokawa Haiku Prize for *Haru no neko*, which has these haiku: "My arm on/the rattan chair—like/ floating in water" and "The pendant—/so large in the middle/of this sweaty body." These poems convey an almost physical sense of an arm resting on the rattan chair, and of a sweaty chest on which a pendant hangs.

This poet directly faces the self and describes it—I feel something brave and clear-eyed in her stance.

> *Takusan no / ware ga umaruru / shabondama*
> Many of / me are born / soap bubbles

Tsugawa Eriko (b. 1968) is a follower of Washitani Nanako and Yamagami Kimio. She was a contributor to *Nanpū*, and led the magazine from 2014 through 2019. This poem is from the prizewinning *Waon* (2006).

Woke up late, I did—
in honor of Meng Haoran
founder of the art

Mizuhara Shūōshi

I woke late on purpose, says the poet, because I venerate Meng Haoran, who made poetry out of rising late in spring.

To sleep soundly past dawn on spring mornings is a wonderful feeling, incarnated in the haiku seasonal image "waking up late." The Tang dynasty poet Meng Haoran (689–740) also knew this feeling. The first two lines of his famous quatrain "Spring Dawn" are: "Spring slumber forgets the dawn/wakens to birdsong everywhere." Sleeping so deeply in spring, he does not notice when dawn comes, but then awakens to the world filled with the song of birds.

Mentioning waking up late and Meng Haoran is like striking a bell that awakens echoes of the poem "Spring Dawn" in the reader's mind. The birds that the ancient poet heard seem to sing in the background of the modern poet's verse. In a minimalist form of poetry like haiku, quotation and allusion play an important role, and this poem is one of the most successful examples.

Asane seri / Mōkōzen o / shiso to shite
Waking up late / Meng Haoran / venerable ancestor making

Mizuhara Shūōshi (1892–1981) was a follower of Takahama Kyoshi and one of the so-called Four S's,* but later criticized Kyoshi and left the group. As the founder of *Ashibi*, he nurtured many distinguished poets, including Ishida Hakyō and Katō Shūson. This poem is from *Ryoshū* (1961).

A newborn fly
already using its wings—to flee
from its foes

Akimoto Fujio

The seasonal image "spring fly" (*haru no hae*) usually means a fly that has lived through the winter and is more or less exhausted. In contrast, the seasonal image "newly born fly" (*hae umaru*), used here, denotes a newborn fly who is full of life and can fly quickly. But it's hard to resist laughing when you see it using that youthful vitality to flee from a predator.

The personification implicit in saying "flee from its foes" (*tonsō*) which usually describes a person fleeing for their life from an enemy, instead of the more common "run away" (*tōsō*), which just means running away in general, adds another, deeper dimension to the humor.

Fujio, one of the leading poets of the New Rising Haiku movement,* was caught up in the Haiku Persecution Incident of 1940–1943, a collective series of arrests of poets affiliated with "anti-establishment" haiku magazines in Kyoto and Tokyo, and spent two years in jail. He was the only poet who continued to write haiku while incarcerated. It is hard to read this haiku without remembering his experience and imagining that he is cheering the fly on as it flees its predator.

Hae umare / haya tonsō no / hane tsukau
Fly born / already making itself scarce / wings uses

Akimoto Fujio (1901–1977) was a founding contributor to Yamaguchi Seishi's *Tenrō* after World War II, as well as founder and leader of *Hyōkai*. This poem is from *Kobu* (1950).

"Stop tickling me!"
On the Enkū Buddha
the kitten's paw

Katō Shūson

The kitten is touching one of the thousands of small wooden carvings of the Buddha made by the monk Enkū (1632–1695) as he traveled around Japan.

Enkū's works are now highly esteemed for their originality and artistic excellence. However, in earlier times children would often take them out of the halls of worship where they were kept and play with them like dolls. In such an age, a curious kitten might well approach and place a paw on the holy image. The voice exclaiming "Stop tickling me!" is that of the Enkū Buddha, but the poet's voice seems to be coming out of the statue, reacting playfully to the touch of the cute kitten.

Enkū was a contemporary of the great poet Bashō,[*1] and Shūson was a great admirer of both.

Kusuguttai zo / Enkūbutsu ni / koneko no te
It tickles! / Enkū Buddha on / kitten's paw

Katō Shūson (1905–1993) was a follower of Mizuhara Shūōshi and was also one of the "humanist" poets.[*2] After he founded *Kanrai*, he nurtured many talented haiku poets, including Mori Sumio and Kaneko Tōta. This poem is from *Fukkoshi* (1976).

The mud-plastered ridge between paddies makes a sweeping curve— right here

Kiyosaki Toshio

The poet feels drawn to the place where the mud-plastered ridge between the paddy fields bends in a sweeping curve.

"Mud-plastered ridge" is a seasonal image. During the rice-growing season, the sides of the ridges between rice fields are plastered with mud so that the water in which the rice plants grow will not seep out.

Normally, we would expect a tranquil farming scene to unfold before us. But "makes a sweeping curve" suggests action and leads you to imagine the actual position of the speaker: he would be standing near a corner of the paddy field, admiring the sweeping curve as it bends around the corner.

When plastering the sides of the ridge, the angled corners are filled in so that they look curved. This is one of the most difficult parts of mud plastering. As I mull over the image of the curved corner, so immediate because of that "right here," I seem to see myself with the farmers, smoothing and shaping as they move along the ridge.

Nuriaze no / gūtto magari / iru tokoro
Mud-plastered ridge's / sweeping curve / is here place

Kiyosaki Toshio (1922–1999) studied haiku with Tomiyasu Fūsei and Takahama Kyoshi, and he inherited the leadership of *Wakaba* from Fūsei. This poem is from *Keifu* (1985).

Mud plastering done
the paddy ridge reflects
some flying thing

Kiyohara Kaidō

The mud plastering of the sides of the ridge between the rice paddy fields is complete and something flying is reflected there.

Once the soil is tilled, the next chore is to plaster the sides of the ridge between the rice paddy fields with mud. This prevents the water in the paddy field from leaking out and the fertilizer from running off. In this poem, the task has been skillfully completed and a flying creature of some sort is reflected in the smooth mud-plaster. But what is this flying creature? The ambiguity—is it a bird? a butterfly?—is intriguing. This is, after all, a ridge plastered with mud, and mud does not reflect in the detail that a mirror might. The ambiguous blur of the flying creature nicely conveys the blurriness of the mirroring surface.

Four busy actions—plastering, completed, reflects, flying—are crowded into this poem, yet it nevertheless feels tight and controlled. As each one enters and exits, giving way to the next in line, I feel the light fluttering of butterfly wings.

> *Nurioeshi* / *aze ni utsurite* / *toberu mono*
> Plastering done / paddy ridge in reflected / flying thing

Kiyohara Kaidō (1882–1948) studied haiku with Takahama Kyoshi and was a contributor to *Hototogisu*. He later founded and led *Mokusei* in his native Fukuoka, and spent several years in Korea, where he edited a haiku column for a Korean newspaper. This poem is from *Kaidō kushū* (1934).

"Go out in the world
so wide, make your mark"
sing the frogs to me

Kosugi Yoshi

There is something amusing in Yoshi's writing about small creatures like frogs encouraging him to action. It works well to wrap his intense ambition to succeed in the gentle humor of this image.

Japanese does not distinguish between singular and plural, so the number of frogs is open to interpretation. One frog singing is a bit weak, so it makes more sense to imagine a chorus of them crying out to the skies.

In the back of the poet's head might have been the old saying, "The frog in the well does not know the ocean." Apparently, Yoshi wrote this poem when he resigned from the haiku group he belonged to. That is, the poem may be saying: I'm leaving the group, which is like the well, and I'm going to be active in the larger world of haiku, which is like the ocean.

> *Yo ni dero to / ware ni kawazu no / nakitatsuru*
> Make your mark / say me to frogs' / loud singing

Kosugi Yoshi (1888–1961) studied haiku with Matsune Tōyōjō and was a founding contributor to Tōyōjō's magazine *Shibugaki*. In 1935, he broke with his mentor and cofounded *Arano*. This poem is from *Yoshi kushū* (1962).

Gripping the gravestone
I washed it well—
then came a minivet's trill

Ishida Akiko

Akiko was the widow of Ishida Hakyō (see page 89). In this poem, she carefully describes the gesture involved in cleaning the gravestone on her visit to her husband's grave. It took a rather long time, but at last she has finished washing the grave. Then she notices a minivet is singing.

The haiku poet Hashimoto Eiji (b. 1947) points out that this poem seems to distantly reverberate against Hakyō's "Frosty grave—/I see it when she lifts me up/in her arms." Her use of the verb "gripping" reminds me of Hakyō's "Lit up by the western sun,/I grip something/in the streetcar." She holds onto the grave almost as if she depends on it to help her live on, just as Hakyō in his poem holds on to something in the streetcar so he can keep standing. Whether consciously or not, her poem surely alludes strongly to her husband's.

The minivet is a small bird about the size of a sparrow and has a high-pitched, metallic trill heard in late spring. Hakyō too must have liked this bird, for he wrote: "When the wind comes/the cypress trees come alive—/the minivet's call."

Haka tsukami / arai owarinu / sanshōkui
Grave holding on to / washing completed / minivet

Ishida Akiko (1915–1975) married the haiku poet Ishida Hakyō when she was 27, and began writing haiku in her 40s while nursing her invalid husband and bringing up their children. First she contributed to Hakyō's *Tsuru,* and after his death, joined Mizuhara Shūōshi's *Ashibi.* This poem is from the complete collection of her works, *Ishida Akiko zenkushū* (1977).

I touch the cuttlefish
with my fingertip—my heart
knows the passing spring

Nakatsuka Ippekirō

The poet touches the raw cuttlefish, perhaps thinking to cook it. The springy, damp feel of it on his fingertip is juxtaposed with his wistful regret at spring's passing.

Regret at the passing of spring is a traditional topic in classical Japanese poetry, and this refreshing way of bringing it into conversation with the matter-of-fact image of touching a raw cuttlefish is very haiku-like. What is also remarkable is the clear contrast drawn between body (the fingertip) and heart within the compass of a single poem.

Composed in 1912, the poem uses literary language but has eighteen syllables—the first segment is six syllables long instead of the usual five. One can read the break from the traditional form as underlining the surprise felt when touching the cuttlefish. This poem is also a forerunner of Hara Sekitei's 1914 "For the purpose of/removing the insides of a cuttlefish—/a woman's hand."

Ika ni fururu / *yubisaki ya haru* / *yuku kokoro*
Cuttlefish touch / fingertip spring / going heart

Nakatsuka Ippekirō (1887–1946) began writing haiku in his teens. He was mentored by Kawahigashi Hekigotō and experimented with such new styles as colloquial and free form haiku. This poem is from *Hakagura* (1913).

The passing spring—
an empty clay pot placed
on the grass

Hasegawa Shunsō

The beautiful season of spring will soon be over. I set an empty pot on top of the verdant grass.

Shunsō's haiku are most often lyrical expressions of feeling, but in this poem he lets a material object, a clay pot placed on the grass, stand in for his emotion. There is a sense of emotional futility. Perhaps his own heart drifting with the passing spring is reflected in the emptiness of the pot. Or we could read the heavy pot pressing down on the tender spring grass as his weariness from day to day.

Shunsō and his wife, who was also a haiku poet, had a bar in the Ginza area of Tokyo, near Izumohashi Bridge, one of the bridges along the canals crisscrossing pre-modern Tokyo. Maybe the pot once held liquor or food but became empty as its contents were used up in the course of his business.

Yuku haru ya / utsuro no kame o / kusa no ue
Passing spring / empty pot / on the grass

Hasegawa Shunsō (1889–1934) worked at Momiyama Shigetsu's publishing company and as an editor of the famed haiku magazine *Haikai zasshi*, and later studied haiku with Watanabe Suiha. Thanks to his friendship with Kubota Mantarō, his small restaurant was visited by many writers and editors, including the novelist and haiku poet Yokomitsu Ri'ichi.* This poem is from *Hasegawa Shunsō kushū* (1936).

Stretched out, my legs reach
far off into the distance
of late spring

Murakami Tomohiko

Stretching out his legs shows that the poet is in a relaxed frame of mind. Nothing in the poem gives a hint of where he is, but I do not want to think of him as being indoors. He should be outside, where he can gaze "far off."

Let's say that on a fine spring day, one of the last days of spring, he is sitting on a grassy patch of warm earth. His legs feel as distant as the far-off mountains, almost like part of them. He senses himself melting into the world but, at the same time, there is the incongruous sense that a part of his body belongs to a different realm of existence.

This is the liminal neither-this-nor-that feeling of late spring.

Nagedashite / ashi tōku aru / boshun kana
Stretching out / legs distant are / late spring

Murakami Tomohiko (b. 1979) studied haiku with Washitani Nanako and Yamagami Kimio and is currently the leader of *Nanpū*. This poem is from the anthology *Shinsen 21* (2009).

Summer

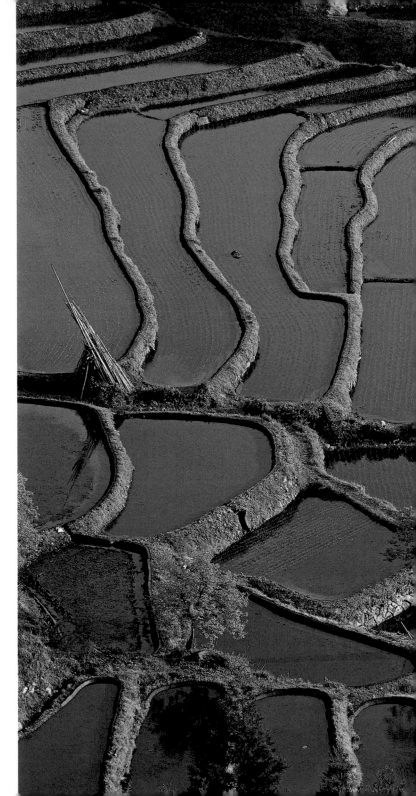

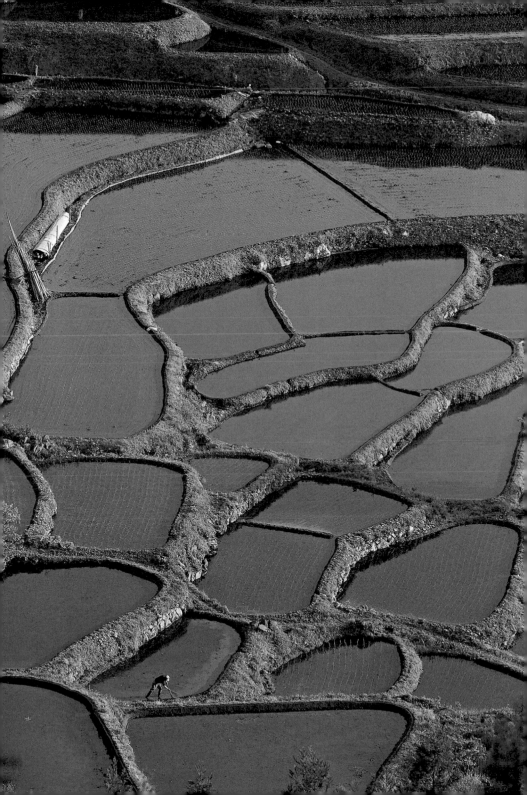

On the lake there is
a harbor and there I spent
the briefest summer

Tanaka Hiroaki

A small harbor on the lake, the kind where a sightseeing boat arrives a few times a day. He stayed there one summer. Looking back at the end of his stay, how short that summer was!

The superlative "briefest" expresses the intensity of his feeling of loss. In the Japanese, the grammatical tense that does this work is the perfective form (*mijikakere*), used for something that was completed in the past. Also, in the Japanese each segment of the poem begins with the syllable *mi*: *mizuumi, minato, mijikakere*. As they repeat, the spaced out syllables echo against each other, suggesting the sound of waves lapping against a pier. You may even see in your mind's eye the clear water sparkling in the late summer light.

I was born in Nagano Prefecture, a mountainous prefecture, so I imagine a small lake in the highlands, but this poet was born in Osaka so for him the nearest lake was Lake Biwa, the largest lake in Japan. But no matter where you imagine it to be, this is the best lake of all the lakes in the world.

When this poem was written, the poet knew that he was dying. The brief summer can be read as a loving memory of his own life.

Mizuumi no / minato no natsu no / mijikakere
Lake's / harbor's summer is / short

Tanaka Hiroaki (1959–2004), a follower of Hatano Sōha, received the Kadokawa Haiku Prize when he was only 22. He founded *Yū* in 2000, but his promising career was cut short by leukemia. His widow, the haiku poet Moriga Mari, publishes a magazine dedicated to the study of his work. This poem is from his last haiku collection, *Yoru no marōdo* (2005).

Many capes
small peninsulas and headlands
awash with summer smoke

Sawa Kōma

The list of three different kinds of landforms that jut into the sea, arranged in order of size (capes to small peninsulas to headlands), suggests a landscape with an intricately indented coastline. You could be looking down on the entire Japanese archipelago.

In summer, the great breakers rush in, washing spray over the capes and other promontories. From afar, the spray looks like smoke. Jutting out into the sea, the land might be waiting for the gods who drift in from beyond. Or the shape could also be a metaphor for the poet waiting for poetic inspiration to arrive from afar. The end of summer is also the season when we remember those who died in the Pacific War. The spray-covered capes, large and small, may also be an image of remembering those dead.

Amata naru / misaki saki hana / keburu natsu
Many are / capes small peninsulas headlands / smoky summer

Sawa Kōma (b. 1944) began writing haiku in college, then became a follower of Takayanagi Jūshin, contributed to his mentor's magazine *Haiku hyōron*, and edited *Haiku kenkyū*. In 1991 he founded *Ensui* and he remains its leader. This poem is from *Fūei* (2008).

144

For the month of May
I'm making my room
into a box of light

Hosoya Ryōryō

May is the beginning of summer and also the time of Golden Week, when there is a string of national holidays. The first half of the month is especially cheerful, thanks to the sunniness and the holiday mood.

In the Japanese, the first segment of the poem breaks in the middle, between "May" (*gogatsu*) and "I" (*waga*). Not cutting at the end of a segment but in the middle like this is quite unusual. You could take the poem to mean that the month of May is what fills his room with light. But I read it as his opening the window and letting the sunlight fill the entire room, so that he is the one who makes the room a light-filled box. And his room can be a metaphor for the heart, the inner world—in which case he wants to fill his own heart with light.

This poet is aware of light because he knows the darkness of the heart. In Japanese, there is a special term for spring-induced depression, "May sickness" (*gogatsu byō*), suggesting that May has its shadows too.

Gogatsu waga / heya o hikari no / hako ni shite
May my / room light's / box making into

Hosoya Ryōryō (b. 1948) studied haiku with Ishikawa Keirō and contributes to *Ichii* and *Kudan*. He is also a well-known pediatrician and specialist in childhood cancer, and has written many books for children and parents. This poem is from his second collection of haiku, *Futsuka* (2007).

Flowerless, the leafy trees—
inside unseen I play
at daytime games

Nagai Kafū

The cherry blossoms have scattered and the trees are burgeoning with bright green leaves under the dazzling noon sun. The poet is enjoying secret pleasures that no one outside knows about. The headnote is: "At a teahouse in Mukōjima Suijin," which marks the poem as autobiographical. Mukōjima is in Tokyo, on the banks of the Sumida River. The area is famous for the cherry trees along the river dike, so the leafy trees in this poem might well be those.

This poem was written in prewar Japan, when teahouses offered food, drink, and entertainment, and Kafū is indulging in wine and women there. He had enjoyed such amusements since his student days and grew even fonder of this "world of flower and willow," as it was called, after living abroad. Disliking everything about modern Japan, he opted out of ordinary society and never held a regular job.

In the dim light of the surrounding leafy cherry trees, the naked bodies of a man and woman are intimately entangled. Each of the three segments in Japanese begins with an "h" sound—*hazakura ya/hito ni shirarenu/hiru asobi.* The hushed sounds hint at secrecy, *himitsu* in Japanese.

Hazakura ya / hito ni shirarenu / hiru asobi
Cherry trees in leaf / others to unknown / daytime games

Nagai Kafū (1878–1959), one of the most prominent novelists of modern Japan, was also a haiku poet. Most of his work is set in the entertainment districts of Tokyo. This poem is from "Jisen Kafū hyaku" in *Omokage* (1938).

Blossoms fallen
the countless skies among the leaves
let loose and party

Shinohara Bon

The cherry blossoms have scattered and now the trees, bare of flowers, are in full leaf. As a strong wind blows through them, the leaves rustle loudly. Standing beneath and looking up, the sky looks as though it is divided into many parts and the clamor seems to be coming from the sky rather than the leaves.

When this poem was composed in 1937, the author was only 27 years old. One of the original things about it was the image of numberless skies between the burgeoning leaves of the flowerless trees. Because the leaves are large and numerous they partition the sky into numberless pieces. Looking up from below, the partitioned sky seems very bright. With "let loose and party" added at the end, the wind rises and each of the many skies moves about and comes alive. Making it the sky that moves, rather than the leaves, is a kind of artifice, but because the leaves are dark and difficult to see clearly, there is a naturalness to it.

This is among the outstanding haiku that use the seasonal image of "cherry trees in leaf" (*hazakura*). The poem is redolent of its author's youth.

Hazakura no / naka no musū no / sora sawagu
Cherry trees in leaf / inside numberless / skies party

Shinohara Bon (1910–1975), president of the publishing house Chuokoron-sha, was active in haiku as a poet and critic, especially during the prewar years. He studied haiku with Usuda Arō and contributed to Arō's *Shakunage*. This poem is from *Sara* (1941).

Neatly sliced into
three pieces—the thin heat of
early summer!

Hashi Kanseki

This is a counterpoint, or *toriawase,* haiku. That is, it juxtaposes two things, in this case the description of preparing a fish in the first two segments and the seasonal image in the last segment.

"Three pieces" is the term for one way to prepare fish in Japanese cooking. It means to divide the flesh into three pieces with a knife: two fillets of flesh and one piece with the backbone. "Thin heat" (*hakusho*) is the relatively mild heat that precedes the rainy season. To me, the image brings out the color and smell of the skin and flesh of the raw fish.

An orthodox reading takes the thing being cut up to be the fish, but other readings are also possible. You can read what is being sliced into three as the poet, or you can read the image of being sliced as a metaphor for the exhaustion caused by the sudden heat. You can even read "three pieces" as the "thin heat" itself being sliced up. With its slippery charm, the poem well conveys the strangeness of the expression "thin heat."

> *Sanmai ni / orosarete iru / hakusho kana*
> Three pieces into / cut up is / thin heat!

Hashi Kanseki (1903–1992) was a well-known scholar of English literature as well as a prolific author of haiku, linked verse, and essays. He founded and led *Byakuen*. This poem is from *Nigitae* (1983), which was awarded the Iida Dakotsu Prize.

The light for night archery
has been placed far off
beyond the grass

Kamikawai Riyō

"Night archery" (*yomato*) is the seasonal image, but it is not included in any of the compendiums of season words that I have to hand. It must be an amusement that was current when this poem was written in 1928 but is no longer played, something like the shooting galleries you see at hot springs resorts and night fair stalls.

Riyō wrote thirteen haiku about night archery in that year, including: "Night archery/everyone and his brother plays—/hot springs visitors!" which shows it was a hot springs amusement. But "The great white feathers are/hallowed and untouchable—/night archery" must be a description of the feathers attached to the arrow, which suggests that it was the real thing, not a mere toy.

In the featured poem, the light which illuminates the target has been placed beyond the summer grass. This subtly suggests that there is a sense of coolness where the speaker stands.

> *Yomato no hi / kusa no haruka ni / okarekeri*
> Night archery's light / grass far off in / has been placed

Kamikawai Riyō (1887–1946) began to compose haiku under the influence of his older brother Momiyama Shigetsu. He relaunched the famous haiku magazine *Haikai zasshi*, which was originally published by his brother, and also founded and led *Aigin*. This poem is from his collected haiku *Riyō kushū* (1930).

Beneath the windmill palm
I sweep fallen
flowers—loneliness!

Murayama Takajo

The headnote is: "Missing my dead mother." When Takajo was 15 her mother fell ill, and Takajo withdrew from her girls' higher school to nurse her through the last year of her life. Her mother died in June, the month when the windmill palm (*shuro*) comes into full bloom and then begins to shed its flowers. As she sweeps the fallen blossoms beneath the tree, the loss of her mother overwhelms her again. She wrote the poem in 1922, two years after her mother died.

The blooms of the windmill palm hang in long racemes of small yellow flowers. Plain and unobtrusive, the flowers are seldom admired or praised. The image of her mother rises from them, deepening her loneliness.

In Japanese the verb *koboruru* can be used to describe either tears or flowers, as can "falling" in English. Is it the flowers she sweeps or her own loneliness?

> *Hana koboruru* / *shuro no shita haku* / *sabishisa yo*
> Flowers spilled / windmill palm beneath sweep / the loneliness!

Murayama Takajo (1904–1926) was one of three siblings who became haiku poets. The youngest, Murayama Kokyō, achieved renown, but the chronically ill Takajo died young. This poem comes from the posthumous *Tōkajō* (1929), edited by Ōmori Tōmei.

Rain is wetting
the crested iris—
on the roof

Murakami Seigetsu

The crested iris is a perennial that blooms in May and whose white and lavender flowers resemble those of the bearded iris. It used to be common to plant it on the roofs of thatched houses. Folk belief held that it prevented strong winds and fires. Nowadays thatched roofs are extremely uncommon but in the Meiji era (1868–1912), when this poem was written, May was the season for roof-blooming iris.

To have flowers blooming on the roof suggests how close the Japanese must once have been to nature and to flowers. For Japanese of the Meiji era, there was nothing special about seeing flowers blooming on a thatched roof. But for us now, it is a startling sight. When we come to the last words, "on the roof," there is a strange sensation as if down and up were changing places.

Masaoka Shiki recorded this poem in the notebook he kept of poems by his disciples.

Ichihatsu ni / ame no furu nari / yane no ue
Crested iris on / rain is falling / roof's top

Murakami Seigetsu (1870–1946) was mentored by Masaoka Shiki, and was a contributor to, and later a selector for, *Hototogisu*. This poem is from Masaoka Shiki's anthology *Shōroban* (1937).

Brief night!
I stole a book to copy it—
all three volumes

Ōsuga Otsuji

There is a book of secret teachings about his art that he desperately wants to read. He cannot progress without reading it, but his teacher says he is not advanced enough and refuses his repeated entreaties. Unable to control himself, he secretly borrows it. The summer night is brief but if he stays awake all night and perseveres, he will be able to copy the entire three volumes and return it to the teacher's shelf in the morning without being discovered.

This is not a record of Otsuji's own experience but a romantic poem of historical fiction. Otsuji and other New Tendency Haiku* poets often wrote such poems in the group's early days. In the background you can sense the strong love of learning of its author, who became an influential haiku critic and theorist.

Otsuji's teacher was Kawahigashi Hekigotō, creator of the "centerless theory" (*muchūshinron*) of haiku, which led Otsuji to desert him and set out on his own path. One gets a sense from this haiku of the tension that can exist between teacher and disciple.

Mijikayo ya / nusumite utsusu / sho san kan
Brief night / stole to copy / book three volumes

Ōsuga Otsuji (1881–1920) made his mark in haiku criticism while still in college with an essay advocating Kawahigashi Hekigotō's New Tendency haiku. He later broke with Hekigotō and joined the group led by Usuda Arō, but later broke with him, too. This poem is from *Nihon haikushō dai isshū* (1909), edited by Kawahigashi Hekigotō.

Mold is growing even
on the stuff she uses
to whiten her face

Morikawa Gyōsui

"The stuff she uses/to whiten her face" must be the traditional *oshiroi* powder foundation. Even this solid cake of makeup has grown damp and moldy.

This poem was composed in 1932, the same year that Gyōsui also wrote such poems as these: "I gather up/the mildewed things/and play with them" and "Mold/in the chopstick case—/what a startled couple!" Mold and mildew must have been everywhere in their home. He also wrote this poem the following year: "My wife woke up/and made a fuss—/rainy season leak." Of course his wife would get upset seeing mold on her makeup, but she must have used it anyway. In 1936 he wrote: "My wife eats/moldy sweets—I watch/in silence." His wife eats sweets even if moldy. There's no way she would have thrown out makeup even if it had grown mold.

The omnipresent mold and mildew symbolized his family's poverty.

> *Kao ni nuru / mono ni mo kabi no / kitarikeri*
> Face on spread / thing on even mold / has come

Morikawa Gyōsui (1901–1976) was praised by his teacher, Takahama Kyoshi, for works depicting the poverty in which he lived. Kyoshi called him "our modern Issa" in honor of the revered haiku poet Kobayashi Issa (1763–1828), known for his poems on his poverty. This poem is from *Kabi* (1937).

A mildewed book—
"Sengyo will not sell for saké"
clearly stamped inside

Uemura Sengyo

There are haiku about a poet's books but surely poems about the seal stamped inside are a rarity. This seal, as is common, is written in formal Sino-Japanese.

The backstory is pretty clear: Sengyo loved to drink and had been known to sell his books so he could buy saké. A book once bartered in that manner was lost forever and must have led to deep regret. This seal is stamped in his book as an avowal of his intention to never sell it for drinking money. The book may be mildewed and soiled but he has read it more than once and will do so again.

The emphatic "clearly" hints at his lifelong effort to balance his twin addictions to books and alcohol.

> *Kabi no sho ni* / *Sengyo fukan shu no* / *in zonsu*
> Moldy book in / Sengyo not exchange saké / seal exists

Uemura Sengyo (1920–1996) came to know Takahama Kyoshi through his first mentor Matsumoto Takashi, and became a contributor to *Hototogisu*. He also founded and led *Misosazai*. This poem is from *Kuma* (1949).

The baby turtle floats
all the way up from the bottom—
then swims off

Takada Masako

This is an immature pond turtle or spotted turtle bought at a night fair or the like. It must have sunk to the bottom and stopped moving its limbs, as if shocked by the water pressure bearing down on it. Then it floats all the way up and, at last moving its limbs, begins to swim.

In pre-modern Japan, such turtles were called "coin turtles" (*zenigame*) because they were exactly the size of the copper coins (*zeni*) that were in circulation then. These turtles have an amazing will to live. If they somehow land on their back, they struggle furiously to right themselves.

In this poem, the turtle has disappeared in the depths and has stopped moving, but there is someone watching who feels concern. When the turtle surfaces, the watcher feels as if a burden has been removed, a feeling expressed in the breezy "all the way up."

The sparkling "k" sounds that are sprinkled throughout the poem (*kame, ko, sukkari, kara*) resonate nicely with the light movements of the little turtle.

> *Kame no ko no / sukkari uite / kara oyogu*
> Baby turtle / all the way up floats and / then swims

Takada Masako (b. 1959) belongs to *Aoi* and was mentored by its leader Kuroda Momoko. This poem is from her prizewinning collection *Kajitsu* (2005).

True love found,
the fireflies
sink down
deep
into
the

grass

Suzuki Masajo

"Fireflies" is a seasonal image associated with night and is often used in haiku about human love. Yet there are very few haiku about love between fireflies; this is a precious example.

One imagines that the bodies of the two fireflies who have sunk into the grass come together on top of the leaves. Their sinking down upon finding love rather than floating upwards is what makes the poem feel like a depiction of actual love and not mere fantasy. But rather than a poem that describes the natural history of fireflies, I sense behind the fireflies the shadow shapes of two human beings in love. The poems that follow this in the collection are: "Love fulfilled/the fireflies leisurely/await the dawn" and "A whisper came—/shall we die?/The firefly's night." Here, too, the fireflies seem to be transformed into two people caught up in an illicit love.

Masajo composed love poems her whole life and out of her encounter with the fireflies this masterpiece was born.

Koi o ete / *hotaru wa kusa ni* / *shizumikeri*
Love attained / fireflies grass into / sink

Suzuki Masajo (1906–2003) was a follower of Kubota Mantarō, and after Mantarō's death, of Mantarō's colleague Azumi Atsushi. After being divorced twice, she started a small restaurant in Tokyo when she was 50. Her independence and artistic talent made her unique for a woman of her time. This poem is from *Miyakodori* (1994), for which she was awarded the Yomiuri Prize for Literature in poetry.

That might be
my murderous soul—
a firefly takes to the sky

Maeda Fura

Fura must have in mind the famous poem by the late tenth-century poet Izumi Shikibu: "In the river firefly/I seem to see/my soul, gone forth/in longing/from my body" (*Goshūi wakashū*).*

Both Shikibu and Fura see themselves in the firefly. However, in contrast to Shikibu's soul, which longs for her lover so intensely that it separates from her body, Fura's soul is motivated by a homicidal wish.

You never know what a human being might be capable of on a moment's impulse. This poem captures that sense of uncertainty.

Hito korosu / ware ka mo shirazu / tobu hotaru
Person kill / I might be / flying firefly

Maeda Fura (1884–1954) was a follower of Takahama Kyoshi, who recognized his talent early on. In 1926, he became the head of the regional haiku group *Kobushi*. This poem, one of his most famous, is from *Shintei Fura kushū* (1934).

The Ashura cormorant
is female, he confides—
my heart breaks

Watanabe Keiko

One of the cormorants trained to catch sweetfish (*ayu*) was especially hard-working, returning with big fish again and again. When the poet asks the cormorant fishing master its sex, she learns that it is female. She feels tremendous pity for a bird who must spend her life using her delicate female body to commit the karmically sinful act of killing, like the Ashura, souls of warriors who are condemned to do eternal battle in the afterlife.

This is a poem about traditional night fishing with cormorants on the Nagara River in Gifu Prefecture. The birds dive into the water from boats, gulping down the shining sweetfish that are lit up by fires suspended over the water from the boats. However, their necks are tied by ropes held by the fishing master so they cannot swallow the fish, and must regurgitate them when they return to the boat. The cormorants' catch, in other words, is stolen by humans. The sadness in Bashō's haiku "Exciting at first/and then sad—/the cormorant boats"[*1] lies in this. Beneath the image of the hard-working female cormorant is the image of a woman, the poet herself.

Cormorant fishing is so ancient an art that it is even mentioned in the eighth-century *Chronicles of Japan* (*Nihon shoki*). Given the long history of cormorant fishing, using the word "Ashura" for the cormorant herself is apt, evoking as it does an ancient world. There is also something about the sinuous beauty of the female cormorant that reminds me of the androgynous-looking Ashura sculpture of Kōfukuji Temple.[*2]

> *Ashura no u / nyotai to kikishi / awaresa yo*
> Ashura cormorant / female body I heard / the pitifulness!

Watanabe Keiko (1901–1984) studied haiku with Watanabe Suiha, then became his wife, and, after his death, the leader of his magazine and group *Kyokusui*. This poem is from her haiku collection *Yoshinobina* (1966).

A tiny squid
with a tiny splotch of ink inside
coming from the west

Ōoka Kōji

Ōoka Kōji was an avant-garde haiku poet who wrote "multi-line" (*tagyō*) haiku instead of conventional single-line ones. In the Japanese, this haiku was originally printed in three lines rather than the usual single line.

"A tiny splotch of ink inside" (*sun no sumi oku*) is a little difficult to interpret. In his note to the poem in *Gendai haiku zenshū 5* (1978), the poet wrote: "I have never seen a squid in an aquarium, but I like to imagine a solid bit of black ink in that transparent body, a body that you could mistake for an alien from outer space." *Sumi oku* is an expression used in calligraphy to describe that first splotch of ink at the head of a line before the brush begins to move. Playing on the double meaning of *sumi* as both squid ink and calligraphic writing ink, the poet suggests that the bit of ink stored within the transparent body of the squid is like a splotch of ink created by a calligraphy brush on the page. "West" is the direction of the Buddhist Paradise, so the poet may be thinking of the squid as having come from the realm of death, that is, of having been reborn.

This is a vignette of nature that evokes the life of a pretty little squid, but also and unexpectedly brings us into the world of calligraphy. In an alien world, I feel a touch of the familiar.

> *Sun-ika wa / sun no sumi oku / nishi kara kite*
> Tiny squid / tiny ink places / west from come

Ōoka Kōji (1937–2003) was a follower of Takayanagi Jūshin and a contributor to Jūshin's *Haiku hyōron*. For many years he ran his own printing press, which published hand-made books of haiku in limited editions. This poem is from *Hanami higata* (1963).

The spider who lives
on iron stairs
makes its wisdom shine

Akao Tōshi

Avant-garde haiku are constructed beyond experience, the words liberated from everyday meaning. The aim is to build a new structural edifice out of words. The result is obscurity but at the same time a strange power. This poem is one of the most famous examples.

The word *tekkai* does not appear in any dictionary, but it must mean a staircase made of iron. Even a spider who dwells in a man-made place like this, apart from nature, can survive by putting its own "wisdom" to work in pursuing prey. "Makes its wisdom shine" compellingly captures a certain kind of existence.

Is it too much to read the spider as a mirror of urban dwellers whose lives are divorced from the riches of nature?

Tekkai ni / iru kumo chie o / kagayakasu
Iron staircase in / lives spider wisdom / makes shine

Akao Tōshi (1925–1981) started submitting his work to haiku magazines while in high school. He became a follower of Takayanagi Jūshin and participated in the founding of *Haiku hyōron*. In 1960, he founded *Uzu,* which he led until his death. This poem is from *Hebi* (1959).

Even on the hand
that holds the dustpan—a spider's thread
at half-light

Suzuki Hanamino

Hanamino was called "the demon defender" of the realist sketch from life* that had been pioneered by the haiku reformer Masaoka Shiki in the late nineteenth century. But in this poem, rather than perceiving a single spider's thread by sight, as is the method in the sketch from life, he perceives the spider's thread through the sense of touch, that is, the way it feels on his skin.

Holding the broom in his right hand and the dustpan in his left, he is sweeping the garden in the half-light of early evening. He has not been lax in looking after it, but the spiders are very active. Their webs dot almost the whole area, and he is surrounded on every side by their threads, which catch onto various parts of his body. Now they have even become attached to his left hand as he wields the dustpan.

The associations multiply: the early evening light of the garden, the smell of the grass and the earth, the heat and humidity. One can imagine the speaker's weariness, and how much he would like to be done with his chore.

> *Chiritori no / te ni mo yūbe no / kumo no ito*
> Dustpan's / hand even on early evening's / spider's thread

Suzuki Hanamino (1885–1942), a follower of Takahama Kyoshi and one of the leading *Hototogisu* poets in the 1920s and 1930s, was also a selector for the well-known magazine *Aomi* based in his home prefecture of Aichi. This poem is from *Suzuki Hanamino kushū* (1947).

Suddenly I see
a vision—maggots swarming
over my corpse

Nomiyama Asuka

An extremely powerful image. This is no peaceful passing away in bed, surrounded by loved ones, that the poet is imagining for himself. Maggots are unlikely to appear on a body unless it was abandoned or only discovered some time after death.

When Bashō was about to depart on the journey that he described in *Nozarashi kikō** he wrote this haiku: "Skulls on my mind,/the wind bites/into my flesh." *Nozarashi* was a euphemism for the skull of a traveler who had died on the road, a fate Bashō found easy to imagine for himself. I cannot help feeling that for Asuka, this poem had a meaning like the one Bashō's poem had for Bashō.

To live with the image of his own corpse in the back of his mind may well have given Asuka's rather short life an added richness.

> *Futo ware no / shigai ni uji no / takaru miyu*
> Suddenly my / corpse on maggots / swarm are seen

Nomiyama Asuka (1917–1970) was a follower of Takahama Kyoshi, a contributor to *Hototogisu*, and later founded and led *Nagarabi*. This poem is from *Manjushage* (1951).

Am I dreaming?
A crane fly alights
on my kneecap

Okamoto Shōhin

The crane fly is a very fragile creature. You could easily break its legs with a simple touch as you idly brush it away.

I imagine the insect perching on the poet's naked knee cap when he is relaxing in his underwear, not when he is fully dressed. The thin legs of the crane fly touching bare skin must tickle. That barely-there touch is what makes the poet wonder if he is dreaming. The shape of the crane fly and the touch of its legs seem somehow ephemeral, so comparing them to a dream is a perfect fit.

Shōhin also wrote: "I blow on/the crane fly and/it flies away—/along with a paper doll."

Yume no gotoku / gaganbo kitari / hiza gashira
Like a dream / cranefly comes / kneecap

Okamoto Shōhin (1879–1939) was a follower of Masaoka Shiki and Takahama Kyoshi, and in his turn nurtured the talent of younger poets like Kubota Mantarō. He later founded and led *Kangiku*. This poem is from *Shiragiku* (1941), edited by Shimomura Kaita.

"Rise, bow, be seated!"
The wind blew
through green leaves

Kōno Saki

She calls out the commands with which class commences in Japanese schools and her classmates obey. Meanwhile, the wind is blowing through the green leaves outside.

This is morning, first period. The speaker is best imagined as the class monitor. As if in response to the voice inside the room, the green leaves outside appear and the wind passes through. Nature and humans both adhere to their respective rules, a unity that is conducive to study and learning.

We can't know what class is about to begin, but the poet, who was still in high school when she wrote this poem, brilliantly captures the opening scene of an actual high school class. According to her own note, she wrote it at the national haiku competition held annually for high school students (Haiku Kōshien) in her hometown of Matsuyama in Ehime Prefecture. The assigned topic was *ao*, which can mean either blue or green.

Kiritsu rei / chakuseki aoba / kaze sugita
Stand up bow / sit down green leaves / wind passed through

Kōno Saki (b. 1981) won first prize in the National High School Haiku Championship (Haiku Kōshien) in 2001. In 2011, she cofounded the online haiku magazine *SPICA* and updates it daily. This poem is from *Hoshi no chizu* (2003).

Ears become leaves
leaves become ears
in the green leaves' darkness

Horimoto Yūki

In the daytime under the deep shade of the trees, something strange happens. The poet's ears turn into leaves on the trees and the leaves on the trees turn into ears.

"The green leaves' darkness" (*aobayami*) is a modern seasonal image, a variation on the traditional "darkness beneath the trees" (*koshitayami*). It evokes the shadowy light beneath trees in full leaf. The poet is having a strange experience. His own ears have changed places with the leaves, and beneath the trees, now thick with ears, sits a man whose own two ears have turned into leaves. The otherworldly scene is worthy of a surrealist painting. As the man and the trees begin to converge, both are altered. Person and tree merge into one. In which case, maybe the sounds heard by the ears attached to the tree can also be heard by the person. Perhaps such strange things are possible at the holy site of Kumano,* where the context suggests this poem was probably composed.

The word "leaves" is repeated three times in this poem, like the continuous sound of the leaves rustling in the wind.

> *Mimi wa ha ni / ha wa mimi ni nari / aobayami*
> Ears leaves to / leaves ears to turn / green leaves' darkness

Horimoto Yūki (b. 1974), after serving as editor in chief of *Kawa*, founded and leads *Sōkai*. He also contributes to the haiku publications *Azusa* and *Kudan*. This poem is from *Kumano mandara* (2012).

My face-washing water
all bumps and hollows—
here comes a swallowtail

Sugiyama Hisako

After waking up in the morning, the poet is washing her face. The water in the washbasin undulates, making the surface uneven. Then a swallowtail butterfly comes flying along.

Face washing is a subject one often encounters in haiku. The action can pinpoint the time as morning, or it can indicate a change of mood or the wish to change one's mood. However, to have it followed by "bumps and hollows" is quite unusual. There cannot be many haiku about face washing that capture the swaying motion of the water. And she is not only describing the way it moves but the unevenness of the water surface as it changes from concave to convex and back again.

When the swallowtail flies into the scene, we realize that the poet is washing her face in an open space like a garden. The way the water is swaying and the large butterfly make me feel a sense of looming uneasiness.

Kao arau / *mizu no ōtotsu* / *ageha kuru*
Face wash / water's bumpiness / swallowtail comes

Sugiyama Hisako (b. 1966) studied haiku with Kuroda Momoko. She is a contributor to Kuroda's *Aoi,* as well as a member of Natsui Itsuki's *Itsukigumi.* This poem is from *Tori to aruku* (2010).

Inside my head
is become
a white summer field

Takaya Sōshū

Modern haiku is typically said to have begun from Masaoka Shiki's realist sketch from life (*shasei*).[*1] Thus, it is meant to describe something external. However, this poem is about something "inside my head," which changes the frame of reference. The poem is also unusual in using neither cutting word[*2] nor classical grammar, but being entirely in the colloquial.

Something has become "a white summer field," but what that something is remains unsaid. Is it simply that a summer field is in front of him? Or has something that existed before undergone a change? It is impossible to tell. I can only say that there is a feeling of too much light, like an over-exposed photograph.

In his own comment on this poem, Sōshū wrote that before he composed it he wrote the words "white summer field" in the middle of a blank piece of paper and stared at them for a week.

Atama no naka de / shiroi natsuno to / natte iru
Head inside / white summer field / is become

Takaya Sōshū (1910–1999) was a follower of Mizuhara Shūōshi but later broke with him. He eventually became one of the principal New Rising Haiku[*3] poets. In the postwar period, he participated in the founding of Yamaguchi Seishi's *Tenrō*. This poem is from *Shiroi natsuno* (1936).

A chicken
hid itself away
in the summer grass

Fukuda Haritsu

Left uncut, the summer grass grew thick and high, and once in amongst it, the chicken became invisible.

The poet must let his chickens run free in the garden, rather than keeping them caged. Of course he takes their eggs and eats their flesh, but he also enjoys relaxing his tired eyes after work by watching them play. The grass must be dense and luxuriant for the chicken, a fairly large bird, to disappear inside it. It would be difficult to imagine this happening with the grass of any other season. And from the fact that the poet let the grass grow so thickly without cutting it, you can assume that he is something of a carefree recluse.

Haritsu worked for the Nippon Shimbunsha newspaper company[*] and was a colleague of Masaoka Shiki, in which case he may well have lived in Tokyo or on its outskirts. Perhaps you could see such scenes in early twentieth-century Tokyo. Of course he might have composed the poem on a trip, or could have been writing about a memory. In any case, I enjoy the simplicity and freshness of the world of haiku from this period.

Natsukusa ni / niwatori ichiwa / kakurekeri
Summer grass in / chicken one / was hidden

Fukuda Haritsu (1865–1944) studied haiku with Masaoka Shiki. He also wrote poems in classical Chinese and published a collection of them called *Shōyoshū*. This poem is from *Shunkashūtō: Natsu no bu* (1902), compiled by Kawahigashi Hekigotō and Takahama Kyoshi.

168

Isn't that an electric current
flowing through
the bindweed flowers?

Mitsuhashi Takajo

At first I was startled: How could anyone imagine the fierce, man-made energy of an electric current flowing through the graceful bindweed flowers? And yet the image seems to express the essential quality of the bindweed.

Bindweed is so strong that unlike the morning glory, to which it is related botanically, its flowers stay open from morning to night, even under the burning sun of midday. Furthermore, it is not a garden cultivar but a weed, with a root and stem system that spreads unstoppably underground. Add to this the light pink of its flowers, and, all things considered, the poet's idea of "an electric current/flowing through/the bindweed flowers" does not seem so far-fetched. Note that she does not assert that there *is* such a current. The way she asks the question, as if talking to herself, has an attractive naturalness.

Reading this poem reminds me of how startling it is to touch an electric current, even a relatively harmless one.

> *Hirugao ni / denryū kayoi / i wa senu ka*
> Bindweed flower through / electric current flows / is it not?

Mitsuhashi Takajo (1899–1972) was one of the Four T's* and was one of the leading women haiku poets of modern times. In the postwar period, she gravitated to avant-garde haiku and published in *Bara*, the magazine founded by Tomizawa Kakio, as well as in Takayanagi Jūshin's *Haiku hyōron*. This poem is from *Himawari* (1940).

Through rippling water
towards the Phoenix Hall
a snake's head glides

Awano Seiho

The three elements of the poem—water, Phoenix Hall, snake—are put together in such a way as to maximize the element of surprise. Riddle follows riddle. First, what kind of water could the "rippling water" of the first segment be? "The Phoenix Hall" in the next segment provides the answer, for this is a famous building that is the main hall of the Byōdō-in, a Buddhist temple in Uji built over a thousand years ago. The water is that of the pond in front of the Phoenix Hall, and the hall must be reflected in its rippling surface.

But the preposition "towards" suggests something is moving in the pond, heading for the Phoenix Hall. What could it be? The third and last segment is the reveal: "a snake's head." A snake is swimming across the pond in front of the Phoenix Hall. Rereading, you see that the very first words, "rippling water," already hint that something is swimming. Now we can add that the head must belong to a rather large snake if it creates ripples, and that impression is intensified by only the head being mentioned. The pair of female and male phoenix statues looking down from the rooftop of the Phoenix Hall represent the world of the Buddha, and the snake swimming towards them is like a threatening demon.

The medieval classic *Tales of Times Now Past* (*Konjaku monogatari*)[1] has frightening stories that this scene could fit right into.

> *Mizu yurete / Hō-ōdō e / hebi no kubi*
> Water rippling / Phoenix Hall towards / snake's head

Awano Seiho (1899–1992) studied haiku with Takahama Kyoshi, founded and led *Katsuragi*, and was one of the "Four S's"[2] of *Hototogisu* in the prewar period. This poem is from *Haru no tobi* (1952).

Oh to be born
a rat snake and immediately
clubbed to death!

Miyairi Hijiri

In contemporary haiku, the desire to be reincarnated as a plant or an animal is a fairly common topic. Such poems typically express the suffering of human life and a longing to experience the life of another creature. They differ categorically from this poem, whose speaker is saying that he wants to be born as another creature so that he can have the experience of being murdered. He feels nothing but despair about life.

There is a contradiction in the poem. When he says "Oh, to be born/ a rat snake," you imagine a newly hatched snake, an infant snake. However, that does not fit with "immediately/clubbed to death!" In order to be clubbed to death, a thing has to be pretty big. He would have to be reborn as a rat snake that immediately became full-grown. I find myself attracted to the illogicality. It makes me think that his despair about life comes from his own almost savage and overwhelming flood of life.

Aodaishō ni / umare sokkoku / utarekashi
Rat snake / to be born at once / be murdered want

Miyairi Hijiri (b. 1947) began writing haiku in his 20s and was published in Iida Ryūta's *Unmo*, but published nothing for six years after his mother's death in 1974. Encouraged by Tsukamoto Kunio* he began to publish again, only to fall silent once more in the mid-1990s. This poem is from *Seibojō* (1981).

Lizards mating—
they take their time,
the male dragging behind

Tagawa Hiryoshi

This vignette of lizards coupling is a finely detailed picture of the animal world. In Japanese, the onomatopoeic *zuruzuru* ("slow and heavy"), used to describe slowly dragging a long and heavy thing, makes the image come alive. The action of these small creatures becomes very real, almost as if seen under a microscope.

The soundscape of the Japanese is shaped by the unusual number of voiced consonants: "g" and "b" (*tokage, kōbi*) in the first segment (which is seven syllables instead of the usual five), with "z" twice (*zuruzuru*) in the second and once (*hikizurare*) in the last. The throaty, voiced sounds vibrate with the weighty feeling of flesh against flesh.

The female is shown in the superior position as these animals copulate, which reminds me of those couples in our own species in which energetic women dominate spineless men. Is the tinge of bitter humor I feel because I am male?

> *Tokage no kōbi* / *zuruzuru to osu* / *hikizurare*
> Lizards mating / slow and heavy male / being dragged

Tagawa Hiryoshi (1914–1999) was a follower of Katō Shūson and a longtime contributor to Shūson's *Kanrai*. He also founded and led *Riku*. This poem is from *Hanamoji* (1955).

The butterfly's tongue
is a watchspring look-alike—
this summer heat!

Akutagawa Ryūnosuke

What the poet calls a tongue is technically the proboscis—a long, tube-like appendage. When not in use it is tightly coiled, but it unrolls to sip nectar from a flower. He compares this to a coiled watchspring such as were traditionally found in watches. Viewed up close like this, a butterfly's face is grotesque and somehow oppressive.

This haiku has two seasonal images, the main one being "heat" (*atsusa*) and the secondary one "butterfly" (*chō*). The butterfly must be the large kind you see in the summer.

The first version of this poem, published in the August 1918 issue of *Hototogisu,* was: "A watchspring look-alike is/the butterfly's tongue—/this summer heat!" (*Zenmai ni/nite chō no shita/atsusa kana*). Two nouns follow hard on each other, making the syntax of this version rather convoluted and cramped. Moreover, instead of the butterfly's tongue, which is the poem's subject, coming first, the watchspring does. That may be why the poet reversed the order of images and rewrote the original poem.

> *Chō no shita / zenmai ni niru / atsusa kana*
> Butterfly's tongue / watchspring resembles / the heat!

Akutagawa Ryūnosuke (1892–1927) is known as the father of the short story in Japan. Many of his works have been translated into English and other languages. He also wrote haiku and tanka. In haiku, he was a follower of Takahama Kyoshi. This poem is from *Chōkōdō kushū* (1927).

There was an old man
and on his head he wore a hat
made all of straw

Imai Kyōtarō

This "old man" appears in a number of poems by Kyōtarō and stands for the poet himself. Summer hats can be fashionable and even the humble *mugiwara bōshi* straw hat can be elegant, but not the one in this poem. Although not falling apart, it has clearly been through a lot, just like its owner. Even so, the owner cannot help being pleased with himself when he wears it.

The second segment of the poem has eight syllables instead of the usual seven: "and on his head he wore a hat." The way the syllables spill over the 5-7-5 grid makes me feel the hat is a little large for his head.

By avoiding startling words and striking expressions, Kyōtarō left us haiku that speak in a low voice and use a simple vocabulary. You can say that he aimed at a lightness of touch suited to our times.

Rōjin ga / kabutte mugiwara / bōshi kana
Old man / wearing straw / hat!

Imai Kyōtarō (1928–2012) was a long-time contributor to *Tsuru* and a follower of Ishizuka Tomoji,* who inherited the leadership of *Tsuru* from Ishida Hakyō. After leaving *Tsuru* in 1995, he founded and led *Uoza*. This poem comes from *Mugiwara bōshi* (1986).

Inside the creel
        it's quiet now—
                the evening primroses have opened

Imai Sei

A creel is a wicker basket used by anglers for their catch. A fish was tossed into one, thrashed around for a while, and then grew quiet. Had the creel been placed in water, the fish would have been calmly breathing rather than thrashing around, so the creel must have been placed on the grass nearby. The other image in the poem is the evening primroses, so this must be a scene of river fishing, perhaps for carp.

The poem, then, describes a death that happens close beside him. What dies is a fish and it dies because the fisherman-poet put it in the creel. In effect, he murdered it. In the phrasing of the poem, the place of this death—"in the creel"—is specified, but the being who has died and grown silent is not. In this omission I feel the poet's sense of sin for having deprived the fish of life.

The evening primroses are blooming in the half-light as if to bring peace to the fish's soul.

> *Biku no naka / shizuka ni narinu / tsukimisō*
> Creel's inside / quiet has become / evening primroses

Imai Sei (b. 1950) studied with Katō Shūson and contributed to *Kanrai*. After Shūson's death, he founded *Machi*. He is also a scriptwriter for movies and TV dramas. This poem comes from *Tanima no kagu* (2000).

My eyeballs go
deep into
cloud-covered peaks

Kyūgyū Nami

Jumping out from the eye sockets, the eyeballs fly off. They go all the way in among the cloud-covered peaks.

The poet is not simply gazing at the mountains from a distance. This is clearly not a world that could exist in reality. But there is more to the poem than that. Giving myself up to the illusion as I read, I feel as if I am in a dream—a waking dream—and enjoy the dizzy sensation as different kinds of clouds touch my eyeballs.

The words "go/deep into" bring to mind this well-known poem by Taneda Santōka:[*1] "Deep I go/deep I go/and still green mountains." In Santōka's poem, the body cannot escape the verdant mountains, but here the eyeballs leave the surface of the earth and enter deep into mountains hidden in clouds. Perhaps Nami's image of cloud-covered peaks came from Santōka's green mountains.

Gankyū no / wakeitte iku / kumo no mine
Eyeballs / go deep into / cloud's peaks

Kyūgyū Nami (1945–2013) was a contributor to *Run* and a member of Morioka Shōsaku's[*2] *Shukkō*. She knew Spanish well and in the afterword to her haiku collection *Watakushi to watashi* (2007), in which this poem appears, she describes how she came to haiku through reading Octavio Paz's Spanish translation of Bashō's *Oku no hosomichi*.[*3]

Granny Mountain and
Leaning Mountain in a sudden
evening downpour

Yamaguchi Seison

The headnote says "Kyūshū Journey." Seison was born up north, in Iwate Prefecture, but this poem is from his journey south to what was for him the unfamiliar area of Kyushu, where he traveled around on horseback.

Granny Mountain (*Sobosan*) is on the boundary between Oita and Miyazaki Prefectures, and is the highest mountain in central Kyushu. The name is said to have been conferred to honor Emperor Jinmu's grandmother, Toyotama-hime, but for someone who does not know that story, the name must bring back nostalgic memories of their own grandmother. Leaning Mountain (*Katamukusan*) is in front of Granny Mountain and is said to lean to one side, almost like a child at her grandmother's knee. The evocativeness of the names draws the reader in, and together with the prominence of the mountains in the landscape, makes the poem come alive.

Deep within the heavy rain, the shapes of the two mountains are dimly visible and the air feels wonderfully cool.

Sobosan mo / Katamukusan mo / yudachi kana
Granny Mountain / Leaning Mountain too / evening downpour!

Yamaguchi Seison (1892–1988), one of the most prominent followers of Takahama Kyoshi, made up the name the "Four S's" for Awano Seiho, Takano Sujū, Mizuhara Shūōshi, and Yamaguchi Seishi, the four leading younger poets of *Hototogisu* of his time. While contributing to *Hototogisu*, he founded and led *Natsukusa* in his hometown of Morioka in northern Japan. This poem is from *Zassōen* (1934).

The rainbow itself
believes
in time

Abe Seiai

Rainbows are strange things. Classical Japanese poets, feeling something ill-omened about rainbows, avoided referring to them, while the ancient Chinese seem to have imagined the rainbow as the incarnation of a dragon.

Seiai is saying that the rainbow itself has a will and is aware of time. The rainbow disappears in an instant. If you take the moment in which it appears as the span of its life, we sense that brief time as concentrated and rich. At the same time, the rainbow must be keenly aware of the imminence of its own end and hence of death itself.

The poem is based on the fantasy of entering into the very mind of a rainbow, but as I read it over and over the seven-colored rainbow comes to seem even brighter. Yes, strange indeed.

Niji jishin / jikan wa ari to / omoikeri
Rainbow itself / time exists / thinks

Abe Seiai (1914–1989), contributed to several of the New Rising Haiku* magazines, and later, in the postwar period, to Takayanagi Jūshin's *Haiku hyōron* and others. He also founded and led *Bin*. This poem is from *Kamonshū* (1968).

The long-horned beetle
has spots to the very tips
of its antennae

Itō Inao

The long-horned beetle's entire body is covered with spots all the way to the end of its distinctive long, thick antennae. This is not a general statement but direct observation. Someone, perhaps an insect-loving young girl or boy, is gazing closely at a long-horned beetle and noticing with fascination how its spots are not just on its body, but extend right "to the very tips of its antennae."

This could be a dead specimen, but to imagine a live beetle that has been caught is much more interesting. As it moves around, waving its spotted antennae, a sense of the mystery of creation wells up. This creature is presented in delicate motion, an image no sculpture could achieve.

The long-horned beetle is a harmful insect that bores into wood, but in the eyes of a child who loves insects, it is an object of enchantment.

Kamikiri no / hige no saki made / fu o moteri
Long-horned beetle's / antennae's end until / spots has

Itō Inao (b. 1949) is a contributor to Minagawa Bansui's* *Shunkou*. He also founded and leads *Ginkan*, which is associated with *Shunkou*. This poem is from his prizewinning collection *Ginkan* (1998).

Huge snowy ravine—
the climbers' trail
a single spotless line

Okada Nichio

A mountain climber is walking through a huge snowy ravine. Many climbers have passed that way before, and their footsteps have created a trail. However, it remains pristine and clean.

The headnote is "Kiso Komagatake," a mountain in southern Nagano Prefecture that is the tallest peak of Japan's Central Alps. At this altitude, there is snow on the ground all year round. The scenery is so magnificent that "snowy ravine" is not enough, and "huge" is added to emphasize the breathtaking expanse. The climber tramps firmly on, enjoying the cool air, so different from the world below; this is the best part of summer mountaineering. Snowy ravines like this are generally muddy from the boots of other climbers. That is why the climber is startled by how clean this trail is.

Four nouns in succession: ravine, trail, line, dirt (*daisekkei*, *fumiato*, *ichiro*, *yogore*). You feel the hard breathing of the climb, which doesn't have room for the explanatory content a verb might offer. In addition, three of the four Japanese characters expressing these words, 踏, 跡, and 路, contain the character for "foot" 足, as though inviting you to imagine the footprints in the snow.

Daisekkei / fumiato ichiro / yogore nashi
Huge snowy ravine / trail one line / dirt none

Okada Nichio (b. 1932), an avid mountain climber, has written a number of haiku about mountains. He is the leader of *Yamabi*. This poem is from *Shinsetsu* (2010).

Tessai's old age—
black waterfalls and
red ones

Takenaka Hiroshi

Tomioka Tessai (1836–1924) was a well-known painter in the Bunjinga or "literati painting" style, which flourished in late-nineteenth-century Japan and was heavily indebted to Chinese landscape painting of the late Ming dynasty. Bunjinga artists painted imaginary landscapes and felt no compulsion to depict reality.

Tessai's best works are considered to have been created in the last years of his life, after he turned 80. The older he got, the freer they became. "Black waterfalls and red ones" describes paintings, but ordinarily a painter would use neither black nor red to depict a waterfall. It's strange to paint a waterfall as red in one case and black in another. The idea of this poem is that Tessai, through growing old, attained a spontaneous freedom to paint a waterfall any color he wanted.

Old age is often perceived negatively, but it was what enabled Tessai to break free of convention. This poem is a hymn in praise of old age.

> *Tessai no / oi kuroki taki / akaki taki*
> Tessai's / old age black waterfalls / red waterfalls

Takenaka Hiroshi (b. 1940) studied with Nakamura Kusatao and contributed to Kusatao's magazine *Banryoku*. After Kusatao's death he founded *Shōrin*. This poem is from *Anamorufōzu* (2003).

From the future comes
a wind—and it blows
the waterfall apart

Natsuishi Banya

A strong wind that comes from a separate dimension, the future, is breaking the waterfall apart. This poem embraces both present and future time. It is a radical departure from the usual descriptive haiku.

A waterfall is, as it were, water falling from heaven to earth. Seen in this way, as something which links heaven and earth, it becomes a natural object of worship. When haiku is written in a single vertical line in Japanese, the waterfall of words also links heaven and earth. In this sense, the waterfall can be read as a metaphor for the poetic form called haiku, and the poem itself can be read as a vision of the changes coming to haiku poetry.

Even in isolation the word "waterfall" (*taki*) has a cool, refreshing feel, and the image of a waterfall being blown apart, fine spray spreading through the air, intensifies the feeling. This poem looks towards the future with a bright sense of expectation.

Mirai yori / *taki o fukiwaru* / *kaze kitaru*
Future from / waterfall blow apart / wind comes

Natsuishi Banya (b. 1955), who began writing haiku at age 14, developed into a devotee of avant-garde haiku and became a follower of Takayanagi Jūshin. He founded and publishes the international haiku quarterly *Ginyu*, and cofounded the World Haiku Association, which has members in thirty countries. This poem is from *Metoroporitikku* (1985).

Pressing my eyebrows
into the cliff I drink—
how pure the water!

Matsune Tōyōjō

A man drinking spring water in the mountains might immerse both hands in the clear water, scoop it up in the palms of his hands, and drink, but that is not what's happening here. The speaker of this poem has no time for such a leisurely action. He gulps down the gushing water steadily streaming from between the rocks of the cliff.

The core of this poem is "pressing my eyebrows into the cliff." It tells us that the climber is standing in such a precarious place that he can hardly balance and is drinking desperately to quench his thirst. Just how his hands and feet are positioned as he leans into the cliff is unclear, but we know that where he stands is unstable.

The projecting rocks of the cliff against which he presses his eyebrows cause pain, but the pain anchors him and reassures him that he is still alive.

Zeppeki ni / mayu tsukete nomu / shimizu kana
Cliff into / eyebrows pressing drink / pure water!

Matsune Tōyōjō (1878–1964) joined *Hototogisu* after meeting Masaoka Shiki, who he was introduced to by his high school teacher Natsume Sōseki. As a judge for the haiku column of the *Kokumin Shimbun* newspaper, he nurtured Kubota Mantarō and others. He later left *Hototogisu* and founded and led *Shibugaki*. This poem is from *Tōyōjō zenkushū*, vol.1 (1966).

Light of the sun and light
of the moon—and the coolness
of a pilgrim's staff

Kuroda Momoko

Night and day she is guided on her way by the light in the sky. The words used for that light, "light of the sun" (*nikkō*) and "light of the moon" (*gekkō*), are also the names of the two bodhisattvas that attend Yakushi Nyorai, the Healing Buddha. Thus another meaning is that she is making her pilgrimage under the protection of the sunlight bodhisattva and the moonlight bodhisattva. She walks single-mindedly, supported by her pilgrim's staff.

The meaning of "the coolness/of a pilgrim's staff" must be that when she leans on the staff, no matter how scorching the heat, it will provide cool relief, like the Buddhist Law itself, which is traditionally compared to a supporting staff. There is also a sense of the oneness of her body and the staff. The staff illuminated by sunlight and moonlight may in fact be an incarnation of the Healing Buddha himself.

In the Japanese, three words have doubled consonants—*nikkō, gekkō, ippon*. When said aloud, this gives the poem a slightly bouncy rhythm, like a pilgrim walking.

> *Nikkō gekkō* / *suzushisa no* / *tsue ippon*
> Sunlight moonlight / coolness's / staff one

Kuroda Momoko (b. 1938) was mentored by Yamaguchi Seison until his death. She founded and directs *Aoi* and actively mentors many younger poets. This poem is from *Nikkō gekkō* (2010), for which she received the Iida Dakotsu Prize.

I'm worth that
whole mob of lazy men
reeking of sweat

Takeshita Shizunojo

Before the war the status and social positions of men and women were very different. This poem is permeated with rage at the discrimination women experienced at work. At the time, Shizunojo was employed at the Fukuoka Prefectural Library. The men with whom she worked were filthy and the smell of their sweat permeated the air. When asked to work they were inefficient and slow, and they constantly herded together, taking shelter in the group.

You can imagine that the poet was the exact opposite of such men. She knows that even alone she can get much more done than that crowd of men working together. Even in the workplace she does not forget her pride in being a woman.

The depiction of working in a library as a kind of physical labor is what makes this intense haiku special.

Ase kusaki / noro no otoko no / mure ni gosu
Sweat reeking / dull men's / group with I rank

Takeshita Shizunojo (1887–1951) was a follower of Takahama Kyoshi. She was the second woman (after Sawada Hagijo) whose haiku was chosen as the best in one section of an issue of *Hototogisu*. This poem is from *Hayate* (1940).

Sweat pouring down
a guy squeezed his eyes tight—wham!
slammed them shut

Kyōgoku Kiyō

The daring use of the onomatopoeic *gyūtto* ("squeezed…tight") is startling. It means to press something strongly, to squeeze it, but my surprise comes from seeing it used to describe the way someone shuts their eyes. Also, usually there is only one "t" as in *gyūto*, but the extra "t" added here increases the intensity. Japanese comics make extensive use of onomatopoeia and in that sense this haiku is like a comic, almost a new kind of haiku.

Why does the person who is sweating close his eyes? Has the sweat gotten into his eyes? Is it too horribly hot? Or is he terribly tired? Is there something he does not want to see? The poem is over before the riddle is solved, but not knowing only makes the poem more striking.

The eyes squeeze shut so tightly they might never open again.

Ase no hito / *gyūtto manako* / *tsuburikeri*
Sweat person / tightly eyes / shut

Kyōgoku Kiyō (1908–1981) was a follower of Takahama Kyoshi. He revived and led the magazine and group *Mokuto*, based in Hyogo Prefecture where his family had been daimyo. This poem is from *Kukutachi*, vol.1 (1946).

The lapis blue of
a candle flame—
summer evening

Yamanishi Masako

We usually think of a candle flame as red or yellow, so I was startled by "lapis blue." This is not a mere figure of speech, but a word that came to her, I think, from carefully observing the candle.

Even in the darkness around a candle there is color, which may vary by season. In this poem it is summer, which perhaps turns the darkness a deep lapis lazuli blue. The blue inside the flame and the blue of the surrounding darkness seem to mirror each other. It feels only right that this scene takes place on a summer evening. The way the poet perceives coolness in the rising heat of a flame is quite wonderful.

The painter Takashima Yajūrō (1890–1975) painted candle flames his entire life. For the lower part of the flame he always used lapis blue. This poem may even have been inspired by seeing his art. Both painter and poet discern a mystery in the candle flame.

> *Rōsoku no / honoo no ruri ya / natsu no kure*
> Candle's / flame's lapis / summer's evening

Yamanishi Masako (b. 1960) began as a contributor to *Kai*, and now leads *Mai*. She also cofounded and contributes to *Hoshi no ki*. This poem is from *Saō* (2009).

Cool moonlight—
the God of Forgetting slips in and out
of my brain

Hayashi Shō

As we age, we often lose track of the names of people and things. It never occurred to me that such a trifling, mundane experience could be the subject of a poem. This poem attributes such memory lapses to "the god of forgetting" (*wasuregami*), a word that isn't in the *Nihon kokugo daijiten*, the multi-volume unabridged dictionary of the Japanese language. Did the poet make it up? If he did, it's an elegant coinage. He may have been using it privately for some time. Be that as it may, I can't help being surprised that there is nothing unpleasant about this god.

As the god slips in and out of the poet's tired brain, the "cool moonlight" shines down, bestowing a feeling of relaxation and refreshment. You feel the poet is at peace with the world.

> *Tsuki suzushi* / *nō o ideiru* / *wasuregami*
> Moon cool / brain goes in and out / god of forgetting

Hayashi Shō (1914–2009) was a follower of Mizuhara Shūōshi, a contributor to *Ashibi*, and editor in chief of Nomura Toshirō's *Oki*. This poem is from his prizewinning *Kōnen* (2004).

Something reflected
in the tombstone—
a summer orange

Kishimoto Naoki

A reflection is visible on a tombstone. Looking around, the poet sees that what is reflected is a summer orange. In other words, he sees the reflected color first and then the thing that gives rise to it. He does not see the reflection and the orange at the same time. This means the orange was not placed on the grave as an offering. It might be hanging from a nearby tree or be an offering on another grave. The tombstone itself must be new for its polished stone to hold a reflection so well.

Does the poet have a personal relationship to the person whose gravestone this is? Where is he positioned physically in relation to the grave? Each riddle breeds another, which gives rise to a kind of unease, of something being off-center.

Naoki's answers to these questions are in his book *100 of my own poems explained.** However, an author's reading of his work need not be the same as that of his readers.

> *Hakaishi ni / utsutte iru wa / natsumikan*
> Tombstone on / reflected is / summer orange

Kishimoto Naoki (b. 1961) studied haiku with Akao Tōshi, Hatano Sōha, and others. He contributes to *Ten'i*, which was led by the late Arima Akito, and to *Shū*, the magazine which succeeded Saitō Kafū's *Yane*. This poem is from his prizewinning *Shun* (1992).

Into a bottle I pour
hot barley tea
then cool it in water

Hoshino Bakujin

Chilled barley tea is a traditional summer drink in Japan. Here the poet takes freshly-made barley tea, and while it is still hot, pours it carefully into a warmed glass bottle. He pours slowly so that the glass will not crack, and screws on the lid. Then, after waiting some time for the filled bottle to cool a little, he places it on its side in cold water.

The bottle is a beautiful amber shape clearly visible in the water. The warm bottle, colored by the barley tea, contrasts with the cold and colorless water; the glass makes a transparent boundary between them. He may also have discovered something new about the texture of a glass bottle. There is a freshness, as though seeing it for the first time.

The poem does not tell us what kind of water is being used to cool the bottle. But this is a poem from the turn of the twentieth century, when there were no electric refrigerators to make ice. In another haiku Bakujin wrote: "Serenely/bubbling away—/pure spring water!" (*Hototogisu*, August 1899). Perhaps he drew the cool water from a bubbling natural spring.

Bin ni irete / mugiyu hiyasu ya / mizu no naka
Bottle in put / barley tea cool / water in

Hoshino Bakujin (1877–1965) studied haiku with Ozaki Kōyō[*1] and Kakuta Chikurei and became one of the leading poets of the Shūseikai.[*2] This poem is from *Haikai shinchō* (1903), edited by Ozaki Kōyō.

For my wife the fillet
for me the whole fish —
loach hotpots

Yoshimura Akira

Visiting a restaurant that specializes in loach (a freshwater fish that is a traditional delicacy in Japan) with his wife, the poet is enjoying a hotpot. His wife chooses one with a fillet of loach, and he chooses one with a whole loach. Side by side they each enjoy their different dishes.

In Japan, eating hot food is traditionally considered a way to cool off during hot weather. Loach in season is particularly delicious cooked in a hotpot. This poem presents two ways of eating loach: filleted, and served whole. The variety suggests something of the special atmosphere of a restaurant devoted to loach cuisine.

Both Yoshimura Akira and his wife, Tsumura Setsuko (b. 1928), were well-known novelists. Each is enjoying what appeals to him or her, and neither tries to impose his or her own taste on the other. This is a glimpse of an intriguing couple.

Tsuma wa hiraki / onore wa maru no / dojō nabe
Wife the fillet / I the whole / loach hotpot

Yoshimura Akira (1927–2006) was a novelist whose works were highly regarded and translated into several languages. He began to study and compose haiku in high school and later he, his wife, and friends gathered regularly to compose haiku. This poem is from *Enten* (2009), edited by Tsumura Setsuko.

I push back hard,
just as unfeeling and cold—
here come the floats

Matsuo Shizuko

The scene is the Gion Festival, held in Kyoto at Yasaka Shrine on July 15, 16, and 17. A great crowd of revelers must have come to watch the large, elaborate floats paraded along the street accompanied by musicians. They jostle and shove to secure a place in the crowd where they can get a good view. When the person next to the poet roughly elbows her aside, she elbows him back just as hard. She is not one to let herself be pushed around.

Haiku at its core is a poetry of greeting, and haiku poems often express empathy in action and words. Given this, it is startling to see the poet frankly portray her own behavior as "unfeeling and cold." But this is part of the freedom that reigns at a festival, when everyday norms of good behavior are temporarily overturned.

This poem captures the feverish atmosphere of the Gion Festival. The author is not a tourist but someone born and bred in Kyoto, writing about her hometown.

Oshikaesu / ware mo jaken ya / hoko o miru
Push back / I too unfeeling and cold / float see

Matsuo Shizuko (1890–1983) began writing haiku after her marriage, mentored by Takahama Kyoshi. She and her husband co-authored three volumes of haiku. This poem is from *Harugotatsu* (1948).

In a patch of shade
beneath an
anti-submarine rocket missile

Inahata Kōtarō

The sea is bright under a strong sun. He stands as if sheltering in the patch of shade cast by the anti-submarine rocket (ASROC) that the battleship is carrying.

The ASROC missile system is carried on battleships and fires rockets attached to the backs of torpedoes. Just before reaching a target and while still in the air, the rocket detaches from the torpedo, which lands in the water, automatically homes in on a submarine, and attacks it at high speed. In armaments jargon the launcher is abbreviated to ASROC, but to make the image vivid, the poet added "missile." Since the Japan Self-Defense Forces use this missile system on their ships, it is natural to imagine the scene as taking place on an SDF ship.

The expression "a patch of shade" (*katakage*) usually describes the shade or shadow cast by a house or wall in bright sunlight; to use it for a modern weapon of warfare is extremely rare. The only place to escape the glare of the sun is underneath the missile—this is the very image of a catch-22 situation.

> *Asurokku / misairu shita no / katakage ni*
> ASROC / missile beneath's / patch of shade in

Inahata Kōtarō (b. 1957) studied haiku with his mother, Inahata Teiko, and is the current leader of *Hototogisu*. This poem is from *Hanbun* (2002).

The enemy soldier
shooting at me shares
the same brutal heat

Katayama Tōshi

"The enemy" is a single soldier shooting at him, hidden in the shadows. The poet feels that both of them are tormented by the same terrible heat. In spite of his own mortal danger, he retains the imaginative capacity to think of the enemy as a human being like himself. This poem makes you feel that even while on the front lines of battle, as Tōshi was when he wrote this poem, he managed to retain a kind of spiritual strength.

The same poet wrote: "The enemy sleeps, I sleep—/The moon shines down/on the battlefield." It is as though the moon, a traditional symbol of friendship in Japan,[*1] can only come into its own when the two soldiers are asleep, their enmity forgotten.

Even on the field of battle he manages to hold fast to the traditional sense of beauty.

Ware o utsu / teki to gōsho o / tomo ni seru
Me at shooting / enemy with brutal heat / I share

Katayama Tōshi (1912–1944) was a follower of Hino Sōjō, a contributor to *Kikan*, and a forerunner of the New Rising Haiku movement.[*2] He died in battle in what is now Papua New Guinea. This poem is from *Hoppō heidan* (1940).

The rock is burning hot
and in the shadow of the rock—
ah, cool snow

Ishibashi Tatsunosuke

The rock is terribly hot, but in its shade some snow remains—a moving sight.

This poem is from *Suichoku no sanposha* ("The vertical walker"), a section of *Sankō* (Mountain-going, 1935). "Vertical" here refers to climbing a sheer mountain cliff face using mountaineering rope, the only way to get to the high-altitude scenery described here. The same section has "The rock is burning hot—/enduring the smell/I shoulder the rope."

A person who lives in the lowlands would be surprised by the great difference in temperature between the surface of a sun-heated rock and the chilly shadow where snow remains at this altitude. The poet greets the startling sight of the snow with the spontaneous "ah, cool snow." The simplicity with which he expresses his feeling and the repetition of the word "rock" is redolent of his youth.

> *Iwa yakuru* / *sono iwakage no* / *yuki aware*
> Rock burns / the rock shade's / snow ah

Ishibashi Tatsunosuke (1909–1948) was a follower of Mizuhara Shūōshi. He is known for his early poems about mountaineering, a subject he introduced in haiku through the poems he published in *Ashibi*. He was later deeply involved in the New Rising Haiku movement* and was one of the haiku poets arrested during World War II for violating the Maintenance of Public Order Law. This poem is from his first collection *Sankō* (1935).

Dawn breaks—
newly born, the cicada nymph
is pale green

Shinoda Teijirō

Dawn, a liminal time between night and day, has the sense of a hallowed moment of new beginnings. One can imagine that the poet was strolling in the dawn woods and saw a faint white movement on a tree trunk. Coming closer to observe, he is surprised to see a cicada beginning to emerge from its chrysalis and stays to watch the whole process. When it has fully emerged it is still pale, the "pale green" of the poem, a lovely color. When the process began it was still so dark he could hardly distinguish colors, but as it becomes lighter even subtle colors can be clearly distinguished.

He does not say "hatched," but "born." Its life as a nymph is over, and it is ready to begin a new life as an adult cicada. The freshness of the cicada's day of birth overlaps with the poet's own remembered youth.

Akatsuki ya / umarete semi no / usumidori
Dawn / being born cicada's / pale green

Shinoda Teijirō (1899–1986) studied haiku with Mizuhara Shūōshi and was a longtime contributor to *Ashibi*. He founded and led *Nobi*. This poem is from *Shinki bara* (1933).

Before you crush it to bits
give
that cicada shell to me

Ōki Amari

This poem is in colloquial Japanese, like a conversational remark. And yet it does not feel at all casual. The tone is urgent and pained.

The speaker is addressing someone who treats the cicada's shell as something of no value, and seems to have roughly crushed a few already. The poems' few words are a protest, prompted by the rage she feels. What has roused that rage? The fact that someone is crushing these beautiful delicate things that nature has created, the shells cicadas discard after they emerge from the earth to breed. The poem astonishes by its tour de force of transforming anger into a hymn to the beauty of creation.

The elegant word for cicada shell, *utsusemi*, with its classical associations of transience and mortality, is not suited to such violent emotion. For this poem, the plain and simple *semigara* is best. The voiced sounds sprinkled throughout the poem (*nigiri, tsubusu, semigara, kudasai*) reverberate like the sound of a cicada shell being crushed.

> *Nigiri tsubusu nara / sono semigara o / kudasai*
> In hand crush if / the cicada shell / hand over

Ōki Amari (b. 1941) cofounded and contributes to *Hoshi no ki*. This poem is from *Seiryō* (2010), which won the Yomiuri Prize for Literature in poetry.

I'm home enjoying
my own bare feet—
what a fine day this is

Suzuki Shigeo

On days when you go to the office you have to wear shoes. A day when you don't need to go to work and you can get by without shoes is pure delight, unless of course you're working from home or busy with housework.

The phrase "enjoying/my own bare feet" suggests the feeling of the soles of his feet touching the tatami, and also the quiet confidence of self-sufficiency and pleasure in his own good health. Rather than spelling all those meanings out, the simple phrase leaves us to imagine the particulars.

Suashi (barefoot) is a relatively new season word similar to, but slightly different from, the usual *hadashi*. Both words mean the same thing, but *hadashi* has rough, dynamic overtones, while *suashi* has a quiet, cultured, and interior feeling. There is no way *hadashi* could replace *suashi* in this poem. One of the pleasures of haiku lies in nuances like this.

> *Ie ni ite / suashi tanoshimu / hi narikeri*
> Home at being / bare feet enjoy / day it is

Suzuki Shigeo (b.1942) was a follower of Ishida Hakyō and is the current leader of *Tsuru*. This poem is from *Yamabōshi* (2007).

Under clear skies
Sado grows dark—
my feet are naked on the sand

Fujimoto Miwako

From a beach in Niigata Prefecture, the poet is gazing out at Sado Island, visible in the distance across the sea. Night is falling there, but it is a clear evening and there is no mist.

The sky around the sun may be colored by the evening glow, but the poet avoids using "sunset" for the seasonal image. Instead, she uses "my feet are naked" (*hadashi*). This is what sets the poem in motion. From the large world of sky and sea in the first two segments of the poem there is an enormous shift of focus to one part of her own body in the last segment. The juxtaposition of the very large and the very small is brilliantly done.

The naked feet tell us that she is relaxing on a sandy beach. She has discovered that the depth of the landscape changes when you let your bare feet touch the earth.

> *Harebare to / Sado no kureyuku / hadashi kana*
> Clear / Sado's darkening / bare feet!

Fujimoto Miwako (b. 1950) is the current leader of *Izumi*. This poem is from her prizewinning collection *Hadashi* (1999).

On the summer ocean
a sailor
has been misplaced

Watanabe Hakusen

In times of peace, the ocean is a place for swimming and similar light-hearted activities. But in this poem the ocean is a place for a warship on its way to battle.

A sailor has gone missing from the warship. Perhaps he met with an accident, or something drove him to commit suicide by jumping overboard? The circumstances are not revealed. What is clear from the word "misplaced" is that the vanished man's existence has no more importance than a misplaced eraser on a desk. There was probably no more than a half-hearted search. The poem captures the inhuman essence of war.

Natsu no umi / *suihei hitori* / *funshitsu su*
Summer's sea / sailor one / misplaced

Watanabe Hakusen (1913–1969), one of the leading poets of the New Rising Haiku movement,* was one of several dozen haiku poets arrested during World War II for violating the Maintenance of Public Order Law. This poem is from *Watanabe Hakusen zenkushū* (1984), compiled by Hakusen's follower Mitsuhashi Toshio.

Swimming practice—
the instructor launches his horse
into the water

Suzuki Uson

Here recruits are being taught to swim. To train his charges, the instructor himself is launching his horse fully into the river. The subject of the poem is "swimming" but not as sport or recreation. It is swimming as a military skill. In times of war it is sometimes necessary to swim across rivers or moats or even through the sea in order to reach enemy lines. Is the instructor who is so resolutely entering the water on his horse a former soldier? You feel his training must be very strict.

Another water-related military art was riding a horse through deep water, making it swim when standing became impossible. As he instructs the recruits in swimming on their own, the teacher himself may be practicing that skill, which was called "horse swimming" (*suiba*).

This poem is very much of the Meiji era (1868–1912), the years when Japan was the victor in two consecutive wars, one with China and the other with Russia.

Suiren ya / uma noriiruru / shihanyaku
Swimming practice / horse mounted entering / instructor

Suzuki Uson (d. 1959) studied haiku with Masaoka Shiki and Kawahigashi Hekigotō. This poem is from *Zoku shunkashūtō: Natsu no bu* (1907), compiled by Kawahigashi Hekigotō.

Treading water
our friendship
grows deeper and deeper

Nakao Sumiko

With the crawl and breaststroke, the swimmer's head ducks in and out of the water so having a conversation is almost impossible. When treading water, however, the head is always above the surface and there are no sudden movements, so a leisurely face-to-face conversation is easy. On the other hand, if the water is too deep to be able touch bottom and you need to tread water to stay afloat, the anxiety and sense of instability is much greater than on land. This shared anxiety can serve to deepen the mutual sympathy that underlies friendship.

The Tang poet Bai Juyi (772–846) said friendship deepens when admiring the beauties of nature together.* Sumiko responds that treading water together does this, too.

This sort of unaffected and simple way of socializing is what haiku is all about.

Tachioyogi / shite yūjō o / fukōseri
Treading water / friendship / we deepen

Nakao Sumiko (1914–1989) was a follower of Akimoto Fujio and a contributor to *Hyōkai*, which eventually ceased publication. She later became a follower of Nagata Kōi and contributed to *Riraza*. This poem is from *Rōkotan* (1987).

Night's child
clothes herself in tomorrow's swimsuit
and sets off walking

Moriga Mari

A child who has a swimming lesson the next day puts on her swimsuit the night before and walks around wearing it.

So eager and happy is she about the coming day and her new swimsuit that she tries the swimsuit on the night before. Thus garbed, she walks around the room. The phrase "sets off walking" suggests the child's vitality. Unable to sit still, she is walking into tomorrow, into the future.

"Night's child" can be interpreted as her still being awake at night, but can also mean a child born of the nighttime, one who only comes into her own then, like a supernatural spirit. The child walking around inside at night in the dark-colored regulation school swimsuit must look like a strange creature indeed.

> *Yoru no ko no / ashita no mizugi o / kite aruku*
> Night's child's / tomorrow's swimsuit / puts on and walks

Moriga Mari (b. 1960) was married to the haiku poet Tanaka Hiroaki. She studied haiku with Hatano Sōha and, after his death, became a contributor to *Momotori*. She founded *Shizuka na basho* to commemorate her late husband's work, and contributes to it. This poem is from her prizewinning *Matataku* (2009).

All the young girls
are wringing out
their navy blue swimsuits

Satō Ayaka

"Young girls" could be either middle school students or high school students, but the term seems more suited to middle school students, that is, girls in their low teens. Since there are a lot of them together, the scene must be at school. Afterschool clubs in Japan are a large part of school life, but rather than a swimming club, in which participation is voluntary, I prefer to read this as the compulsory swimming that is part of physical education classes.

The young girls have just emerged from the dressing room near the school swimming pool, wearing their neat school uniforms again. Having finished washing their swimsuits at the sink, they are now wringing them out. Wringing the swimsuits takes a certain amount of force. As they do it, the weariness built up from swimming creeps over them.

This is a vivid vignette of a moment at the end of the swimming period. The poet was in her early twenties when this poem was published, young enough to remember such moments well.

Shōjo mina / kon no mizugi o / shiborikeri
Young girls all / navy blue swimsuits / wringing out

Satō Ayaka (b. 1985), as a young student, received the grand prize of the National High School Haiku Championship (Haiku Kōshien). She contributes to Sato and Kagami, and cofounded and runs Manbō with Seki Etsushi. This haiku is the first poem in her prizewinning Kaisō hyōhon (2008).

Summer lassitude begins
tonight and the mothering is
"all sold out"

Katō Chiyoko

Summer in Japan is hot and humid. Energy flags, appetites fade, and people lose weight. In weather like this, mothering is beyond her.

This poem is from the early 1960s, when Japan was still recovering from the devastation of World War II. There was no air conditioning in summer, food and clothing were still in short supply, and shops were often sold out of everyday goods. Physically and economically, the populace was barely getting by. In this context, "all sold out" must have been a familiar and often-encountered phrase. No matter how her children beg her to do this or that for them, she can't respond. She may even have used those exact words to her children: "The mothering is all sold out."

The humor is there, and so is the pain.

Natsuyase hajimaru yo wa / okaasan / urikire desu
Summer thinness begun night / mother / sold out

Katō Chiyoko (1909–1986) took up haiku after marrying the haiku poet Katō Shūson. She was one of the cofounders and editors of *Josei haiku*, a magazine for women's haiku. This poem is from *Toki* (1962).

Roasting eggplant
cooling it down — we chat about
the beloved dead

Ikeda Sumiko

Yakinasu, a succulent Japanese dish, is traditionally made by broiling eggplant over an open flame, then peeling off the charred skin and quickly cooling the eggplant in water. It is a dish with a haiku taste. There is something playful, light-hearted, and earthy about the way it is made: you don't just broil the eggplant, you broil it and then you cool it and when it is cool, you flavor it.

This season word tells us it is late summer, the time of year when World War II ended, so "the beloved dead" might be connected to the war. The poet's father was a military doctor who was deployed to the Chinese front and died there in August 1944 when she was only 8 years old. Her mentor, the haiku poet Mitsuhashi Toshio (1920–2001), never stopped protesting war in poems like "They'll repeat/the same terrible mistake—/autumn evening."

Talking about the dead one, whoever it is, brings him close. It is also possible that roasted eggplant was one of his favorite foods.

Nasu yaite / hiyashite tamashii / no hanashi
Eggplant roasting / cooling dead soul / talk

Ikeda Sumiko (b. 1936) wrote fiction and free verse from her teens, but did not begin writing haiku until she was close to 40 years old. She currently contributes to *Sendan*, *Ani*, and *Men*. This poem is from her prizewinning *Tamashii no hanashi* (2005).

When I look into the center
of the sunflower
the sea fades away

Shiba Fukio

At the seaside, he looks up at a tall sunflower. Looking more closely, he stands gazing at the pistil and stamen that make up the center. Then he notices that the sea seems to have disappeared, and there is only the sunflower.

The appeal of this poem comes from the statement "the sea fades away." Of course the sea has not really disappeared. That would be impossible, but his attention has wandered from the sea, which at first attracted him because he had not seen it for some time. Now the sunflower, this huge flower, totally engrosses him.

The poem makes you feel the uniqueness of the sunflower, which is so large that it can hide even the sea from view.

> *Himawari no / shibe o miru toki / umi kieshi*
> Sunflower's / pistil and stamen look when / sea disappeared

Shiba Fukio (1903–1930) first received attention for the haiku he published in his early 20s. He became a promising contributor to *Hototogisu*, but when he died unexpectedly at 26 he left only a few hundred haiku behind. This poem is from *Teihon Shiba Fukio kushū* (1970), one of the several editions of his complete works published posthumously.

Autumn

The tin-can phone
connected me to the autumn
of the ancients

Settsu Yukihiko

The poet and his friend were playfully talking to each other through a tin-can phone when somehow his friend's voice phased out and he felt he was connected to an autumn of another age, when people now long dead were still alive.

The idea of the poem is that this primitive toy, the tin-can phone, brings past and present together. Sometimes when we are reading old poems they also give this feeling. So here the tin-can phone might also be a buried metaphor for the act of reading itself. On the other hand the tin-can phone links people through space, and the phrase "autumn/of the ancients" carries the same idea of linking people, but those who are separated in time. One way and another, the feeling of trying to erase separation between people flows beneath the words of the poem.

Yukihiko died while still in middle age and this poem was written near the end of his life. Takayama Reona (b. 1968), one of Yukihiko's younger haiku colleagues in *Ani*, used it as the preface to *Urutora* (1998), his own collection of haiku. He must have wanted to link himself to Yukihiko's life and works. In that sense this poet has already become one of the ancients, looked up to by many younger poets today.

> *Itodenwa / kojin no aki ni / tsunagarinu*
> Tin-can phone / ancients' autumn to / linked

Settsu Yukihiko (1947–1996) came to prominence in 1974, when he was selected for the "50 Haiku Competition" of Takayanagi Jūshin's magazine *Haiku kenkyū*. He also co-founded several haiku magazines, the last in 1980, called *Ani*, which became a major base for avant-garde haiku. This poem is from *Settsu Yukihiko zenkushū* (1987).

The demon of autumn
sat down on a rock
and kindled a fire

Tomizawa Kakio

Who is the demon? Is it a spirit of the dead or an imaginary monster? At most, we can say that it is something that is no longer human if it ever was. And yet it is a demon of autumn, that elegant season, so it has not totally left behind this world and everything in it.

And what is the fire for? It is not for warmth, or to burn something up. In practical terms it is a useless fire, although it might be one of the fires lit for Obon, the festival of the dead, to welcome spirits and see them off. But the ashes from this fire will remain on the rock.

This poem was written in 1941, during the Pacific War, but the critic and haiku poet Origasa Bishū (1934–1990) wrote that it made him think of a landscape left after a nuclear bomb. We, on the other hand, cannot help but see the Fukushima nuclear disaster in the flames.

> *Ishi no ue ni* / *aki no oni ite* / *hi o takeri*
> Rock's top on / autumn's demon sits / fire has lit

Tomizawa Kakio (1902–1962) was one of the central figures of the New Rising Haiku movement* in the prewar period, cofounder of several postwar modernist haiku magazines including *Bara*, and a central participant in Takayanagi Jūshin's *Haiku hyōron*. This poem is from *Hebi no fue* (1952).

Walking in the nest
are bees, feet lightly thrumming
at noon in autumn

Usami Gyomoku

Let me read in slow motion, segment by segment. The first segment makes you ask: What or who is walking? And what kind of nest are they in? Is it even possible to walk in a nest? Riddle begets riddle.

With the next segment, the riddles are solved: it is bees that are walking in the nest and the sound is made by their feet. One can write about non-human footsteps, of course, but it is startling to find the word used about bees. The parts of this poem are knit together in a pleasing music by the vowel sound "a" in *aruku* (walk), *hachi* (bee), *ashioto* (footsteps), and *aki* (autumn). The seasonal image at the end, with the clear light and dry air of an autumn noon, wraps the whole scene in a silence broken only by the faint footsteps of the bees, which seem to have stirred up a kind of fragrance in an ineffably strange world.

This poem was composed in the Kiso Mountains of Nagano Prefecture, which Gyomoku often visited.

Su o aruku / hachi no ashioto / aki no hiru
Nest on walk / bee's footsteps / autumn's noon

Usami Gyomoku (1926–2018) was a calligrapher as well as a haiku poet. He began writing haiku at the suggestion of his father when he was 19, soon became a contributor to *Hototogisu* and other haiku magazines, and ultimately cofounded *Shin* in 1984. This poem is from *Sōshin* (1989).

The living spirit
steps nimbly about
hither and yon

Hosokawa Kaga

Today is Obon, the festival of the dead. In addition to welcoming back the spirits of the dead, there is also a custom of fêting the very oldest members of the family, the "living spirits." The way the old person in the poem is depicted stepping nimbly about makes for a wonderfully witty contrast with the solemnity of the occasion. The onomatopoeic *hyoko hyoko* to describe the way she walks is a wonderful touch.

According to the poet, the "living spirit" is his own mother. The poem was written in 1974, when the custom of fêting the oldest members of the family at Obon may have been more widely practiced than it is now. In the afterword to the collection of haiku in which this poem appeared, Kaga wrote of his deep feelings for his mother: "In my earliest memories, my mother was always there, struggling valiantly in the midst of our poverty. Now in her later years she has been given peace, and for that I am profoundly grateful."

While feeling such deep tenderness, he made a poem of pure description, recording his mother's portrait for all time.

Ikimitama / *hyoko hyoko aruki* / *tamaikeri*
Living spirit / nimbly walks / graciously [honorific]

Hosokawa Kaga (1924–1989) studied haiku with Ishida Hakyō and Ishizuka Tomoji* and contributed to *Tsuru*. After retirement from his government job he founded and led *Hatsuchō*. This poem, written in 1974, is from his prizewinning *Ikimitama* (1980).

Walking through the wild grassy fields
getting damp—
Festival of Souls

Shimosaka Sumiho

This poem lacks a strong cut or caesura, so one reads it smoothly and without pause. Boundaries melt in the mind as they do on the page, and there is a sense of crossing paths with the dead as the poet walks through the fields. *Tamamatsuri*, festival of souls, is another name for Obon, the festival of the dead.

At first glance the wild grasses in a field may look dry, but sometimes the leaves are dew-laden and the hem of your clothes may get damp. To me, the dew on the leaves—invisible yet unquestionably there—might even suggest the unseen spirits of the ancestors who are welcomed back to this world on this day.

The poet does not say what gets damp, and the ambiguity is effective, for the word "damp" is naturally associated with tears. You can also think of the dampness as coming from tears shed for the beloved dead.

Kusahara o / ayumeba nurete / Tamamatsuri
Grassy field through / when walk dampening / festival of souls

Shimosaka Sumiho (b. 1963) studied haiku with Saitō Kafū and contributes to *Shū*. She is also editor in chief of *Kuntsuaito*, led by Yorimitsu Masaki.* This poem is from her prizewinning *Gankō* (2012).

I wash the grave—
because the water is
so sweet now

Shimizu Keiko

She is washing the gravestone at Obon, the festival of the dead, the time to visit family graves and freshen them up. The season is autumn, but the weather is still warm and the water now tastes especially good.

Everyone takes care that grave-washing water is clear and clean, but ordinarily the taste is a matter of no moment. That is because there is no way for the deceased whose bones rest in the grave to drink it. However, the poet writes that she is washing the gravestone because the water has become delicious. There is a definite humor. You can almost envision the dead one who dwells in the grave contentedly sipping the water as it trickles down. Her feeling of love for the deceased is also evoked. The shift in register from classical grammar to the colloquial "so sweet" (*oishiku*) is also part of the charm of this poem.

Haka arau / *mizu ga oishiku* / *naritareba*
Grave I wash / water delicious / has become and so

Shimizu Keiko (1911–2005) began writing haiku under the influence of her brother-in-law Akimoto Fujio and contributed to his magazine *Hyōkai*. She later became a contributor to *Riraza*. Her most productive period was between the ages of 62 and 90, when she published four collections of haiku. The poem here is from her prizewinning *Ame no ki* (2001).

Threading swiftly in and out
I rowed downstream to watch —
the fireworks!

Matsuse Seisei

The poet is watching fireworks from a boat going downriver. The boat-man may be the one who is doing the rowing, but the poet writes as if he himself is, which gives an easy swing to the verse. At first he was watching from upstream, but he felt somehow dissatisfied. So he rowed downstream to where the pyrotechnicians were busily setting the fireworks off from the riverbank, and now he is looking back from downstream.

Koginukete means "while rowing, threading among [other] boats," and implies energy and vigor. Fireworks originated from ceremonial fires lit on the last day of Obon, the festival of the dead, to see off the spirits, so there are many subdued poems about them, but this poem is youthful and has a feeling of speed.

> *Koginukete / kawashimo ni miru / hanabi kana*
> Rowing in and out / downriver at see / fireworks!

Matsuse Seisei (1869–1937) was a follower of Masaoka Shiki, as well as an editor of *Hototogisu*. He also wrote tanka and classical Chinese poetry and was a *haiga* (haiku-paint-ing) artist. His *Tsumaki* (1904–1906, four volumes) is the oldest example of a haiku collec-tion by a single poet published during the author's lifetime. This poem is from *Shunkashūtō: Aki no bu* (1902), compiled by Kawahigashi Hekigotō and Takahama Kyoshi.

One evening cicada calls
when the other falls still—
so far away!

Nakamura Kusatao

We are in a forest on an early autumn evening after a clear bright day. An evening cicada that was shrilly chirping for a long time goes silent and another begins to chirp, the sound coming from far off. This successive chirping does not feel like a coincidence. As if fearing to fall silent, when one cicada stops chirping, another one takes up the song.

The silence of a cicada signifies death and the deepening of autumn. The cicada's song seems to be saying, "I'm not dead. Here I am, alive and well." It can't be coincidental that one takes up where the other leaves off. You can't help but be moved by the sympathy between the two cicadas so distant from each other.

Separated though they are, the early autumn twilight enfolds both.

> *Higurashi no / naki kawarishi wa / haruka kana*
> Evening cicada's / cry in succession / far off!

Nakamura Kusatao (1901–1983) first studied haiku with Takahama Kyoshi and contributed to *Hototogisu*. Widely read in Western literature, philosophy, and religion, he became an influential figure in postwar debates about haiku and founded and led *Banryoku*. He is often grouped with Ishida Hakyō and Katō Shūson as a "humanist" poet.* This poem is from *Chōshi* (1936).

We called the little hill out back
Cicadaland—
and it's still mine

Andō Tsuguo

He is always thinking of his hometown, and every time he does so, the early autumn chirping of the evening cicadas on the little hill behind his house echoes in his heart.

The hill the poet evokes is not a concrete reality before his eyes. It belongs to memory. It cannot always be his, any more than memory can be eternal. But the poet's affirmation of the reality of the impossible is, I dare say, what gives this poem the feel of a true haiku.

For someone who lives far away from where they grew up, their hometown becomes a special place. Just to think of it at times of suffering or sadness can be a comfort. For this poet, his home town of Tsuyama in Okayama Prefecture was summed up in the little hill behind his house that he and his family called Cicadaland.

> *Higurashi to / iu na no urayama o / itsumo motsu*
> Evening cicada so / named mountain behind / always I hold

Andō Tsuguo (1919–2002) was a haiku and free form poet, as well as a prolific scholar of comparative literature and Japanese poetry who published numerous works about Matsuo Bashō[1] and other classical poets. He studied haiku with Katō Shūson and later joined Ōoka Makoto in the development of the modern poem sequence (*renshi*).[2] This haiku is from *Urayama* (1972).

In the new coolness
so well wrung out—
a dishcloth!

Kume Masao

Autumn has begun but in the daytime the heat is still oppressive. There is a clean white dishcloth on the table, rinsed and well wrung out. All the newly cool air seems to be gathered up and concentrated there.

The seasonal image "new coolness" (*shinryō*) is the fresh coolness you feel at autumn's beginning. A well-wrung dishcloth is a very apt accompaniment to that sensation.

Who did the wringing? I would like the answer to be the poet himself. That way "so well wrung out" is not a mere observation, but an action taken after the poet himself has tossed the cloth into water and rinsed it. His still-damp hands feel the cool air directly. Read this way, the setting would be the domestic surroundings of his own home.

Shinryō no / *kataku shiborishi* / *fukin kana*
New coolness / tightly wrung out / dishcloth

Kume Masao (1891–1952) was a novelist. His haiku nom de plume was Santei. He participated in Kawahigashi Hekigotō's New Tendency Haiku movement,* but broke with him when Hekigotō abandoned fixed form, seventeen-syllable haiku. Later, he was active in Kubota Mantarō's haiku gatherings. This poem is from *Kaeribana* (1943).

Even on this night
pregnant with lightning
come, it's time to sleep

Nakamura Teijo

The world of seasonal images is not without seeming contradictions. "Thunder" is a summer image, but its companion, "lightning," belongs to autumn. On the surface this seems strange, but thunder manifests in towering cumulonimbus clouds as a frightening boom, while lightning, which seems to race across the distant sky, was traditionally thought to presage a good autumn rice harvest and was a venerated natural phenomenon.

Inazuma, "lightning," is written with characters that mean "husband of the rice," and may even have reflected the belief that lightning bolts "inseminated" the rice plants. The old belief lives on in this poem. And so does the joy that comes from seeing lightning flash across the sky. Watching it, the poet is reluctant to sleep, but nevertheless tells herself that the time has come.

There is a kind of serene sensuality about this poem.

> *Inazuma no / yutaka naru yo mo / nubeki koro*
> Lightning / plentiful is night even / should sleep time

Nakamura Teijo (1900–1988), a follower of Takahama Kyoshi, was one of the so-called Four T's,* the leading female poets of postwar haiku. After the war she founded and led *Kazahana,* through which she nurtured many female haiku poets. This poem is from *Teijo kushū* (1944).

In the bottom
of the washbasin—
a watermelon seed

Shinozaki Hisako

What is a watermelon seed doing at the bottom of a washbasin? How did it get there? If you let yourself start thinking about this strange conjunction, questions arise. Did someone use the basin to catch seeds while they were eating a slice of watermelon? Maybe the poet herself did. Or an unnoticed seed got stuck to her cheek and then fell into the washbasin when she washed her face. But how could anyone not notice that? It is all quite unsettling. Whatever the backstory, the seed is clearly somewhere it is not meant to be. It could be a buried metaphor for the poet's own anxious feeling of not being where she is expected to be. Maybe she feels as oddly out of place as this watermelon seed in a washbasin. I see the basin as white enamel, and the watermelon seed as black, which makes it stand out all the more.

Senmenki no / soko ni suika no / tane hitotsu
Washbasin's / bottom in watermelon's / seed one

Shinozaki Hisako (b. 1975) studied haiku with Kagiwada Yūko and is a contributor to *Miraizu*. This poem is from *Chōshinsen 21* (2011), a haiku anthology by 21 emerging poets under the age of 50.

Everyone waiting together
for the typhoon—
that feeling

Nakata Yoshiko

A big typhoon is coming. The weather forecast predicts that peoples' homes will be buffeted by fierce wind and rain. Their lives may even be at risk. As everyone waits together, they are busy preparing as best they can by boarding up their windows and so on. Perhaps "everyone" is a family or fellow students at a school. Or it could even mean the entire country.

Please note that this is not a scene of everyone waiting together for a typhoon. This is the *feeling* of that waiting. The poem is not about one particular experience but rather a feeling that has developed through accumulated experiences. It describes the intense communal feeling all share when confronting something overwhelming. Perhaps this is how people felt in earlier times during war.

And what are we awaiting now?

> *Taifū o / minna de matte / iru kanji*
> Typhoon / everyone waiting / feeling

Nakata Yoshiko (b. 1959) first studied haiku with Katsura Nobuko and contributed to *Sōen*. After Katsura's death she joined *Sōju*, led by Uda Kiyoko. In 1998 she cofounded *quatre*, and she currently runs the magazine. This poem is from her first haiku collection, *Wakusei* (2002).

As the winds swirl
the water I drew and brought in
sways on and on

Baba Ikuko

Water drawn outside in the midst of a storm and brought into the house continues swaying in the bucket for some time.

This is not water you get from turning on a faucet in the kitchen. Another poem by Ikuko shows us that considerable strength is needed to get water: "In the new coolness of autumn/ I used all my strength/ to draw water." In the featured poem, perhaps she is drawing water from a well. Or it might be a hand-operated pump. Before the storm gets really bad, she goes into the garden and fills a bucket with enough water to tide her over.

Even when she puts the bucket down on the floor the water continues to sway, as though reflecting the power of the storm. I feel as though the constantly changing shape of the clear water is the external expression of the poet's own inner unease amidst the gathering storm.

Nowaki naka / kumi koshi mizu no / yure yamanu
Windstorm in / dipped and brought water / sways without stopping

Baba Ikuko (1918–1994) studied haiku with Kaneko Isekikō,* later became a follower of Mizuhara Shūōshi, and was a contributor to *Ashibi*. This poem is from her prizewinning *Kai no oto* (1985).

I sip a bit of saké
for the dad I am
this autumn night

Ōgushi Akira

"My response to the telegram from home announcing the baby's birth," reads the headnote. When the happy news he was eagerly awaiting arrives from his hometown, he raises a glass to toast the birth of his first child. The poem itself is a kind of heartwarming toast to the newborn as well, but strangely it does not include any direct mention of the child's birth. He writes as if his drink might be merely a way to deepen the enjoyment of a lovely autumn evening. Perhaps this reticence is a way of shyly cloaking his intense joy. At the same time, there is a quirky humor in the way the father provides an unadorned self-portrait in words for the newborn baby.

Drinking saké on an autumn night inevitably calls to mind the famous tanka by the modern poet Wakayama Bokusui (1885–1928): "On autumn nights/when the saké flows over/pearl-white teeth,/how wonderful to/drink alone in the quietness." In saying "a bit of saké," Akira may have wanted to set himself apart from Bokusui, who was a notorious drinker.

Sake mo sukoshi wa / nomu chichi naru zo / aki no yo wa
Saké a bit / drinks father I am / autumn night

Ōgushi Akira (b. 1937) studied haiku with Ōno Rinka. After Rinka's death he founded and became leader of *Momotori*. This poem is from his prizewinning *Asa no fune* (1978).

I stand up to go drink
hot water one room over—
the long night!

Okamoto Hekisansui

The poet must have been sitting at the table after dinner, reading and writing. Feeling thirsty, he stands up to go to the next room for a drink of hot water—not cold water, but hot, which gives a sense of the chilliness of the air. In the same way, the very small distance he crosses to reach the next room emphasizes the long, silent hours of the night.

Many haiku from the Meiji era (1868–1912) deal with simple feelings and impressions. Of course Hekisansui also wrote such poems, but this poem is simply a report set down without any strong emotion. The very lack of emotional content was something new.

Hekisansui formed the Mita Haiku Society with Momiyama Shigetsu and others, and mentored Kubota Mantarō. The first hints of what Mantarō's haiku became are here in this haiku by Hekisansui. Clearly inspired by Hekisansui, Mantarō later wrote: "I add cold water/to the hot—/what a long night!."

> *Tsugi no ma e / yu o nomi ni tatsu / yonaga kana*
> Next room to / hot water drink to stand up / night long

Okamoto Hekisansui (1878–1942) studied haiku with Masaoka Shiki and selected poems for *Hototogisu* from age 26. In the 1910s he grew apart from *Hototogisu* and moved to composing seasonal free form haiku. This poem is from *Hekisansui kushū* (1907).

The sky opens
wide and wants to laugh—
the flowering fields!

Watanabe Suiha

The poet is precise in his use of language: he does not say that the sky laughs, he says that it *wants* to laugh. That is, he does not record the action, he records the feeling: on this sunny day, the sky is feeling cheerful and bright.

Rather than personification, we should read this as the poet's perception of the sky's will and emotion. The best word to use would be animism. Suiha's mentor, Takahama Kyoshi, wrote in *Susumubeki haiku no michi* (1918), "One of the distinctive traits of Suiha's haiku is to see inanimate objects as having feelings." This haiku is a perfect example of what Kyoshi meant.

> *Ten byōbyō / waraitaku narishi / hanano kana*
> Sky far and wide / wants to laugh / flower field

Watanabe Suiha (1882–1946) was a follower of Naitō Meisetsu and later of Takahama Kyoshi, and became an influential member of *Hototogisu*. He also founded and led *Kyokusui*. This poem is from *Hakujitsu* (1936).

Two paths meet and find
each other among
the autumn grass

Kinoshita Yūji

In a field where a breeze is softly blowing through autumn grasses, one path encounters another.

The image feels somehow familiar to me, as if I saw it once in a decorative Rinpa* screen painting. There are only two empty paths, without a sign of humans, yet "meet and find each other" is an expression usually reserved for people and suggests a lovers' rendezvous. The scene feels imbued with the poet's own deeply felt longing for companionship.

Yūji's teacher Kubota Mantarō wrote the following poem: "The dew-laden path/again divides/into two ways." Mantarō's poem is about places where the road divides, but insofar as the road stands for feelings, there is a tie to Yūji's poem. Mantarō's poem was written in 1944; Yūji's poem was written at least fifteen years later.

> *Akikusa no / naka aiaeru / michi futatsu*
> Autumn grasses / among meet / paths two

Kinoshita Yūji (1914–1965) was an accomplished poet of modern verse when he began writing haiku during World War II. After the war he joined the group led by Kubota Mantarō. He also founded and led *Shunrai*. This poem is from the posthumous collection *Teihon Kinoshita Yūji kushū* (1966).

A hut of early afternoon—
I tear it down and
all is silver grass

Yasui Kōji

Early afternoon is a peaceful time of day when nothing happens. A hut of early afternoon might be suspended in eternal time. At the least, we feel that for this hut, time will drift peacefully by until sunset. Instead, the hut is suddenly destroyed. And not through a natural process but intentionally, by the poem's speaker.

What is this hut? Is it a base for a fisherman or a shepherd's summer hut? In that case, why would someone need to tear it down? Will there be no fishing or grazing from next year? After the hut is torn down, there is nothing but the waving plumes of autumn silver grass (*susuki*) lit up by the afternoon sun, and an overwhelming sense of the power of nature.

This haiku begins and ends in mystery.

Hirusugi no / koya o kowaseba / mina susuki
Past noon / hut tear down / all silver grass

Yasui Kōji (b. 1936) was a follower of Nagata Kōi and a contributor to *Riraza*. He also contributed to Takayanagi Jūshin's *Haiku hyōron*. This poem is from *Afugaku* (1974).

A diamond of dew—
one drop
on top of a rock

Kawabata Bōsha

A single drop of dew that makes you feel the hardness of a diamond is simply sitting there on a rock.

Dew of course is made of water, but here it is perceived as being as hard as a diamond, as the Zen priest Dōgen (1200–1253) said of the Buddhist dharma: "Frozen, it becomes harder than diamonds, who could break it?"[*1] Dōgen is writing about ice whereas Bōsha is writing about dew, but as the poet and critic Nagata Kōi suggested,[*2] in a sense here Bōsha has absorbed and gone beyond Dōgen.

By incorporating Buddhist terms and references in his haiku, Bōsha gave deep expression to the essence of things beyond physical sight.

> *Kongō no / tsuyu hitotsubu ya / ishi no ue*
> Diamond's / dew one drop / atop a rock

Kawabata Bōsha (1897–1941), once an aspiring painter, became a follower of Takahama Kyoshi and, eventually, one of the leading poets of *Hototogisu*. This poem is from *Kawabata Bōsha kushū* (1934).

Water sound and
insect song and
my own heart, beating

Nishimura Kazuko

The sound made by the water—I imagine a quietly flowing stream—
must be rather subdued if the sounds of the insects and her own beating
heart can be distinguished through it. Rather than describing the surroundings, the poet focuses on the layers of sound. She might be beside
the stream and listening closely with eyes shut.

The poem is constructed of three elements, each a sound. Ordinarily,
use of the same character twice in a poem is frowned upon but here, as
though deliberately breaking that taboo, she uses 音, the kanji for
"sound," three times. The fact that each appearance has a different pronunciation (*oto, ne, on*) shows the author's artistry.

As I repeat the poem aloud, the entire poem itself begins to feel like
the sound of a beating heart or a voice at prayer.

Mizuoto to / mushi no ne to waga / shin'on to
Water sound and / insect's sound and my / heart sound

Nishimura Kazuko (b. 1948) is a follower of Kiyosaki Toshio. She cofounded and co-leads
Chi-in with Namekata Katsumi.* This poem is from her prizewinning *Shin'on* (2007).

Cricket peers down
deep into the bowels
of the earth

Yamaguchi Seishi

Ordinarily the cricket is loved for its touching song, but the silent and solemn cricket in this poem is described in terms of its appearance. Far from such lighthearted activities as looking for a mate, this cricket is peering down into a crevice in the earth. What might it see? There can't be anything there but an all-encompassing darkness. And yet the cricket cannot stop staring. The image exudes malaise and a profound loneliness.

Yamaguchi Seishi wrote many haiku about insects. One of the most famous, from *Tōkō* (1932) is: "Crunching and munching/the praying mantis eats up/the face of a bee." This is a cruel scene of one insect devouring another, and the stark perception of the bee's face as an inanimate object is brilliant. But it is a poem of observation.

The cricket poem, in contrast, is a virtual self-portrait, written during a period when war was at hand and the poet himself was gravely ill.

Koorogi ga / fukaki chichū o / nozokikomu
Cricket / deep earth within / peeks into

Yamaguchi Seishi (1901–1994) was a follower of Takahama Kyoshi and one of the so-called Four S's[1] of *Hototogisu*. He later became a leading poet of the New Rising Haiku movement.[2] In 1948 he cofounded *Tenrō*, through which he contributed to the revival of haiku in postwar Japan. This poem is from *Shichiyō* (1942).

The tiny stinkbug
            can't save up, so lets loose
                        with a mighty fart

Aijima Kyokō

This is a portrait of the life of a stink bug. The Japanese name *hehiri-mushi* literally means "fart releasing bug." In haiku, it can apply to any one of several kinds of beetle that emit a foul smell when disturbed or attacked. The stink bug in this poem may be unable to store anything of any size up in its tiny body but, as its name predicts, it can still let out a huge fart.

The stink bug unable to "save up" also evokes the life of the common people who lived from hand to mouth, and for whom this politician poet clearly had sympathy. Around the same time he also wrote: "The stink bug/has broken the wind/that it should," and "The stink bug/raises its butt/and gives forth."

> *Hehirimushi* / *takuwae mo naku* / *hanachikeri*
> Stink bug / savings without / lets go

Aijima Kyokō (1867–1935) was a follower of Masaoka Shiki and Takahama Kyoshi, and was also a member of Japan's House of Representatives. This poem is from *Kyokō kushū* (1932).

Waiting for the moon
I pop the cork
from a bottle of champagne

Hoshino Tsubaki

The poet is waiting with friends to witness the rising of the autumn harvest moon, a traditional Japanese custom. As their meal begins, she pops the cork on a bottle of champagne for the first drink. The choice of posh champagne rather than ordinary beer makes the meal as special as the venerated moon. The concreteness and onomatopoeia combined in the phrase "pop the cork" skillfully suggests both the spirited flight of the cork and the excited anticipation of the poet and her companions.

The poet and her guests could be sitting outside in the garden, but it feels more natural to think of them waiting indoors. By moonrise they may be enjoying the conversation and their delicious meal so much that they forget about the moon. "I think of you most when admiring the snow, the moon, and the flowers," wrote the Tang dynasty poet Bai Juyi.* His sentiment hums beneath the words of this poem.

> *Tsuki o matsu / shanpan no sen / pon to nuki*
> Moon waiting / champagne cork / pop taking out

Hoshino Tsubaki (b. 1930) was the oldest daughter of Hoshino Tatsuko. After her mother's death, she inherited the leadership of *Tamamo*. At present she is *Tamamo*'s leader emeritus. This poem is from *Tsubaki shikishū* (2008).

A tempest blows through
the taro plants and through
my house, echoing

Murayama Kokyō

Taro, or *satoimo*, is a starchy root plant that is grown all over Japan. This small, round, hairy tuber is a humble food prized for its nourishing qualities and often appears in home cooking, especially in the autumn. The leaves of the taro are quite large, especially in comparison to its underground tubers. In this poem, the leaves beyond the open window are swaying and rustling as a strong wind blows through them. The same wind blows in through the window, making the whole house resound.

Clearly this is no mansion but a small and simple dwelling. However, the poet is not lamenting his poverty. In total sympathy with nature, he delights in hearing the sounds his house makes in the wind. Wealth would distance him from nature, but poverty brings it near. This is the medieval aesthetic of *wabi* and *sabi*, "the beauty of lack." Kokyō lived it out in his own life.

The poem was composed in 1956, the year after Kokyō moved to Nerima on the edge of Tokyo. His house there was set amid a rural landscape that was often buffeted by stormy winds.

Imo arashi / *wagaya fukinuke* / *hibiku nari*
Taro tempest / my house blows through and / echoes

Murayama Kokyō (1909–1986) studied haiku with Shida Sokin* and later was a contributor to Ishida Hakyō's *Tsuru*. He also led *Sagano* and wrote many books on haiku and haiku poets. This poem is from *Saikyō* (1962).

Wings, and then
the torso crosses—a giant
gold-ringed dragonfly

Kinbara Tomonori

What this poem describes is not revealed until the last segment. First we have wings, then they float out of his field of vision and a torso replaces them. At this point the reader is helpless to imagine anything other than a huge monster materializing, something like a winged dragon. But no, the next instant brings "gold-ringed dragonfly," and the portrait is complete. A huge gold ringed dragonfly had passed by. The progressive unfolding creates an intensified sense of this insect's unusually large size.

The gold-ringed dragonfly (*Anotogaster sieboldii*) is the largest dragonfly in Japan and can grow to a length of almost 4 inches (over 10 centimeters). Reversing the usual order of description vividly recreates the surprise the poet felt when the dragonfly winged its way past him.

Hane no ato / *dō ga yokogiri* / *oniyanma*
Wings after / torso crosses / gold-ringed dragonfly

Kinbara Tomonori (b. 1962) was a follower of Saitō Kafū and a contributor to Kafū's *Yane*. This poem is from the prizewinning *Hakushoku* (2009).

Cicada and dragonfly both
live
without water —
the wind at dusk

Hayashi Kei

One evening when there is a strong wind, the poet is suddenly struck by how winged insects like cicadas and dragonflies survive with almost no water as they fly about. For these aerial creatures, dryness and death are not connected. This simple fact is the door to awareness of a mystery, the mystery of the many different ways there are of being alive.

Placing the words for the two autumn insects, cicada and dragonfly, side by side encourages you to imagine the differences in the feel of their wings and bodies and also in the sounds they make. It also sparks consideration of what it means for creatures of different kinds to live together.

Japanese haiku are conventionally printed in one long vertical line, but this unusual "multi-line" (*tagyō keishiki*) haiku was purposely written out in four short vertical lines, and has nineteen rather than the usual seventeen syllables. In Japanese the lines march across the top of the page from right to left, leaving a large expanse of blank space beneath them that seems to have been swept clean by the strong, refreshing wind.

Semi mo / *tonbo mo* / *kawaite ikiru* / *kaze no kure*
Cicada and / dragonfly both / dryly live / wind's evening

Hayashi Kei (b. 1953) first came to prominence when his haiku was selected in the "50 Haiku Competition" of Takayanagi Jūshin's *Haiku kenkyū*. He participated in the founding of the international haiku magazine *Ginyu*, and later cofounded the haiku magazine *TATEGAMI*. This poem is from *Kaze no kuni* (2004).

In autumn tides
it floats, a comma on the waves—
Ganryūjima

Imai Chizuko

The small island of Ganryūjima lies in the Kanmon Straits between the main Japanese islands of Honshu and Kyushu. It is known as the site of the historic duel between the two samurai Miyamoto Musashi and Sasaki Kojirō in 1612. This poem registers the poet Chizuko's surprise when, for the first time, she saw this island that she knew only by name and never thought she would see in reality.

Another poem about the Kanmon Straits is this famous haiku about the nearby port of Moji by Chizuko's mentor Takahama Kyoshi: "Say 'spring tides'/and without fail I always think/of Moji."

The word for 'autumn tides' is usually pronounced *akishio*. However, since it recalls the 'spring tides' (*shunchō*) of Kyoshi's poem, I choose to echo that poem by pronouncing this word similarly, in the less common way, as *shūchō*. This also adds to the musicality of the poem, for *shū* in the first segment echoes nicely against the *ryū* of the second and the *chu* of the third. The rhythmic repetition evokes the sounds of the tide.

Shūchō ni / Ganryūjima wa / chu to arishi
Autumn tides in / Ganryūjima / a comma looked like

Imai Chizuko (b. 1928) is the daughter of Imai Tsurujo, who was a niece of Takahama Kyoshi. Chizuko was in charge of taking dictation from Kyoshi in his later years, and was also a contributor to *Hototogisu* and a member of *Tamamo*. Together with Fujimatsu Yūshi and Fukami Kenji, she founded *San*. This poem is from her prizewinning *Sugiyuku* (2007).

I swiftly wash
the split sardine
in the lapping waves

Takigawa Gubutsu

He must be sitting in a boat at sea, preparing a sardine that he caught in a net. He splits the live fish open with his bare hands and discards the entrails, then quickly rinses the gutted fish in the waves that lap against the boat.

For the dish called *saki-namasu* (literally "split fish"), such sardines would be flavored with a mix of vinegar and miso, but in this situation you would simply want to eat the raw fish just as is. The salt in the sea-water makes a perfect seasoning.

What a refreshing and exhilarating feeling this dish would give, just as though you had taken nature itself in the form of the sea into your own body. The repeated "sa" sounds in *saki-iwashi* (split sardine) and *satto* (swiftly) are cooling and pleasant.

> *Saki-iwashi* / *satto kuru nami ni* / *araikeri*
> Split sardine / quickly coming waves in / I wash

Takigawa Gubutsu (1858–1944) was a close friend of Kakuta Chikurei and participated in the Shūseikai*[1] from its formation. A public prosecutor, he ultimately served as the president of the Kyoto District Court. This poem is from *Haikai shinchō* (1903), edited by Ozaki Kōyō.*[2]

Mackerel sky—
for the dog, the interesting things
are other dogs

Nagashima Yū

Here we have a dog, probably being taken for a walk by its owner, under a sky dappled with cirrocumulus clouds. The dog itself is not described. The focus is on the connection between the dog and other dogs, "the interesting things." When another dog approaches, the dog reacts strongly. I imagine it either straining at the leash to get closer (perhaps it knows the dog or wants to get to know it) or barking out of fear or hostility.

Somehow this haiku strikes me as a picture of the essential nature of a dog, and, by extension, the essential nature of all living creatures. Except for people, that is. We humans often have an excessive interest in our own selves rather than in others. Could it be that there is something fundamentally unhealthy about the human spirit?

Using "mackerel sky" as the seasonal image was an excellent decision. The other, more common, word for this kind of cloud is *iwashigumo* ("sardine sky"), which is five syllables. Using the four-syllable *sabagumo* works better because it allows for a cutting word,* in this case *ya*, and the slight break thus created nicely underlines the contrast between the person, who is looking up at the clouds, and the dog, who is not.

Sabagumo ya / inu no kyōmi wa / hoka no inu
Mackerel sky / dog's interest / other dogs

Nagashima Yū (b. 1972), a well-known novelist, began writing haiku in 1994 and was a contributing founder of *Kōshinfū*. After the magazine suspended publication, he founded *Bōten* in 2014, and is currently its coordinator. This poem is from *Haru no ojigi* (2014).

Even the sponge gourd
becomes a Buddha—
hurry up, don't lag behind

Masaoka Shiki

The poem is prefaced with the Tendai Buddhist saying, "The trees, the grasses, and the land all become Buddhas." This means that insentient beings are innately enlightened and endowed with the Buddha nature. The saying was often quoted in Noh plays and became one of the spiritual pillars of traditional Japanese poetry.

In the last days of his life, his body ravaged by tuberculosis, Shiki is lying in bed and gazing out his window at the sponge gourd (*Luffa cylindrica*) in his garden, when he remembers the saying. "Hurry up, don't lag behind," Shiki tells himself, meaning that if a sponge gourd can become a Buddha, so can he. It's a pun: in Japanese "Buddha" can be a euphemism for the dead, so he is also embracing his own imminent death. The remark has the flavor of a Buddhist sermon and at the same time the earthy yet elegant wit of haikai.

Shiki's modern side, as a reformer of the haiku,* tends to be emphasized today, but in the last years of his brief life his view of life and death was a traditional one. The sponge gourd, whose juice was gathered daily as a remedy for his phlegm-stuffed throat, also appears in the final three poems he wrote as he was dying, including this one: "The sponge gourd/ is blooming—here lies/a phlegm-stuffed Buddha."

> *Hechima sae / hotoke to naru zo / okururu na*
> Sponge gourd even / Buddha becomes / late don't be

Masaoka Shiki (1867–1902), more than any other poet or critic, was responsible for haiku's survival into the modern period. His signature style as a poet was the realistic sketch from life and his central assertion as a critic was that haiku is literature in the modern sense of the word. This poem is from *Shiki zenshū*, vol. 3, published posthumously in 1930.

Sweet olive fills the air
and
the distant tide is rising

Ishibashi Hideno

On a day in late autumn, sweet olive (*Osmanthus fragrans*) is in bloom and its fragrance fills the air. Far off in the distance, the tide has quietly come in.

The poem can be read as a realistic sketch from life.[*1] In that case, the poet is standing on a hill and the bush with its fragrant blooms is nearby, while far off in the distance she can see the sea at full tide. However, I prefer to read it like this: Through her sense of smell, the poet becomes aware of the sweet olive, which must be blooming nearby. At the same instant, she intuitively senses that the tide has risen in the distance. Faint though they are, she perceives the sound and smell of the ocean.

In the Japanese the logic-transcending leap between the widely separated sweet olive and the distant tide is accomplished by the hardworking particle *ni* (translated as "and"). The flowers and the tide together fill the space that the poem conjures up and a tentative, taut relationship between them is born. Strangely enough, that space is one of serenity.

Mokusei ni / tōki ushio no / michinikeri
Fragrant olive and / far tide / is coming in

Ishibashi Hideno (1909–1947) began writing haiku in college but did not formally study it until she joined the haiku group led by the novelist Yokomitsu Ri'ichi.[*2] Later she became a follower of Ishida Hakyō and a contributor to his *Tsuru*. She was married to the influential haiku critic and scholar Yamamoto Kenkichi.[*3] This poem is from *Sakura koku* (1949).

This refreshing feeling—

in my body

a faint buoyancy

Higano Yuki

Buoyancy is a scientific principle that anyone is aware of when they go swimming, because it is what keeps them from sinking. The experience is too common for there to be anything new to discover in it. A poem is unlikely to materialize there. This haiku, however, does not take place in water but on land, and reimagines the idea of buoyancy in a novel way. The poet senses the mass and even the texture of the air that her body has displaced.

She begins by writing about the simple pleasure of the clear autumn air, but she does not end there. There is a keen awareness of the existence of her own body within the Earth's atmosphere, and a recognition of the mystery of her own physical existence.

Sawayaka ya / karada ni kasuka / naru furyoku
Freshness / body in faint / is buoyancy

Higano Yuki (b. 1977) studied haiku with her father Takahashi Etsuo* and is the editor in chief of his magazine *Umi*. This poem is from her first haiku collection, *Inori no ten* (2007).

Coldly crisply
a tissue sticks straight up
from the tissue box

Azukizawa Yūko

In late autumn, when everything is chilly, the immaculate whiteness of the tissue sticking up straight from a box of facial tissues is a magnet to the eye. Each sheet of tissue in turn stands up ready to be plucked from the box, until the very last sheet is reached. Because the poet could perceive this completely normal sight with new eyes, she found a new subject for haiku.

Another way to look at it is to say that the tissue's soft fluffiness has enfolded the chilly air, and its straightness reveals the shape of the air. In that sense, the way the tissue stands up straight may even embody the shape of the poet's own resilient and flexible spirit.

Hiyayaka ni / tisshu hako yori / chokuritsu su
Coolly / tissue box from / straight stands up

Azukizawa Yūko (b. 1957) studied haiku with Hatano Sōha and belonged to his *Ao*. After the demise of *Ao*, she stopped writing haiku for some time. However, in 2002 she participated in the founding of Shimada Gajō's* *Sato* and is still a contributor. This poem is from *Migime* (2010).

If the water takes on
any more clarity than this
it will be wounded

Ueda Gosengoku

The seasonal image in this haiku is "clear water" (*mizu sumu*), which evokes the deepening of autumn through the increasing clarity of the water. But what body of water is this? The expression "will be wounded" cannot apply to real water such as a pond or stream. The thought comes: Must this really be only water? The word "wounded" is surely more appropriate for the human heart. Thinking about it like this creates a link between the seasonal image and the world of feeling.

In the haiku collection where this poem appears it is preceded by: "The maple leaves shine/on twin springs—the older and/the younger sister." The headnote for the two poems is "At Kita-Karuizawa," an area known for its natural beauty and hot springs. So it turns out that a body of real water gave the poet the idea for this poem which so richly suggests the weather of the heart.

> *Kore ijō / suminaba mizu no / kizu tsukamu*
> This more /clear if water / will hurt

Ueda Gosengoku (1933–1997) began writing haiku as a junior high school student. While in college, he joined Akimoto Fujio's *Hyōkai*. In 1973 he founded *Aze* and was its leader until his death. This poem is from *Fūkei* (1982).

The water is clear and
the strips of seaweed long
and horribly dirty

Iwata Yumi

The seasonal image "clear water" (*mizu sumu*) suggests a cheerful feeling. In terms of the weather, the water somehow seems clearer as the autumn chill increases. At the same time, there is joy at the arrival of the beauties of autumn and pleasure in its gradual deepening.

Most haiku that include this seasonal image simply elaborate on these feelings in various ways. Compared to them, this poem is a complete outlier. There is not the slightest pleasure in it. Gazing down at the clear water, the poet notices long strips of seaweed drifting on the current in the water's depths. Focusing more closely, she realizes that some kind of sediment is clinging to them.

This is a terrifying poem, an image of desolation at the extreme of seeing and being.

Mizu sumite / nagaki mo no sono / yogore yō
Water clear / long seaweed its / dirtiness

Iwata Yumi (b. 1961) studied haiku with Hatano Sōha. After Sōha's death, she joined Kuroda Momoko's *Aoi*. Since 2017 she has also contributed to *Shū*. This poem is from her prizewinning *Hanataba* (2010).

The sky looks so clear
I think I could pass
right through

Wada Kōzaburō

Autumn has deepened and the sky is cloudless and clear. For all its vastness, this sky feels as near and accessible as a local vacant lot. There is a dreamlike, floating feeling and a great sense of serenity.

Reading this haiku, I was reminded of Tanaka Hiroaki's "There is no/ stairway to the sky—/the flowering rice." Although Hiroaki can imagine stairs that would take him to the sky, he is definitely earth-bound. Kōzaburō, on the other hand, feels much closer to the sky, at times even a part of it. There is something almost frightening about the mood of this poem.

In the afterword to the book where it appears, the poet writes that he had recently had two successive operations for a brain tumor. He seems to have emerged from this experience with an expanded and clarified poetic world. I pray for his full recovery, and look forward to his further development.

Tōrinuke / dekisō ni sora / sunde ori
Pass through / could as though sky / is clear

Wada Kōzaburō (b. 1954) studied haiku with Nozawa Setsuko and was editor-in-chief of her haiku magazine *Ran*. In 2002 he founded *OPUS*. This poem is from *Aozora* (2007).

Even after
the autumn rainbow disappears
our eyes search the sky

Yamada Hiroko

On its own, "rainbow" is a summer image, but there are also the sea sonal images "spring rainbow," "autumn rainbow," and "winter rainbow," each with its own nuance. In autumn the air is dry, so rainbows are relatively infrequent. They also tend to be paler and briefer than those of other seasons. An autumn sky looks much the same whether such a rainbow is still there or has disappeared, but an afterimage may remain for the watcher after it vanishes.

Of all the different kinds of rainbows, those of autumn have the greatest air of mystery. In that sense, autumn is the only appropriate season for this haiku. People were looking up at the rainbow and now even after it fades from the sky they keep straining to see it, as if longing for the beauty they had enjoyed. The poet, who met an unexpected death, seems to merge with this ephemeral rainbow.

Aki no niji / kietaru ato mo / aogaruru
Autumn rainbow / disappeared after even / is looked up at

Yamada Hiroko (1934–2010) was 12 years old when her haiku was published in a local literary magazine. She joined *Hototogisu* in her 30s, and later founded and led *Enkō*. This poem is from *Kusazemi* (2003).

Autumn wind—
everything I see
is haiku

Takahama Kyoshi

This is a haiku about composing haiku—a daring meta-poem. The poet may mean that he makes everything he sees into a haiku, or that everything he sees turns by itself into a haiku, or even both. What matters is the avid desire, even obsession, that surely lies behind this pronouncement. I doubt if any other haiku poet before or since Kyoshi has been so forceful or so full of self-confidence.

The autumn wind is a melancholy wind that seems to shadow the landscape. That is precisely why everything it touches can become a haiku. Another way to read the poem is as an affirmation of the power of the seasons to inspire poetry.

Akikaze ya / ganchū no mono / mina haiku
Autumn wind / in eyes things / all haiku

Takahama Kyoshi (1874–1959), a haiku poet and a novelist, was a follower of Masaoka Shiki and became editor of *Hototogisu*, the haiku magazine founded by Shiki's other major disciple, Yanagihara Kyokudō. Through *Hototogisu* Kyoshi fostered many new poets, including a number of women. He saw haiku as a poetry of nature, and insisted on the necessity of the seasonal image. This poem is from *Gohyakku* (1937).

Would there were
a person come to kill me
in the autumn wind!

Hara Sekitei

Here the wind can only be the wind of autumn, not that of any other season. He wants to be caught up and annihilated in this wind that withers plants and sends small creatures to their deaths.

This poem, composed in 1914, stands at the outer limit of subjective language and expression in haiku. The poet's note for it and the poem after it reads, "A feeling came to me as I closed my eyes and when I opened them again the feeling grew still stronger." The other poem is: "Shall I set my own/house on fire?/The autumn wind…" The tone of desperation is almost inconceivable.

While the priest of the temple where he was boarding was away at the sect's head temple, Sekitei and the priest's wife fell in love and eloped to a town in another prefecture. But in his hoped-for murderer there is no hint of the priest. A process of abstraction is at work. Sekitei wrote an equally fine poem in the same year: "Autumn wind—/a different pattern for each of/two plates."

Akikaze ni / korosu to kitaru / hito mogana
Autumn wind in / kill to come / person would there were!

Hara Sekitei (1886–1951) was a follower of Takahama Kyoshi and became one of the leading haiku poets of the early nineteenth century. In 1921 he founded *Kabiya* and led it until his death. This poem is from *Hara Sekitei zenkushū* (1990).

The autumn wind—
one person there is who is not
worth murdering

Nishijima Bakunan

The note says: "I neither love nor hate the woman who deserted me." The note and the poem point to his violently vacillating feelings towards a woman who spurned him. The poem suggests that his emotions have somewhat calmed, but it is hardly normal to say that someone "is not worth murdering." It is tantamount to confessing that he once harbored a serious desire to murder her.

This is the autumn wind that brings death to plants and small creatures. Does that same wind bring home to the poet the inevitability of death even without his intervention? In this poem, one of the most extreme modern haiku about love, the autumn wind smells of blood.

Akikaze ya / korosu ni taranu / hito hitori
Autumn wind / killing not worth / person one

Nishijima Bakunan (1895–1981) was a follower of Iida Dakotsu and a founding contributor to Iida's *Unmo*. After Dakotsu's death, he stayed with the group and helped Dakotsu's son Ryūta run the magazine. This poem is from *Hito-oto* (1941).

Blown by
the autumn wind
a door opens

Shinohara Ontei

Perhaps this is an unlocked double door, attached rather loosely to the hinges by a weak spring. It would be the entrance to a café or a shop, opening slowly in the wind. These days automatic doors are the rule, but I remember the time when you could lightly push on a door like this and step into a shop.

The autumn wind lends a sense of loneliness to the scene. If someone driven by longing for human company went inside, they might find themselves in another world. Yet in the poem only the door opens; nothing is said about whether someone enters or not.

The plain words suggest more than they say and leave me with a sense of disquiet.

> *Akikaze ni / fukarete hiraku / tobira kana*
> Autumn wind by / blown opens / door!

Shinohara Ontei (1872–1926) was a haiku poet and novelist. He studied with Masaoka Shiki, and after Shiki's death became a follower of Takahama Kyoshi and a contributor to *Hototogisu*. He founded and led *Dojō*. This poem is from *Ontei kushū* (1927), edited by Shimada Seihō.

I think myself
a bell that rings when lightly struck—
the autumn wind

Kubo Yorie

The phrase "A bell that rings when lightly struck" is used to praise someone who is quick-minded and responsive. It often implies sensitivity as well. You would need great self-confidence and pride to use it about yourself, but the poet prefaces the comparison with "I think," as if to say she only thinks of herself that way, but she might be wrong.

The seasonal image of the autumn wind suggests loneliness, even isolation. These associations give depth to the subtle suggestion that her innate sensitivity and intelligence are going to waste. It is rare to write about oneself with such richly contoured nuances.

Yorie's husband Kubo Inokichi was a doctor, and the couple were the center of a literary salon in Fukuoka which included the tanka poet Yanagihara Byakuren (1885–1967). According to the contemporary poet Kai Michiko's essay on Yorie in *The World of Women's Haiku,** Inokichi had a romantic involvement with Byakuren which hurt Yorie deeply.

> *Uteba hibiku / ware to omou ya / aki no kaze*
> When struck make a sound / I so think / autumn wind

Kubo Yorie (1884–1941) knew Masaoka Shiki and Natsume Sōseki in her childhood, when they were young men boarding at her grandfather's house, and she is mentioned in works by both. She later studied haiku with Kiyohara Kaidō, became a follower of Takahama Kyoshi, and contributed to *Hototogisu*. This poem is from *Yorie kubunshū* (1928).

The autumn wind—
all the soldiers' wives
babies strapped to their backs

Hasegawa Kanajo

This is one of five haiku titled "Military families" composed by Kanajo in 1937, the year the Second Sino-Japanese War began. These poems depict the everyday lives of the wives of soldiers sent to fight in China. The wives, whose children are still so small they are strapped on their mother's backs, are bravely going about their work. The children are so young that they will have no memory of their father if he is killed in combat.

The autumn wind is, above all, a wind of loneliness. You feel something is imminent but there is no sense that it will be the promised day of shining victory. This poem shows us daily life in wartime through a woman's eyes.

Akikaze ya / mina ko o oeru / hei no tsuma
Autumn wind / all children carry / soldiers' wives

Hasegawa Kanajo (1887–1969) began to write haiku after marrying the haiku poet Hasegawa Reiyoshi,⁺ a follower of Takahama Kyoshi. She also joined Kyoshi's group and became one of the leading female members of *Hototogisu*. When Reiyoshi founded *Kareno*, she contributed to the magazine, and later founded and led *Suimei*. This poem was published in the feminist magazine *Kagayaku* in October 1937.

There is nothing that is
not the autumn wind—
heaven's deep blue

Takahashi Masō

When the poet looks up at the clear autumn sky, it is a deep blue. From earth to sky all kinds of winds, some strong some weak, are blowing in different directions, but all are part of the autumn wind.

As the poet reflects on this, a feeling of deep desolation comes over him. Everything on earth is enfolded in the blowing winds of autumn. Whether alive or not, the fate of everything—and the poet's flesh itself is no exception—is the same: decay and nothingness. Broadly speaking, you could even say that everything blowing in the autumn wind is part of it, too.

This is one of the poems Takahashi Masō composed on his deathbed. As he looks on this world for the last time, all things seem to be transparent. He himself seems to melt into the autumn wind and disappear.

Akikaze ni / arazaru wa nashi / ten no kon
Autumn wind / is not not / heaven's deep blue

Takahashi Masō (1907–1946) studied haiku with Hara Sekitei, who gave him his haiku nom de plume. He was a medical doctor with a promising future but died at the age of 40. This poem is from the posthumous collection *Akiyamagoe* (1951).

Of itself the autumn wind
blows, of itself
the potter's wheel spins

Kawakita Handeishi

I have lived, says the poet, in accordance with the autumn wind, not opposing it. I have followed the spinning of the potter's wheel to create form out of clay.

This poem is Handeishi's concise poetic statement of his ideal of life and art, which begins with transcending the self. To follow the autumn wind—to align one's way of being with nature—makes intuitive sense, but he also states that it is not he who spins the potter's wheel but that he merely follows its natural turning. Reading this poem after seeing Handeishi's pottery, I felt that it was this attitude that produced the natural shape of his tea ceremony bowls.

Handeishi is ranked with Kitaōji Rosanjin (1883–1959) as one of the two greatest potters of the modern period. Haiku was one of his hobbies, and I was fortunate enough to attend an exhibit of his work which included examples of his poems written in his own hand. Both the calligraphy and the poems themselves were superb.

Akikaze no / *fuku mama rokuro* / *mawaru mama*
Autumn wind / blows as kiln / goes around as

Kawakita Handeishi (1878–1963) studied haiku with Kajishima Issō,* a follower of Matsuse Seisei. He contributed to Issō's *Kaitsumuri* and *Fuyuki*, and was also mentored by Yamaguchi Seishi. He did not publish a haiku collection, but 275 of his poems are included in the exhibition catalog *Handeishi-ō kaikoten* (1971). This poem is from another exhibition catalog, *Kuwakita Handeishi no subete* (2009).

Autumn wind—
my index finger
is whose grave?

Terayama Shūji

First, there is the surprise at the connecting of finger and grave. The specific finger is the index finger, which might have been the one used to point to someone who was thereby driven to their death. In that sense, the index finger would become that person's grave.

Or you could think of it like this: Open your hand and you see that each finger has two joints. The shape is reminiscent of a pagoda-shaped grave marker (*gorintō*). Besides the index finger, each of the other four fingers could also be someone's grave. In which case you can think of the five fingers together as a small cemetery and the two hands together as a large one. The hands become a perfect image of a sacred ground like Osorezan, the mountain near the poet's hometown which was believed to be a gathering place of the dead.

The autumn wind passing through the spread fingers is a faint sign from the dead. The poem speaks of how heavily the existence of the dead weighed on Shūji.

Akikaze ya / hitosashi yubi wa / dare no haka
Autumn wind / index finger / whose grave

Terayama Shūji (1935–1985) was one of the most influential avant-garde writers and dramatists in postwar Japan. He began writing haiku and tanka in his teens, and eventually broadened his pursuits to include modern style poetry and drama, establishing a theater company and directing movies. This poem comes from *Kafun kōkai* (1975).

In the painted scroll of Hell
the women are pure white—
the autumn wind

Mutō Noriko

Many pictorial depictions of the various Buddhist hells where sinners are punished are designated Japanese National Treasures, carefully kept in museums. However, if we imagine the poet looking at this in a museum, the image of the autumn wind is out of place. I prefer to think of the poet having come across one of those typical hell scrolls from an earlier century tucked away in an anonymous temple somewhere in the Japanese countryside. In such paintings color is used to distinguish the sexes, the men being depicted as dark and the women as white.

The whiteness of the women suggests that while alive they led a life that spared them from strong sunlight or heavy labor, or even old age. What sins could such women have committed? There is something incongruous, even ridiculous, about including them in this scene of punishment.

The autumn wind and the color white have a strong mutual affinity. They also bring to mind Bashō's* haiku, "Whiter/than the stones of Stone Mountain/is the autumn wind."

> *Jigoku-e no / onna wa shiroshi / aki no kaze*
> Hell picture's / women are white / autumn's wind

Mutō Noriko (b. 1949) studied haiku with Usami Gyomoku. She was a contributor to *Shin* and a founding contributor to Hasegawa Kai's *Koshi*. In 2011 she founded *Enza*, which she currently leads. This poem is from *Shuka* (2003).

Autumn wind—
I wipe down the pillar
looking at the pillar

Okamoto Hitomi

As the poet is cleaning her house she hears the autumn wind blowing outside, but she is wiping down a pillar and her hands and eyes are focused on that alone.

This is a housework haiku. But it is something more as well, for a strong urge to purify the home suffuses the poem. I can visualize the well-rubbed and polished pillar, like the hallway floor, glowing darkly from all the smoke it has absorbed from cooking and heating fires over the years.

The words "autumn wind" and "looking" bring to mind Takahama Kyoshi's "Autumn wind—/everything I see/is haiku" (page 254), which the poet may also have had in mind. For Kyoshi, when the autumn wind blows everything that he sees becomes a haiku, but if this poem is seen as a response to Kyoshi then she is saying that when wiping down a pillar, you must forget about haiku and look only at the pillar. The poet's strong focus chimes well with the insistent blowing of the autumn wind.

Akikaze ya / hashira fuku toki / hashira mite
Autumn wind / pillar wiping when / pillar looking

Okamoto Hitomi (1928–2018) studied haiku with Tomiyasu Fūsei and his protégé Kishi Fūsanrō.* She later founded and led *Asa*. This poem is from *Yabumi* (1990).

The wind changes—
all things release
their autumn voices

Fubasami Fusae

The direction of the wind has changed. Everything caught up in it releases its autumn voice.

"Autumn voices" (*aki no koe*) is a difficult seasonal expression. It is probably derived from "Poem on the Voices of Autumn" by the Song poet Ouyang Xiu. The critic Yamamoto Kenkichi's[*1] summary of Ouyang Xiu's original Chinese is: "the mysterious voices of heaven and earth, lonely and frightening, heard in autumn when things brush against each other." In this season the air is clear and distant sounds carry. You listen alertly, and what you hear are these voices, that is, the sounds of autumn.

The "autumn voices" are not merely an idea; the expression also describes the flute-like resonance created when the actual wind reverberates against an object. These are the sounds that Fusae's poem beautifully expresses. All things touched by the wind raise their voices, expressing an animistic life force. These are the voices of autumn in all their joy and loneliness.

Kaze kawaru / *mono mina aki no* / *koe hanatsu*
Wind changes / things all autumn's / voices release

Fubasami Fusae (1914–2014) first studied haiku with Kamikawai Riyō, then joined Iida Dakotsu's *Unmo*. She was a founding contributor to Ishihara Yatsuka's[*2] *Aki*, and later its leader emeritus. This poem is from *Hakuku* (2012), for which she received the Iida Dakotsu Prize at the age of 99.

Already my feet
step on darkness
in the autumn dusk

Kusama Tokihiko

On an autumn evening, when the days are getting short, dusk seems to come early. Suddenly, when the poet looks down, he notices that his feet are already shrouded in darkness.

Dusk is already all about him, but the darkness is concentrated around his feet. How surprising it is that the degree of darkness should differ depending on your distance from the ground. There is something beautiful in this. When you look up again, the darkness will have spread further around you, perhaps already flooding over all you see. You witness time's flow before your very eyes.

The fourteenth-century monk Yoshida Kenkō wrote of the quickness with which death comes upon us in his *Essays in Idleness*: "People know that they will die, but death will surprise them while they believe it is not yet close. It is as if we gaze at the far-off ebb-tide flats while even now the sea is rising to flood the rocks we stand on."* The tide rises with a speed beyond human imagination and I feel the same swiftness in the way night comes on in this poem.

Ashimoto wa / mō makkura ya / aki no kure
Beneath my feet / already darkness / autumn's dusk

Kusama Tokihiko (1920–2003) first studied haiku with Mizuhara Shūōshi, and later became a follower of Ishida Hakyō and contributed to *Tsuru*. He was actively engaged in efforts to spread haiku overseas from 1987. This poem is from *Sakurayama* (1974).

In the autumn dusk
straddled by
Tsutenkaku Tower

Uchida Misa

The poet is looking diagonally up at Tsutenkaku, a 108-meter high tower in the center of Osaka's entertainment district, built in 1912 in imitation of the Eiffel Tower.

The tower's twin pillars that she looks up at certainly do resemble vast legs that would seem to be straddling her, but "to straddle" also suggests to stand over someone contemptuously. To be straddled and looked down on is not an experience anyone enjoys, so I was taken a little aback by the use of the word here. The fact that she accepts being straddled by Tsutenkaku Tower suggests the affection she feels for this landmark.

The scene is the middle of a vibrant entertainment district, and the blinding neon of the cheap restaurants all around highlights the melancholy of the autumn dusk.

Aki no kure / Tsūtenkaku ni / matagarete
Autumn dusk / Tsutenkaku Tower by / being straddled

Uchida Misa (b. 1936) was influenced by the haiku of Tsubouchi Nenten,* and when Nenten founded *Sendan* in 1985, she joined the group. She is also a founding contributor to Suzuki Takako's *Mon.* This poem is from *Gyoganseki* (2004).

Autumn dusk—
the bones of a huge fish
are gathered in by the sea

Saitō Sanki

As night comes on, the ocean tide is trying to reclaim the skeletal remains of a huge fish washed up on the shore.

The seasonal expression "autumn dusk" (*aki no kure*) brings to mind the famous "Three Evening Poems"[*1] of the thirteenth-century *Shinkokinshū*, each of which uses a different image to express the lonely beauty of nightfall in autumn. These three waka are among the earliest expressions of the medieval sense of beauty. Saitō Sanki was a leading poet of the New Rising Haiku movement[*2] but he was imbued with this medieval aesthetic.

The scene in this poem is desolate. There is no human presence. The huge fish is now nothing but bones, and even those bones are on the verge of disappearing into the sea. Soon they will return to the void. I feel a deep sense of emptiness, like that which will pervade the world of the near future when humanity is extinct. While inheriting the tradition of the "Three Evening Poems," Sanki presents a new kind of autumn nightfall.

Aki no kure / *taigyo no hone o* / *umi ga hiku*
Autumn nightfall / huge fish's bones / sea pulling

Saitō Sanki (1900–1962) began writing haiku in his 30s and became a leading figure in the New Rising Haiku movement. He was arrested during the 1940 government crackdown on untraditional haiku poets and was forbidden to publish haiku. After the war he reactivated the movement with like-minded poets, helped Yamaguchi Seishi found *Tenrō*, and later founded and led *Dangai*. This poem is from his last collection, *Henshin* (1962).

Just a bit—
the time it takes for birds to cross the sky—
saké at noon

Yajima Nagisao

As he is enjoying a bit of saké in the daytime, he remembers that there are two ways to write "a bit" (*chotto*). One way is with characters that mean "one inch" (一寸) and expresses space, and the other is with characters that mean "birds migrating" (鳥渡) and expresses time—the time it takes for a flock of migrating birds to cross the sky overhead. Playing with words can spice up a drink before sundown quite nicely. To watch a flock of birds enact the phrase "a bit" as you sip your drink must be tremendous fun.

Nagisao's mentor Ishida Hakyō composed this poem: "As swiftly as/ the geese overhead/the buckwheat was harvested." Here the quickness with which the migrating geese pass overhead is compared to the speed with which the buckwheat is cut and harvested. Nagisao might have had his mentor's poem on his mind. To me, the two poems seem variations on a theme.

> *Chotto to wa* / *tori wataru ma ya* / *hiru no sake*
> Just a bit / bird crossing while / daytime saké

Yajima Nagisao (b. 1935) was a follower of Ishida Hakyō. After Hakyō's death he joined *Kanrui*, led by Katō Shūson. In 1994 he founded *Fukurō*, which he still leads. This poem comes from the prizewinning *Kudarano* (2008).

Birds heading south
above the celadon blue
of Mount Tsurugi

Okada Teihō

Superb celadon ware was produced in China during the Song period (960–1279). The rarest glaze, invented at imperial command, was a pale blue described as "the blue of the sky seen through a rift in the clouds after rain." It was the product of the potters' effort to match nature's coloring.

Teihō chooses the word "celadon blue" from the vocabulary of ceramics in order to describe the transparent blue depth of the autumn mountain when seen from a distance. The worlds of ceramics and nature come together to beautiful effect.

Mount Tsurugi is a peak in the eastern part of Toyama Prefecture, on the northern edge of the Tateyama range of the Japan Alps. As the poet gazes at it from afar, the migrating birds of autumn would be flying high over the peak.

Tori watari / *uka tensei no* / *Tsurugidake*
Birds migrating / celadon blue / Mt. Tsurugi

Okada Teihō (b. 1926) was a follower of Mizuhara Shūōshi and is a contributor to *Ashibi*. This poem is from *Tenkei* (2010).

One day the sky
was birds birds and more birds—
passing through on their way south

Sudō Gojō

These would be small migrating birds that head south in autumn: Daurian redstarts, waxwings, bramblings, thrushes, and the like. There are so many of them that they blot out the sky.

Haiku focuses on the present, and it is quite unusual to refer to the past by saying "one day." But this poem is evidently a reminiscence about the poet's amazement on a certain day when the sky looked nothing like its usual self. Another odd thing is the somehow awkward way those successive nouns, "day," "sky," and "birds," follow one upon the other. But here, too, the effect is to emphasize the poet's unaffected amazement.

In fact, the very things that make the poem seem awkward at first turn out to be what makes it express so well the poet's joyful astonishment at the workings of nature.

Aru hi kotori / sora o ootte / watarikeri
One day small birds / sky hiding / passed migrating

Sudō Gojō (1872–1915) was a poet of haiku and tanka and was a mathematics teacher by profession. He studied haiku with Masaoka Shiki, who praised his talent. This poem is from *Gojō kushū* (1929).

As I climbed the slope
a monkey hit me—
with a nut from a tree!

Iwaya Sazanami

The poem's speaker is trudging up an extremely steep hill when some menacing monkeys appear. However, he does not stop and when he nears them, one of the monkeys hurls something at him. The shock and the pain almost make him lose his balance. It turns out to be a nut, perhaps an acorn or a beechnut. For a monkey, such a thing is a precious staple, carefully secreted away in the hollow of a tree. Using it for ammunition shows how desperate the monkey felt.

The monkey must be part of a group, while the speaker is alone. Alone or not, he is not going to turn back. Once he passes out of the monkeys' territory the danger will be over.

This poem has the happy feeling of an adventure story for children.

> Soba yukeba / saru ni utareru / konomi kana
> Steep slope when went / monkey by hit / nut!

Iwaya Sazanami (1870–1933) was a children's book author and a novelist. He cofounded the haiku group Murasakiginsha with Ozaki Kōyō[1] and also joined the Shūseikai.[2] This poem is from Sazaranami (1932).

My love for him
is like the ripest apple—
so full so beautiful

Nakagawa Tomijo

Is there another haiku whose speaker sings so lyrically about being deliriously in love? Such haiku may exist, but if they do they are certainly outliers, for the subject is more suited to tanka than haiku.

The manner of expression is also unconventional. The seasonal image "apple" is used as a simile, but no real apple appears in the poem. In an ordinary haiku, this lack of concreteness would make you feel something lacking, but not with this poem. The redness of an apple and its sweet-sour taste make an apple the perfect comparison. Then there is the closing "beautiful," a word whose use is effectively banned in haiku as sentimental.

Bending the rules of haiku as she pleases, a young woman proudly sings the fullness of her love.

Waga koi wa / *ringo no gotoku* / *utsukushiki*
My love / apple like / beautiful

Nakagawa Tomijo (1879–?) began to write haiku under the influence of Takemura Shūchiku,* who boarded in her home in Kanazawa and was a follower of Masaoka Shiki. She later moved to Tokyo and met Shiki, who recorded the meeting in a haiku and praised her poetry. This poem is from *Meiji haiku* (1901), edited by Shūchiku.

Guardian persimmon
may you be
a natural light for all time

Shiga Yasushi

"Guardian persimmon" refers to the custom of leaving a single persimmon on the tree after all the other fruit has been picked, as a prayer for a good harvest in the coming year. The single fruit left on the tree, shining in the twilight, is a kind of light made by a natural object, as opposed to electric or other artificial light.

The guardian persimmon has been a close part of daily life since the days before electric and fluorescent light, illuminating and encouraging people as they go about their daily life. Nowadays, when our lives are lived under electric light, it will not do to forget the modest glow of the guardian persimmon—for it is in that subtle natural brightness that we find our true happiness. That is what the poem means.

Its expression may be knotty to untie, yet in its strong prayerful wish for the life-giving force of nature to be restored, this poem is clear as day.

Komorigaki / banko e yūki / akari nare
Guardian persimmon / for all time organic / light be

Shiga Yasushi (b. 1944) is a regular contributor to the haiku magazine *LOTUS*. This poem is from *Henshō shiin* (2008), which also includes the long essay on Yasushi by Yasui Kōji titled (in translation) "Vertical Language Haiku."

Oh!
There it is, my life—
a snake gourd

Masaki Yūko

Haiku is sometimes said to be a poetry of surprise, but this is the first time I have encountered a haiku that actually includes as one of its words the colloquial "Oh!" of surprise.

Here the exclamation expresses a feeling of being taken aback, as though you heard or saw something you weren't meant to hear or see. The pronoun "it" follows, and then the definition of "it" as "my life." But you don't know what "it" stands for until the third segment, when "the snake gourd" (*Trichosanthes cucumerina*), bright red fruits hanging from its vines, is revealed.

Her life is not an idea or concept here, but a concrete thing that exists vividly outside her. This somehow makes me feel that she is at a critical turning point.

> *A'— sore wa / watashi no inochi / karasu-uri*
> Oh that / my life / snake gourd

Masaki Yūko (b. 1952), encouraged to compose haiku by her older brother, Masaki Kōichi, joined *Oki* and studied with Nomura Toshirō. She later became a contributor to Shibuya Michi's *Shibi*. This poem is from her prizewinning *Shizuka na mizu* (2002).

Whirlpools spin between
two islands that share
the autumn festival

Imai Tsurujo

Travel back and forth between these two nearby islands is always frequent and becomes especially so at festival times. However, the swift currents and large whirlpools between the islands make the crossing a perilous one. This is a wonderful birds' eye view of a vibrant sea festival, the boats courageously plunging through the whirlpools as they come and go. Only the scenery is described, but it is easy to imagine the islands' inhabitants on the boats and their various dramas.

According to *The World of Women's Haiku,** this poem was composed during the festival for the ocean gods held in 1949 by fishermen in the Kurushima Straits, which is one of the Seto Inland Sea's most perilous areas. Tsurujo lived near the straits at the time, having been evacuated there during the war, and the poet Takahama Kyoshi and his companions came to visit her and attend the festival. The poem would have been written as a kind of welcome for Kyoshi, and its broad sweep and strong sense of movement must have pleased him greatly.

> *Uzu hedate / aki no matsuri no / shima futatsu*
> Whirlpool between / autumn festival / islands two

Imai Tsurujo (1897–1992), who was Takahama Kyoshi's niece, studied haiku with him and contributed to *Hototogisu*. This poem is from her haiku collection *Mei no yado* (My niece's place, 1958), whose title was taken from a poem Kyoshi wrote when he came to visit her: "A long trip and / a cold night, but seeing my niece / is worth it."

Fling
every chrysanthemum there is
into her coffin

Natsume Sōseki

The poet's note is: "Composed as a funeral offering for Kusuoko as I lay ill."

Ōtsuka Kusuoko (1875–1910), a well-known writer and translator who was also admired for her beauty, was the wife of Sōseki's good friend, the philosopher of art Ōtsuka Yasuji. When she died suddenly of pleurisy on November 9, 1910, at the age of 35, Sōseki, who was hospitalized in Tokyo at the time, sent his wife to offer condolences in his place. His own illness must have made the loss of his young friend affect him especially strongly. The tone of this poem, with its use of the imperative, is almost harsh. The image of the chrysanthemum, emblem of long life, gives an added poignancy to the tragedy of death at a young age.

An early draft was: "Into the coffin/fling chrysanthemums—as many/as there are." But in that version the coffin is there from the beginning so there is no surprise. Having "coffin" at the end creates a much stronger effect.

Aru hodo no / kiku nageire yo / kan no naka
All there are / chrysanthemums throw / coffin within

Natsume Sōseki (1867–1916), a follower of Masaoka Shiki in haiku, is primarily known as one of the greatest novelists of the modern period. *Kokoro* and a number of his other novels have been translated into English and other languages. This poem is from one of the earliest editions of Sōseki's complete works, *Sōseki zenshū* (1917–1919).

Like a tiger its cub
I prized that spinning top you've got
up your sleeve!

Kawahigashi Hekigotō

This haiku is quite condensed, but the meaning, unfolded, is: In our game of spinning tops, you have gone and won the top that I prized with as much passion as a mother tiger prizes its cub, and that always brought me good luck and victory. I'm mortified that my precious top is now tucked away in your sleeve.

The old-fashioned spinning top is used in a children's game that is rather like a sumo match for tops, in which two players compete to see whose top can knock the other's off a small circular platform. Here, the image can be read as foretelling the future of haiku. The speaker could be seen as Hekigotō himself, and the addressee as Takahama Kyoshi, the two poets who vied with each other to inherit the mantle of their friend and teacher Masaoka Shiki. In fact Hekigotō eventually withdrew from haiku, and Kyoshi became the ruler of the haiku world.

The image of a top in the haiku that Kyoshi wrote at Hekigotō's death must be related to this poem: "He was like/ a quickly spinning top that could turn/ on a dime."

> *Tora no ko no / bai o nanji ga / tamoto kana*
> Tiger child's / spinning top your / sleeve!

Kawahigashi Hekigotō (1873–1937), together with Takahama Kyoshi, was one of the two most prominent members of Shiki's haiku reform movement. Later, he diverged to become the central figure in New Tendency Haiku,* and ultimately moved on to free form haiku. He was also a prolific essayist and a world traveler who visited Europe and North America as well as China and Mongolia. This poem is from *Zoku shunkashūtō* (1906).

For spinning tops—
a checkered straw mat
on the upside down washtub

Momiyama Shigetsu

They are playing at spinning tops on a woven checked mat spread over an upside-down washtub. Because this game was traditionally played during the Chrysanthemum Festival, which took place on the ninth day of the ninth lunar month, spinning tops (*bai uchi*) is a seasonal image.

  Such woven checked straw mats were called *ukiyo goza*, floating world mats, and were clearly used in the seventeenth century, since one is mentioned in a short story published in 1694. But I wonder if they were used later as well. I don't know if the poet knew the word from his own experience or if he learned it from literature, but the beauty and the sense of the passage of time evoked by the name could not be achieved by any other word.

> *Bai uchi ya / tarui no ue no / ukiyo goza*
> Spinning tops / barrel on top of / woven checked mat

Momiyama Shigetsu (1878–1958) studied haiku with Masaoka Shiki and then Takahama Kyoshi, and then established himself as a publisher of literary works, focusing on haiku. His pioneering magazine *Haikai zasshi* (1917–1930) was for a time the only competitor to *Hototogisu*. This poem is from *Edo-an kushū* (1916).

My name means to walk
holding a severed head—pushing
through rough sedge grass

Shibuya Michi

Kanji are mysterious things. The poet's first name is "Michi," written with the familiar character *michi* 道, meaning path or road. This character is made up of two parts, 辵 meaning "to walk," and 首 meaning "head." According to Shirakawa Shizuka's pioneering etymological dictionary of kanji based on ancient Chinese bronze inscriptions (*Jitō*, Heibonsha, 1984), the character for *michi* originally meant to walk holding a head, perhaps the head of someone from another tribe. He hypothesizes that the head of someone from another tribe was once a magical charm with the strong power of warding off terrible things that could happen while traveling outside your own area.

The first and second segments of the poem are descriptions of the poet's first name, Michi, as explicated by Shirakawa's deconstruction of the character. In the last segment, there is a dramatic shift. Suddenly, the poet is not just talking about her name and how it is written. She is a woman pushing her way through the fields where the rough sedge grass grows and she is carrying a bloody, freshly severed head.

Inspired by her investigation into the etymological meaning of her own name, the poet has come up with a striking self-portrait.

Watakushi wa / shinnyū ni kubi / kayano o wake
I / walk with head / sedge grass fields dividing

Shibuya Michi (b. 1926), a distinguished practitioner of avant-garde haiku and the modern haiku sequence, began writing haiku as a medical student. She pursued a double career as a pediatrician and a poet for many years, founding *Shibi* in 1996. In 2010 she received the Grand Prize of the Modern Haiku Association for lifetime achievement. This poem is from *Sokeishū* (1991).

He cuts
the tattered lotus leaves—
in deep water the sickle goes in

Terashima Tadashi

When the lotus plants in a lotus pond die in late autumn, their big, tattered leaves present a piteous sight. From the seventeenth century on, haiku poets have found them a fertile topic for poetry. For lotus farmers, however, the messy leaves are a nuisance when digging up the edible roots in winter, so they need to lop off the leaves and stems and dispose of them in advance.

This poem vividly depicts the strenuous physical labor of a farmer. "He cuts the tattered lotus leaves" gives the impression that he is cutting away only the leaves. Then, moving on to "in deep water the sickle goes in," we realize, as if sharpening the focus, that he is reaching deep into the water to cut the stems near the bottom of the lotus plants. A subtle description, superbly done.

> *Yarehasu o / karu mizu fukaku / kama o ire*
> Tattered lotus leaves / cut away water deep / sickle put in

Terashima Tadashi (b. 1944) studied haiku with Abe Midorijo and joined Midorijo's *Komakusa*. She died in 1980, but he has remained a contributor to the magazine. This poem is from *Nanigenaku* (2006).

I rejoice and they fall
in streams from the trees—
look at those nuts!

Tomiyasu Fūsei

Why is the poet rejoicing? It must be because he came upon nuts falling from a tree. And then when he is rejoicing about the one tree, many more start to fall from a nearby tree as well. It is as if his rejoicing causes more nuts to fall: trees and human are affecting each other. There are many descriptions of trees in modern haiku but how many depict the poet sharing joy with trees? To me, this feels not so much an expression of naivety or a childlike mind as a primordial communion.

This is the kind of cheerful poem that you enjoy repeating out loud. The four plosive "k" sounds (*yorokobeba/shikiri ni otsuru/konomi kana*) scattered among the three segments suggest the sound of nuts falling and hitting the ground.

If you recite this poem beneath an oak tree in autumn, the acorns might start tumbling down.

> *Yorokobeba* / *shikiri ni otsuru* / *konomi* kana
> When I rejoice / steadily fall / nuts!

Tomiyasu Fūsei (1885–1979) was a follower of Takahama Kyoshi and a contributor to *Hototogisu*. He also led *Wakaba*, the haiku group originally formed at his workplace, the Japanese Ministry of Communications, and developed it into one of the largest haiku groups in Japan. Because of his extreme fondness for plants, he was sometimes called "the gardener Fūsei." This poem is from *Kusa no hana* (1933).

And now through water
it is falling, drifting down—
a nut from the tree

Suzuki Takao

Since the poet can see the nut as it falls through the water, the water must be crystal clear and deep. I imagine it falling from a large tree growing beside a pond. "And now through water" implies that before falling through the water, the nut had fallen through the air. Once the nut has broken through the surface of the water, the speed of its fall slows somewhat and the nut starts to drift. A process that begins high up in the tree and continues until midway through the pond is described with elliptical precision. This process must be repeated again and again as the nuts fall, but only the fall of a single nut is described. Also, it "is falling, drifting down," but the moment of touching the bottom is left undescribed. This nut will be falling and drifting forever.

The poem begins from reality but takes us to a space of mysterious serenity.

> *Suichū o / sara ni ochiyuku / konomi kana*
> Water in / again falling / a nut!

Suzuki Takao (1928–2013) was a follower of Ishida Hakyō and, after Hakyō's death, Nomura Toshirō. He founded and led *Mon*. This poem is from his prizewinning *Sennen* (2004).

The fallen chestnut decides
where to settle—
a hollow in the earth

Inoue Seigetsu

After wandering from place to place around Japan, Seigetsu settled in Ina, a town in Shinano in central Japan, where he found a temporary home and like-minded poet friends. In that sense, the chestnut is an image of Seigetsu's life itself. The theme of roaming is also reminiscent of the wandering poets of the Edo period (1603–1867) typified by Matsuo Bashō.[*1] At the same time, the vivid description of the chestnut settling into a hollow in the earth looks forward to Masaoka Shiki's early twentieth-century realism. It may not be overstating things to say that this haiku links two different eras of poetry.

Chestnuts were the most important tree for the prehistoric people of Japan's Jōmon period (ca. 10,000–ca. 300 BCE). The chestnuts themselves were used for food and the wood for building. Today Ina is known for the many Jōmon period artifacts that have been excavated there, which were yet to be discovered during Seigetsu's lifetime. Perhaps Seigetsu unconsciously sensed how special Ina was.

Ochiguri no / za o sadameru ya / kubotamari
Fallen chestnut / where to settle decides / hollow in earth

Inoue Seigetsu's (1822–1887) life and works were an influence on the later poets Akutagawa Ryūnosuke and Taneda Santōka.[*2] This poem is from *Nagori no mizukuki* (1885), a haiku anthology compiled by Seigetsu.

A chestnut bug
apologetically
wiggles its way out

Tsujita Katsumi

Sometimes when you are given fresh chestnuts and leave them spread out to dry on a piece of newspaper, an insect larva bores a hole from inside and crawls out. This happens even though you had not noticed any holes when you spread out the chestnuts, and is because the egg was laid inside the chestnut while the chestnut was still small. It might be the larva of a weevil or a moth.

The fun of this poem comes from the word "apologetically." When the chestnut bug hatched, it was inside the chestnut and had nothing to eat but the flesh of the chestnut that surrounded it. It just ate what was there, so there is no reason for it to feel guilty towards humans. Yet the way it wags up and down as it emerges from the hole looks for all the world like a person bowing in earnest apology.

Chestnuts were a staple food for people of the prehistoric Jōmon period (ca. 10,000–ca. 300 BCE) in Japan. I can imagine someone from that world watching a bug emerge from a chestnut with precisely the same feeling as this.

Kuri no mushi / *sumanasasō ni* / *ide kitaru*
Chestnut bug / apologetically / emerges

Tsujita Katsumi (b. 1931) studied with Yamaguchi Seishi and Akimoto Fujio, and was a contributor to Seishi's *Tenrō* and Fujio's *Hyōkai*. He published several haiku collections, and after retiring from his job as a middle and high school teacher, he founded and led *Han*, of which he is now the leader emeritus. This poem is from *Shōmei* (2002).

Chestnut, shapeshifter—
twist yourself into
Baldy the Scary Monster!

Ishii Rogetsu

The poet is challenging the chestnut, which exploded with a large pop when he was roasting it: "If you can make such a big noise, you should be able to turn yourself into Baldy the Scary Monster—come on, let's see you do it." Baldy the Scary Monster (Ōnyūdō) is one of the many Japanese monsters called *yōkai*. The loud noise the chestnut made as it popped open startled the poet so much that he imagined a monster suddenly materializing before his eyes.

The chestnut also features in "The Crab and the Monkey" (*Saru kani gassen*), a folktale widely known from mid-eighteenth century children's books. When the villainous monkey draws close to the hearth for warmth, the chestnut, out to avenge the crab killed by the monkey, explodes and gravely injures him. The chestnut in the folktale and the chestnut in this poem both have will and agency and have a central role in the story.

You can see this poem as an expression of the longstanding Japanese taste for the supernatural. You can also read it as an expression of animism. Either way, the poet feels a mysterious life in the chestnut.

Kuri hanete / Ōnyūdō to / bakete mo miyo
Chestnut leaps / bald-headed monster / shapeshift show me

Ishii Rogetsu (1873–1928), who studied haiku with Masaoka Shiki, was a founder of the regional haiku magazine *Haisei* and became a central figure in the spread of Shiki's style of haiku in northeastern Japan. This poem is from *Rogetsu kushū* (1930) and is also included in *Shin haiku* (1898), edited by Masaoka Shiki.

All the things in our house
are old colors—
I repaper the shoji

Kōzai Teruo

Everything in the house has acquired an old color, says the poet. In preparation for winter, I repaper the shoji screens.

As someone who was born in the 1950s, I remember very well the "old colors" that Japanese houses had then. Almost everything was made of old wood and of earth, and as time passed acquired a blackish patina. Looking back now, those houses were attractively simple and plain, and there was something secure and solid about their aesthetic. Replacing the paper in the shoji meant imposing the new white of the paper on the old colors of the house. It made the house seem fresh and rejuvenated.

This poem was composed in 1965, the year after the author had lost his second son, a senior in high school, in a mountaineering accident. For the reader who knows that, the whiteness of the shoji may also be a witness to the father's grief.

Ie no mono / issai koshoku / shōji haru
House things / all old colors / shoji I repaper

Kōzai Teruo (1917–1987) studied haiku first with Takeshita Shizunojo and later, for many years, with Nakamura Kusatao, including participating in the founding and editing of Kusatao's *Banryoku*. This poem is from *Soshi* (1972).

Autumn fades—
ripples rise on the surface
of a small rain puddle

Ozawa Hekidō

For "rain puddle," the poet uses the archaic word *niwatazumi*. A breeze has arisen, sending ripples across the puddle. Anyone would notice ripples on the surface of a large body of water, but to discover them moving over something as small as a puddle requires a special kind of attention. In the background is the fading autumn, season of regret; the poet's sense of loss and loneliness seems to take shape in the ripples on the water's surface.

This is an example of the seasonal, fixed form haiku that Hekidō favored in later life. Even for such a haiku, it is extremely restrained, with not a wasted word. I much admire its classical tone.

> *Yuku aki ya / sazanami no tatsu / niwatazumi*
> Going autumn / ripples rise / rain puddle

Ozawa Hekidō (1881–1941) studied haiku with Kawahigashi Hekigotō and became one of the leading New Tendency Haiku* poets, mentoring Akutagawa Ryūnosuke among others. However, Hekidō later returned to seasonal, fixed form haiku. This poem is from his *Hekidō kushū* (1960), edited by Takii Kōsaku, which won the Yomiuri Prize for Literature in poetry.

Winter

Each and every one
a new world yet untrodden—
the winter stars

Takayanagi Katsuhiro

The human race has achieved unprecedented prosperity and tremendous population growth. In the process, we have despoiled the environment and condemned many animals and plants to extinction. And now we are even putting our own existence at risk. Yet our power is limited to the earth. We have reached the moon, but so far our reach does not extend to the stars in the sky.

This poem makes you realize the pathetic impotence of this proudly flourishing race of ours. However, the poem is not about despair. I imagine the profile of a young man looking up at the star-filled sky. You feel the limitless possibilities of the young man himself and of the entire human race. When he says "untrodden," he is not thinking of himself alone but of the human race as a whole.

The scale of this poem is vast. And winter is the right season for the poem. Without that sense of chill, the affirmation of the first two segments might seem easy sentimentality.

> *Kotogotoku / mitō narikeri / fuyu no hoshi*
> Each and every one / untrodden are / winter's stars

Takayanagi Katsuhiro (b. 1980) studied haiku with Fujita Shōshi,* contributed to Shōshi's *Taka*, and after Shōshi's death became the editor in chief of the magazine at age 25. He is also a scholar of haiku. This poem is from his first collection of haiku, the prizewinning *Mitō* (2009).

Saké made talk come easy
for Hakyō—Hakyō Day
is coming soon

Itō Hakuchō

Hakuchō's good friend, the renowned haiku poet Ishida Hakyō, was known for being unsociable, morose, and taciturn, except when he had a flask of saké in front of him. Then, as if by magic, he was transformed into a convivial person who greatly enjoyed drinking and talking with others in his poetic circle. Now the anniversary of Hakyō's death, "Hakyō Day" (November 21), is coming up.

In the Japanese, "Saké made talk come easy" modifies the name "Hakyō", but as the rest of the poem unfolds this word reveals itself as the first word of the following "Hakyō Day." (In Japanese this effect is achieved without having to repeat the word.) This is how an introductory phrase (*jokotoba*), a figure of speech often used in classical Japanese poetry, works. Here it makes the reader think of the person twice, in two different ways, once alive and once dead, thus increasing the intensity and depth of the poem.

A haiku written for the anniversary of someone's death should convey either a sense of grief at personal loss, or esteem for the works left behind. In this poem, we feel Hakuchō grieving for the cheerful Hakyō who enjoyed celebrating life with his fellow poets.

Sake nakuba / mukuchi no Hakyō / ki mo chikashi
Saké without / taciturn Hakyō / death day near

Itō Hakuchō (1926–2008) studied haiku with Tanaka Umajirō,* who was close to Ishida Hakyō and also one of the founding contributors to Hakyō's *Tsuru*. Hakuchō participated in the founding of Umajirō's *Shigi*. On the second anniversary of Umajirō's death, he revived *Shigi* and became its leader. This poem is from *Chirori ni suguru* (2004).

The Asuka Buddha's face
is oval today too—
daikon drying

Saitō Kafū

Buddhism was introduced into Japan from Korea in the sixth century CE and the first full-scale Buddhist temple in Japan, Asuka-dera, was built in 588. The oldest datable image of the Buddha in Japan, completed in 609, is the statue of the Asuka Great Buddha enshrined there.

The Asuka Buddha is distinguished by its large eyes, slight smile, and elongated face. This poem's description of the face as oval is precisely right, and "today too" adds a playful note, as though the speaker worships the image every day but never stops marveling at the sameness of its face. The seasonal image of drying daikon radish adds life to the poem.

A farmer who is hanging the radishes to dry from the eaves of his house nearby might be looking in at the Buddha's image during a work break. In that case, the description of the Buddha's face can be read as his thought.

Asuka butsu / kyō mo omonaga / daiko hosu
Asuka Buddha / today too long-faced / daikon dries

Saitō Kafū (1931–2017) was a follower of Yamaguchi Seison. He founded and led *Yane*. This poem is from his prizewinning *Tsuji haikai* (2010).

The sky above
so far away for the living—
a young hawk soars

Uda Kiyoko

The sky above looks very far away to those on earth, but the young hawk flies there with ease.

With the vivid phrase "the sky above is so far away for the living," the poem posits a sharp distinction between the living and the dead. The living can look up at the sky but can never touch it. The dead, in contrast, are omnipresent throughout the world, and fill the sky. You could even say that the heavens are a home for the dead.

The word translated as "young hawk" is *morogaeri*, which has the specific meaning of a three-year-old hawk. Hawks can live for decades so it may have years of life left to fly about the heavens. This young hawk makes me think of Kiyoko's younger friend the novelist Nakagami Kenji.* Kenji died in 1992 and the collection where this poem appears contains several poems in his memory. *Morogaeri* is partly homonymous with *kaeri*, "returning" or "the return," as if she sees in the hawk the spirit of her dear young friend.

Tenkū wa / seija ni fukashi / morogaeri
The sky / living beings to deep / three-year-old hawk

Uda Kiyoko (b. 1935) was a follower of Katsura Nobuko and editor in chief of *Sōen*, the magazine of Nobuko's group. After Nobuko's death she founded, and still leads, *Sōju*. This poem is from *Zō* (2000), for which she received the Iida Dakotsu Prize.

Lit up by sun
the hawk flies and will fly until
it is bits of bone

Terada Kyōko

As the hawk flies across the sky, it is lit up against the sun so that (the poet imagines) you can see its bones. Its will is so strong that it will keep flying until it dies, the flesh falls away, and the bones disintegrate. The image evokes the fierce determination to live that sustained the poet during the chronic tuberculosis she suffered from her 20s onward.

Flying appears twice in this poem. The first time, "the hawk flies," describes an actual scene. In the second, "will fly until it is bits of bone," it is a fantasy and a wish: the hawk will still fly even after it has died and is no more than bone. "Flies" (とぶ) is spelled out in the graceful hiragana script but "will fly" (飛ぶ) uses the more concentrated and visually complex kanji, as if for added emphasis—nothing will stop this bird.

> *Hi no taka ga / tobu koppen to / naru made tobu*
> Sun's hawk / flies bone fragments / becomes until flies

Terada Kyōko (1922–1976), a follower of Katō Shūson, was one of several women poets who emerged from Shūson's *Kanrai*. She also participated in the founding of Mori Sumio's *Sugi*. This poem is from her prizewinning *Hi no taka* (1967).

On a dazzling bright winter day
become fine dust
I will take my leave

Sōma Senshi

This is one of the last poems Senshi wrote as he was dying, published in the final year of his life. The first draft was "On a dazzling winter day/ leaving nothing behind/ I will take my leave." Only the middle segment differs, but in the earlier draft the middle segment is an assertion of will and intent—he declares that while regretting his departure from this world, he will leave nothing behind in it.

In contrast, in this poem will is not involved at all. Once his body is cremated and turned to smoke, it will be no more than the thing called fine dust, and in that transfigured form he will depart this world. He envisages his death with perfect clarity.

The seasonal image "dazzling bright winter day" (*tōrei*) is even brighter than the more common "sunny winter day" (*fuyubare*) and gives an impression of transparency. It makes me think that even as dust, he is gazing down on the mountains and rivers.

> *Tōrei no / mijin to narite / saran to su*
> Dazzling bright winter day / fine dust turned to / leave I will

Sōma Senshi (1908–1976) was a follower of Mizuhara Shūōshi and a contributor to Shūōshi's *Ashibi*. He was also mentored by Ishida Hakyō and contributed to Hakyō's *Tsuru*. This poem is from *Sanga* (1976).

Winter warmth—
the stick of butter
still in its paper wrapping

Nakamura Yasunobu

On an unseasonably warm winter day, a stick of butter is left in its paper wrapping, as though to keep it from melting. The stick of butter is described as a concrete object in plain words. Butter carries connotations of the luxurious Western-style food that is now part of the everyday Japanese diet, but this poem is not about the pleasures of food and eating. When the temperature rises, butter melts. I think the poet chose "winter warmth" as the seasonal image to bring out this uneasy sense of the changeable and uncertain. Winter should by nature be cold, and when it is warm there is a pervasive air of unease.

Fuyu nukushi / *batā wa kami ni* / *tsutsumarete*
Winter warmth / butter paper in / is wrapped

Nakamura Yasunobu (b. 1971) was a contributor to Kaneko Tōta's *Kaitei* until it suspended publication in 2018. He is now a contributing member of the haiku magazine *Ani*, and cofounder of the online haiku magazine *haiku&me*. This poem is from *Shinsen 21* (2009), an anthology featuring the work of twenty-one promising young poets.

Dried mud between
his eyebrows—
the rugby player!

Mimura Jun'ya

Rugby is traditionally a winter game, played by two teams of fifteen players each who compete to see who can score tries by placing an oval ball over the other team's goal line. It is a rough sport played in all weathers. In haiku, both the sport and the players are winter seasonal images. The word *mayu no ne* can mean either the eyebrow(s) or the area between the eyebrows. Here it means the latter.

In this poem, as a player was running around the muddy playing field the mud flew up and hit his face. The young man was so caught up in the game that he did not wipe the mud off and so it has dried on his face. There is a feeling of manliness about this portrait.

> *Mayu no ne ni / doro kawakiiru / ragā kana*
> Eyebrows in / mud dried / rugby player!

Mimura Jun'ya (b. 1953), who is also a professor of classical Japanese literature, was mentored by the *Hototogisu* poets Shimomura Hibun,* Kiyosaki Toshio, and Inahata Teiko, and is a contributor to that magazine. In 1997, he became the leader of *Sazanka*. This poem is from his haiku collection *Rugby* (2011).

Sudden winter showers —
the train station's
east exit and its west one

Azumi Atsushi

The note to this poem is "Den'enchōfu Station," a train station in a residential district of Tokyo. This tells you what station inspired it, but readers over the years have come to read the poem without reference to the note, as depicting any large train station in a city.

The simple dichotomy of east and west leaves room to imagine many stories. In pre-cellphone days, a rendezvous could be aborted if you misremembered the exit where you agreed to meet. You might wait on and on before you gave up and went home. In fact, in his comment on this poem the author explained that just such an experience lay behind it. Thinking of how quickly an early winter shower can come and go, I can imagine that at the west exit it's raining but by the time you arrive at the east exit it has stopped. Then, when you go back to the west exit the rain has started again.

The originality of this poem lies in its juxtaposition of the early winter "passing shower" (*shigururu ya*), a classical poetic image much loved by Bashō[1] for its overtones of evanescence, with the train station of a modern metropolis.

Shigururu ya / eki ni nishiguchi / higashiguchi
Sudden winter shower / station in west exit / east exit

Azumi Atsushi (1907–1988) first studied haiku under Tomiyasu Fūsei. He later joined Hino Sōjō's *Kikan* and was involved in the New Rising Haiku movement.[2] In the postwar period, he cofounded *Shuntō* and eventually inherited its leadership from Kubota Mantarō. In addition to his poetry, he is known for his essays. This poem is from *Furugoyomi* (1954).

I'm one of the cheaply made
mass-produced generation —
winter skylark

Takano Mutsuo

In Japan those born at the beginning of the postwar period, between 1947 and 1949, are called the "early baby boom" generation. The poet is one of them, but here he focuses on another aspect of the immediate postwar period, one that Japan was also known for, by playfully substituting the term "cheaply made mass-produced generation." The idea of a surge in the birth rate overlaps with the idea of a surge in the manufacture of cheap "Made in Japan" goods.

There is a rueful smile of self-deprecation at the thought that this generation could not produce much that is worth admiring. Yet juxtaposed to this is the winter skylark, which does not fly as high as the spring skylark but gives an impression of proud solitude. In the poet's choice of this seasonal image, I sense his sympathy and hope for the generation whose hard times he has shared.

> *Ware wa sosei / ranzō sedai / fuyu hibari*
> I cheaply-made / mass-produced generation / winter skylark

Takano Mutsuo (b. 1947) first studied haiku with Kaneko Tōta and became a leading member of Tōta's *Kaitei*. When Satō Onifusa founded *Kogumaza*, he joined the group and edited its magazine, and in 2003, after Onifusa's death, became its leader. This poem is from *Mushi no ō* (2003).

On the next rice field over,
the ridge casts a shadow—
winter rice fields

Kurata Kōbun

On a clear winter day, the shadow of the dividing ridge between rice fields falls on the adjacent field. There is no one to be seen.

"Winter rice field" (*fuyuta*) is a field after harvest, left unplowed. The earth may be trampled by the reapers, there is probably a lot of uneven stubble, and rice straw may be strewn about. All this is elided, and only the shadow that falls onto the neighboring rice field is described. What is left? The glare of the strong winter sunlight and the unpeopled landscape, for farmers and their families do not go into the fields at this season. Then there is the next field over—and the next and the next, the fields stretching on and on, and everything waiting for the spring planting season to begin.

> *Tsugi no ta ni / aze no kage aru / fuyuta kana*
> Next rice paddy over / ridge shadow is / winter rice paddy

Kurata Kōbun (1940–2014) was mentored by Takano Sujū. Encouraged by Sujū, he founded *Fuki* when he was only 32 and was its leader for the rest of his life. He was also a professor of Japanese literature. This poem is from *Jifu hibo* (1976).

How horribly cold
it was in 1936
on 2/26

Nara Fumio

On February 26, 1936, a group of young Imperial Japanese Army officers in Tokyo attempted a coup d'état and assassinated several leading officials. Their attempt, known as the 2/26 Incident, failed, but resulted in the military solidifying its position, thus hastening the coming of the Pacific War.

The poet is remembering his high school days when, like virtually all Japanese high school students, he memorized important historical dates by matching the digits to a phrase. Here, "1936" is matched to "horribly cold" (*hidoku samui*): *hi* is short for *hitotsu*, "one;" *ku* is "nine;" *sa* is short for *san*, "three;" and *mu* is short for *muttsu*, "six." I myself was taught to memorize 794, the date of the founding of Heian-kyō (now Kyoto) as the capital of Japan, by using the phrase *nakuyo uguisu Heian-kyō*, "the bush warbler sings in Heian-kyō." Here, the first word (meaning "sing") represents the date: *na* is short for *nana*, "seven;" *ku* is "nine;" and *yo* is short for *yottsu*, "four;" thus seven-nine-four.

Besides being a fun way to remember important dates, such mnemonic phrases often convey something of the atmosphere of a period and can be quite poetic. "Horribly cold" reminds us that the weather that day, when Tokyo was buried under a huge snowfall, was freezing cold and even suggests the chill dread of the times, when war was looming. The poet Fumio was in fact born in that very year. Perhaps this poem framed around numbers came into being as he contemplated that coincidence.

> *Hidoku samui to* / *oboeshi kono hi* / *ni ni-roku*
> Horribly cold as / remembered this day / Feb. 26

Nara Fumio (1936–2018) studied with Nakamura Kusatao and worked as a selector for Kusatao's *Banryoku*. This poem is from *Sojō* (2005).

The winter tree
rips to shreds the winds
from the sky

Shinohara Hōsaku

In a lonely landscape, the branches and leaves of a tall tree are singing in the wind. The poet personifies this, as though the tree had a will of its own. The effect is startling.

In the image of the tree ripping the wind to shreds, I feel a determination not to retreat no matter how difficult the circumstances. This tree stands alone, enduring its solitude with a valiant heart. The figure of the poet seems to be projected onto the tree. Such an attitude must have enabled Hōsaku to persist in his path as a New Rising Haiku[*1] poet.

The featured poem uses a seasonal image ("winter tree"), but Hōsaku constantly experimented with seasonless haiku as well. He composed outstanding haiku such as "Breathing blue/ all the way down through my lungs/ I sail the seas," and "So young she was/ when she became a mother—/ her clouded eyes." Seasonless though they are, they are fresh and vibrant. Yet I feel that his poems with seasonal images, like this poem, are even more lyrical.

> *Ōzora no / kaze o saki iru / fuyuki ari*
> Sky / wind is ripping / winter tree there is

Shinohara Hōsaku (1905–1936) was a New Rising Haiku poet who participated primarily in Yoshioka Zenjidō's[*2] *Amanogawa* and his own *Kasabi*. His promise was cut short by his early death. This poem is from the posthumous *Shinohara Hōsaku shū* (1957).

Branch of the winter tree
gradually thins until only
air is there

Masaki Kōichi

As I look at the branch of a winter tree, says the poet, I see that the closer it comes to the tip the thinner it gets, until finally it disappears entirely.

He lets his eyes slowly trace a single branch of a leafless winter tree. The part attached to the trunk is thick, but little by little the branch narrows. The description carefully follows the movement of his eyes. Beyond the very tip, his eyes come to rest on empty space—the last words register this nothingness. As the branch ends, there is a sense of spreading space beyond.

The branch of the tree could be an image of this poet's life. Kōichi died of illness at a relatively young age, his life gradually dwindling like the branch's gradual thinning. The words "until only/air is there" seem to float unanchored, a premonition of his own approaching death. Reading this poem I follow its author's line of sight and also experience vicariously his last days.

Fuyuki no e / shidai ni hososhi / tsui ni nashi
Winter tree's branch / gradually thin / finally nothing

Masaki Kōichi (1942–1992) was a follower of Nomura Toshirō. This poem is from *Masaki Kōichi kushū* (1993), edited by his sister Masaki Yūko, who is also a haiku poet.

If I freed the fire in
my heart how bright these
withered fields would burn

Inagaki Kikuno

Before me spreads an expanse of leafless trees and withered fields. If I were to release the fire of love that is burning in my heart, that wintry landscape would burst into flames.

A love poem, of course. "These withered fields" suggests that it is a desperate love, one that has no hope of being requited. Perhaps there is some reason that it is doomed; for example, the object of her love is already committed to someone else. In spite of this, or rather, because of it, the fire in her heart only burns the more fiercely, and her feelings for the object of her desire grow even stronger. The coldness of the situation is in stark contrast to the heat of passion within her. But for now she resists taking any action that would release the fire in her heart; that is, any action that would express her feelings.

Has such intense passion ever been recorded in a haiku?

> *Kono kare ni* / *mune no hi hanachi-* / *naba moemu*
> This withering in / heart's fire freed / if would burn up

Inagaki Kikuno (1906–1987) first studied haiku with Ōba Hakusuirō,* then, as a longtime contributor to *Shuntō*, with Kubota Mantarō and Azumi Atsushi, who was Mantarō's successor as leader of *Shuntō*. Before she became a haiku poet, she was a well-known movie actress. This poem is from her prizewinning *Fuyunami* (1966).

Winter desolation—
what speaks is
the caged bird

Takahashi Awajijo

Something spoke in the long silence. However, it was not a person but a caged bird. Beyond the window, all is wintry desolation as far as the eye can see.

Solitude and longing are the subjects of this poem. The speaking bird implies the absence of any other human besides the poet herself. But since this bird speaks rather than sings, it must be a bird that imitates the human voice, like a parrot. Even keeping such a bird suggests an underlying loneliness. Awajijo lost her husband only a year after their marriage, and there is a sense in this poem of her experiencing again the pain left by his absence.

The seasonal image "winter desolation" is usually used about an outdoor scene, but here it seems to permeate the indoors also, and even the inner life of the poet herself.

Fuyuzare ya / mono o iishi wa / kago no tori
Winter desolation / something spoke / caged bird

Takahashi Awajijo (1890–1955) first studied with Takahama Kyoshi. She later became a follower of Iida Dakotsu and a contributor to his *Unmo* as well as to Abe Midorijo's *Komakusa*. This poem is from her first haiku collection *Kaji no ha* (1937).

The small bird died
leaving behind its cage and a view of
withered fields

Ameyama Minoru

His little bird has died and now he can see through to the fields outside the window. In a cage set beside the window he kept a small bird. He used to delight in watching it while it was alive, but now that it is dead his gaze shifts to the scene beyond the cage. The desolation of the wintry landscape suits the aftermath of the bird's death. A poem which well conveys the sense of absence left by death, mere bird though it was.

The combination of dead bird and wintry fields creates a somewhat imaginary, almost abstract, landscape image, but the strongly present image of the cage anchors the poem in reality.

The consonant "k" sounds throughout this poem. Each segment of the Japanese begins with it (*kotori, kareno, kago*), it appears again in the second segment (*yoku suku*) and yet again within the third segment (*nokoru*). You can almost hear the sounds the bird made in its cage while it was alive.

Kotori shini / *kareno yoku suku* / *kago nokoru*
Small bird dead / withered fields easily seen through / cage remains

Ameyama Minoru (1926–2000) was a haiku poet and scholar as well as a well-known microbiologist. He was deeply inspired by Shiba Fukio and wrote a biography of him. He was also close to Andō Tsuguo and Kaneko Tōta. He originally belonged to *Kaze*, but eventually left and continued to write and publish haiku independently. This poem is from *Shōchōshū* (1971).

The winter waves
wave against the winter wharf—
in and out

Katō Ikuya

Haiku is a brief form, and using the same word or phrase more than once is discouraged. However, in this poem "winter waves" appears twice in the Japanese, but pronounced in two different ways and as part of two different phrases. The way this sleight of hand works is that the word "waves" (*nami* 波) of the first segment overlaps visually with the second segment's "wharf" (*hatoba* 波止場), which is written with characters that mean "wave stopping place." The overlap expresses the continual motion of the waves coming in one after another.

This overlap is a little like the *kakekotoba* (pivot words) of classical Japanese waka, in which one word or part of a word both ends a grammatical segment and becomes the first word of the following one. However, with *kakekotoba*, sound (the pronunciation) provides the pivot, while here it is sight (the character itself). The first "wave" is pronounced *nami*, while the second is pronounced *ha*.

These complications bring to mind the spatial illusions in the work of the Dutch artist M.C. Escher (1898–1972), such as the drawings in which steps seem to go both up and down. Here the incoming waves and the outgoing waves are intermingled.

> *Fuyu no nami* / *fuyu no hatoba ni* / *kite kaesu*
> Winter waves / winter wharf to / come and go

Katō Ikuya (1929–2012) first studied with his father, who was a traditionalist haiku poet and also a haiku scholar. Later he was influenced by the New Rising Haiku movement,* participated in Takayanagi Jūshin's *Haiku hyōron*, and cofounded the avant-garde haiku magazine *Unicorn*. He was also a poet of modern verse. This poem is from *Kyūtai kankaku* (1959), his first collection of haiku.

Reflected in
the silvery skin of the *hatahata* —
the flames!

Ishida Katsuhiko

Hatahata (Japanese sandfish, *Arctoscopus japonicus*) is caught in the winter months along the coast of the Sea of Japan, especially in Akita Prefecture. It is about 15 centimeters long with a flattened body, and the flesh is considered so delicious that it is designated as Akita's official prefectural fish.

This poem describes the *hatahata* just as it has been placed on a charcoal grill. But rather than simply stating that unexceptional fact, the poet draws our attention to the way the flames are reflected on the silvery skin of the fish. Were the fish not plump and fresh, the flames would not reflect well, so this phrase not only tells us that the grilling has just begun but also suggests that this fish is going to be delicious. A reader who knows about *hatahata* will see in the mind's eye the scaleless and silvery body speckled with brown.

One of the pleasures of travel is eating local products, and the poet must be waiting eagerly for the fish to be cooked. I feel this anticipation behind the intense observation of the poem.

> *Hatahata ni / utsurite itaru / honoo kana*
> Sandfish on / reflected are / flames!

Ishida Katsuhiko (1920–2004) was a follower of Ishida Hakyō and a contributor to Hakyō's *Tsuru*. After Hakyō's death, he participated in the founding of *Izumi*, which was led by another former *Tsuru* member, Kobayashi Kōji,* and also became its editor. This poem comes from his prizewinning *Shūkyō* (2000).

The gurnard fish
dreams in
ultramarine

Ōtake Seiji

The gurnard is said to walk slowly along the ocean floor using the finger-like spines underneath its large pectoral fins. It also emits a croaking sound using its swim bladder.

In the daytime, the deep blue of the ocean depths must fill the gurnard's field of vision. At night this must become pure darkness, but if the fish dreams (and who is to say that it does not?), the dream would be deep blue like the ocean, and contain nothing else either animate or inanimate. This speaks of the dreamy nature of this fish and of its solitary life. Somehow I feel that this at the same time expresses the poet's own inner life.

This is not a simple objective description; the poet imagines himself as a living fish, and the process of composition begins from there.

Hōbō ni / konjō no yume / arinikeri
Gurnard in / deep blue dream / there was

Ōtake Seiji (b. 1937), as a member of *Shuntō*, studied haiku with its leader Azumi Atsushi first, and later with Naruse Ōtōshi.* After Ōtōshi's death, he cofounded and co-led *Reki*. This poem is from his prizewinning *Shōka* (2009).

I'm slurping up
an oyster when the oyster
licks my tongue

Bōjō Toshiki

Live oysters, just shucked, are considered a delicacy, but the oyster in this poem is not content with simply being someone's meal. This oyster has a will of its own and counterattacks, licking the human's tongue.

This is a witty poem, but that is not its only intent. It also aims at evoking the mysterious and subtle feel of a raw oyster on your tongue. At the same time, it is a reminder that our food is also a living creature, a life.

As I repeat this poem to myself, I savor the aliveness of the oyster incarnated in the onomatopoeic *sururi to*, which evokes the oyster's slipperiness.

> *Kaki susuru / sururi to shita o / name ni kuru*
> Oyster slurp / slippery tongue / lick to come

Bōjō Toshiki (b. 1957), is the grandson of Takahama Toshio* and the great-grandson of Takahama Kyoshi, and is a contributor to *Hototogisu* as well as the leader of *Kachō*. This poem is from his first collection of haiku, *Zero* (1998).

With a heavy book
near at hand
I settle in for winter

Satō Kōroku

He may be secluded indoors for the winter, but his thirst for learning is undiminished. He has placed a heavy book nearby and looks into it often.

I wonder what book it could be, in this house which must have many others on its shelves, including many lighter books. This heavy book might be a dictionary or other reference work, in which case placing it nearby would be for the purpose of looking things up often. Or it could be an ordinary book which happens to be big and heavy. Things slow down in the winter, so this would be a good chance to finish reading such a book. Whichever it is, this person seems to be somewhat physically inactive but highly active mentally, so the image of settling in for winter suits him well. The poem as a whole gives off a feeling of pleasure.

> *Omoki sho wa / tejika ni oite / fuyugomori*
> Heavy book / near at hand placing / winter hibernation

Satō Kōroku (1874–1949) was a follower of Masaoka Shiki, a passionate supporter of Shiki's haiku reform, and a lifelong friend of Takahama Kyoshi. He was also a popular writer of young adult fiction, while continuing to write and publish haiku independently. This poem is from *Kōroku kushū* (1950).

The golden screen
so swiftly folded—now you see it
now you don't

Iijima Haruko

"Golden screen" is a winter seasonal image because screens were originally used as protection from the cold wind, but this screen must be at the front of a heated banquet room in a hotel. After the party is over, the hotel employees fold the screen up and take it away. The poet is exclaiming at the dexterity and speed with which they can fold up this large and bulky object, so quickly that it leaves a golden afterimage behind. I have the feeling of having been shown the reality of life's uncertainty and evanescence.

According to the poet, the event described here occurred at the party that followed a formal meeting of the haiku group *Take*, an affiliated group of *Taka*. Being a member of both groups, I must have witnessed the scene, but I have absolutely no memory of it.

> *Kinbyōbu / nan to subayaku / tatamu koto*
> Golden screen / how quickly / they fold up

Iijima Haruko (1921–2000) was a follower of Fujita Shōshi* and was a founding member of *Taka*. In addition to her poetry, she was a critic who contributed significantly to the development of women's haiku. This poem is from *Yatsugashira* (1985).

The whole day
slipped by in silence
in sight of the shoji

Hasegawa Sosei

Since he is recollecting the whole day, it must be evening or nighttime, with the Japanese paper screens (shoji) glowing in the lamplight. He cannot remember that anything unpleasant happened the entire day.

When the poet composed this verse he was hospitalized. Even in a hospital you cannot avoid frequent interactions with people. It is a place where an infinite number of unpleasant things might occur. And yet, his feeling is that it has been a quiet, uneventful day. This means that his spirit is serene and he is calmly aware of his surroundings. The white paper shoji glowing in the lamplight takes on its color and fills his sight.

I think of this as an image of the serene interior of the poet himself.

> *Shizuka naru / ichinichi narishi / shōji kana*
> Quiet is / one day became / shoji!

Hasegawa Sosei (1907–1946) studied with *Hototogisu* poets including their leader, Takahama Kyoshi. He participated in a magazine that advocated New Rising Haiku* but ultimately parted ways with it. Drafted during the Sino-Japanese War but demobilized due to illness (tuberculosis, of which he eventually died), he is known for his haiku about war. This poem is from *Teihon Sosei shū* (1947).

even coughing
alone

Ozaki Hōsai

Even when I cough, there is no one to take notice. I am all alone.

After graduation from the University of Tokyo (then Tokyo Imperial University), Hōsai worked at a life insurance company. However, he could not accustom himself to the company, which maintained strict control over the lives of its employees, and this, together with his fondness for liquor, led him to quit. He then moved to an insurance company in Korea (at the time a Japanese colony) but liquor again led to failure and he was fired. He began a business in Manchuria, another Japanese colony, but ill health made him return to Japan. Then he became a temple assistant at Chion-in Temple in Kyoto but was forced yet again to leave because of his drinking. Finally, he ended up on the island of Shōdoshima in the Seto Inland Sea, as the sole occupant of a tiny hut in the mountains above Saikōji Temple, where he ate little and grew steadily weaker until after several months he died.

This free form haiku of extreme brevity is almost shocking, especially to readers who think of haiku as a fixed form of seventeen syllables. Yet I do not know another haiku in which a cough echoes so forlornly and in such solitude. Hōsai could not adjust to society; in this poem, you hear the true voice of his soul.

Seki o shite mo hitori
Coughing even alone

Ozaki Hōsai (1885–1926) was a follower of Ogiwara Seisensui* and a contributor to Seisensui's free form haiku magazine *Sōun*. Yoshimura Akira, the novelist and haiku poet, wrote a fictionalized biography of him. This poem, probably the best known free form haiku there is, is from his only haiku collection *Taikū* (1926), posthumously edited by Seisensui.

The lady coughs and
I join her in coughing
though we're no connection

Shimomura Kaita

A woman I happened to be sitting next to coughed. I coughed after her, but that was our only connection. I'll never meet her again.

Was this a chance meeting in some enclosed public space, such as a train? The slightly archaic "lady" (*nyonin*), unlike other words available in Japanese (such as *onna, josei, fujin*) expresses a sense of respect and admiration. She must have been beautiful and had something special that drew him to her. The "I" of the poem felt an inexplicable delight when she coughed and he happened to cough right after her. However, when he reflected that his only connection with her was that they had coughed almost in unison, the little thrill of delight faded.

A vivid portrait of the subtle shadings of erotic emotion.

> *Nyonin seki / ware seki tsurete / yukari nashi*
> Woman coughs / I cough together / connected not

Shimomura Kaita (1910–1966) joined Okamoto Shōhin's *Kangiku* when he was only 15. He contributed to and edited the group magazine until it ceased publication, and later he founded and led *Kongō*. He ultimately dissolved it and quit haiku, only to return twelve years later, this time as a free form haiku poet. This poem is from *Kōhai* (1947).

I cough—the sweet fragrance
of death rising
from my body

Yamagami Kimio

This is the cough of someone who is mortally ill. Each cough worsens his condition and brings him a little closer to dying. But death seems to hold no terror for him. It has a lovely "sweet fragrance."

How can this be? As his illness has progressed, the elements of death have increasingly permeated his body, a fact he quietly recognizes. He may even be longing for death to bring a quicker end to his suffering. The phrase "sweet fragrance" also hints at incense, suggesting that thoughts of the incense offerings at his own funeral may also be in his mind.

In this sickbed haiku, one of the finest examples of its kind, death and life face each other in unforced intimacy.

Seki o shite / shi no kōbashisa / waga mi yori
Cough making / death's fragrance / my body from

Yamagami Kimio (1931–2014) studied haiku with Mizuhara Shūōshi and Yamaguchi Sōdō* and eventually became the leader of *Nanpū*, which Sōdō had begun. This poem is from his prizewinning *Shiijishō* (2002).

Remade in the shape
of an old man
I blow my runny nose

Hatta Kogarashi

If he has metamorphosed into an old man concentrating on blowing his runny nose, then what is his usual form? Is he usually unaware of it as he goes about his daily routine? Perhaps his usual self-image is the way he remembers himself as a child or a young man. But then he takes out a tissue to blow his runny nose and suddenly realizes that he has reached old age.

The poem makes you see that moment clearly. Something without defined shape suddenly takes on the fixed shape of an aged human. Or a youthful self-image is suddenly transformed into an aged one. It is poignant to think that the watery dribble running from his nose would make him suddenly aware of old age, becoming the means of an inner transformation.

Insofar as it deals with such a transformation, this is a fantasy haiku, but it is far from being warm and fuzzy. It provides a glimpse of the truth of what is called old age.

> *Rōjin no* / *katachi ni natte* / *mizubana kamu*
> Old man's / shape becoming / runny nose blow

Hatta Kogarashi (1925–2012) studied haiku with Hasegawa Sosei and Yamaguchi Seishi, cofounded the magazine *Bankō*, and contributed to *Raigyo*. This poem is from his prize-winning *Kagamizai* (2010).

Mother is dead
so I want the winter clothes
she is wearing now

Nagata Kōi

When his mother was alive she needed winter clothes to survive. He never thought he would find himself saying he wanted to have them. But now that his mother is dead she no longer needs her thick winter kimono to keep her warm. On the other hand, he really needs them to protect himself from the cold. The heartlessness makes you think he might be ready to peel the clothes off his mother's corpse, but it succeeds in expressing with great directness the difference between his mother when alive and his mother now that she is dead.

Kōi wrote other seemingly unfeeling poems about his mother. Two other examples are: "Morning glories—/ when I've visited one hundred times/ mother will die" and "Winter sparrows—/ something remains/ to make mother die." Paradoxically, overwhelming affection for his mother may have impelled him to compose such poems.

Haha shineba / *ima kitamaeru* / *fuyugi hoshi*
Mother is dead so / now she wears / winter clothes I want

Nagata Kōi (1900–1997) studied with Ono Bushi* and Hara Sekitei, then later joined Ishida Hakyō's *Tsuru*. In the postwar period, he joined the newly founded *Tenrō*, the magazine led by Yamaguchi Seishi. In 1949 he founded *Riraza*, which he ran until his death. This poem is from *Romeishū* (1952).

The hoeing calluses
on my five fingers
almost split the gloves

Koide Shūkō

For many years he has cultivated his land with a hoe, and all his fingers are callused from the repetitive labor. Now when he puts on his work gloves his thick fingers fill the gloves so tightly they almost split at the seams.

There is no entry for the term "hoeing callus" (*kuwadako*) in my dictionary, but it is obviously a word to do with farming and the earth. He probably has calluses on both hands. Calluses like his don't come from mechanized farming. They are evidence of having confronted the earth with no more than a single hoe—a simple, almost primitive, hand tool.

During the farming off-season in winter, he is staring at these gloves that covered his hands earlier in the year. He describes what he sees precisely as it occurs to him. These fingers of his would laugh at the uncallused hands of a pen-wielding intellectual who never digs the earth. What he sees in these gloves is not only his callused fingers but the pride he takes in his calling as a hard-working farmer.

Kuwadako no / goshi tebukuro ni / michimiteri
Hoe calluses / five fingers gloves in / fill up fully

Koide Shūkō (1926–2006) studied haiku with Ishihara Yatsuka* and later became the third leader of *Kōjitsu*, the haiku group based in his home prefecture of Chiba. This poem is from *Tsuchikure* (1969).

Yarn choosing—
the red I desire is different
from all the ones here

Yamashita Chizuko

She is in a shop, choosing yarn. Several shades of red are available but the red that she had in mind and yearned for is different from all of them. In a word, this shop has nothing for her.

The poem records an intense feeling: the impossibility of being satisfied with what is available, a kind of fierce thirst. Rarely, if ever, does a haiku describe a surge of emotion as sharp as this. Yet the poem presents more than simply emotion—we also glimpse a visual landscape behind its words. In the background is the yarn store, full of many colors of yarn including a wide variety of reds, and as if buried among them is the figure of a woman choosing. The huge number of choices is part of her deep despair.

Such a sense of being at odds with the world is unusual in haiku, where the exterior world is usually intimately linked to the poet's inner world.

Keito eru / hoshiki aka to wa / dore mo chigau
Yarn choosing / desired red / each differs from

Yamashita Chizuko (b. 1950) was active in *Ran*, the group founded by Nozawa Setsuko, and in Imai Sei's *Machi*. She then founded *Rin* and now also contributes to *Kudan*. This poem is from *Happu* (2002).

From out of the north wind
a finger emerged
pointing at me

Hashizume Sajin

To point a finger at someone is to criticize them severely. It never indicates admiration or praise. The poet is in a crowd when he notices a mysterious finger pointing at him. He cannot see whose finger it is, nor can he even make out a figure behind it. His eyes focus on the fingertip, which is pointed at him in a clearly malevolent way. A stormy, cold north wind is blowing, making him feel even worse.

Most of the human figures who appear in haiku are very friendly and kind. However, what is described in this poem is an anonymous and malign figure. That is where its originality lies.

Behind this poem I sense the disorder and upheaval that followed World War II in Japan.

> *Kitakaze no / naka ware o sasu / yubi o miki*
> North wind / inside I at pointing / finger I saw

Hashizume Sajin (1913–1986) studied haiku with Saitō Sanki and helped edit Sanki's *Gekirō*. Later he studied with Yamaguchi Seishi and contributed to *Tenrō*. After moving around from job to job for years, he found his vocation as the head of a circus. This poem is from *Gokyū* (1975).

I am on cordial terms with
a number of drafts
who visit my room

Aioigaki Kajin

A draft is, as everyone knows, a breeze that blows into a house. Traditional Japanese houses were constructed in such a way that drafts were ubiquitous, coming in through the doors, the paper screens that divided the house into rooms, and the cracks in the walls. Houses today are so well sealed that experiencing drafts is rare, but the author of this poem obviously knew them well.

The invisible breezes that seem to haunt the place where he spends most of his time are described as if they were material things, almost people. The formal quality of "on cordial terms" (*jukuchi*) and "a number of drafts" (*sūjō*), both words composed only of kanji, also elevates the register. The gap between that elevated diction and the drafts themselves, which bespeak poverty, gives rise to a humorous mismatch. In the poem before this one in the collection, there seem to be even more drafts: "The drafts occupy/every chink and corner of/my room."

> *Sukimakaze* / *sono sūjō o* / *jukuchi seri*
> Draft / several of them / I know well

Aioigaki Kajin (1898–1985), a follower of Mizuhara Shūōshi, became an important member of *Ashibi*. In the postwar period, he co-led the regional haiku magazine *Unasaka*. This poem is from *Bibōshū* (1955).

After a while the broom
I used to sweep away the frost
falls

Nomura Toshirō

After using a broom to sweep away the frost in front of the house, the poet propped the broom against something; it stays standing for a while and then it falls down. Since he used it to sweep outdoors, it must be a bamboo broom, which requires a firm grasp and vigorous movements. By the time he finished sweeping all the frost away, the handle would have become warm. If he had simply waited, the frost would have disappeared naturally as the sun rose higher, so his sweeping also suggests a kind of hot impatience.

I imagine him leaning the broom against a wall when he was done, in the same place as always. Maybe he intended to sweep more later. But then the broom falls. Is there a connection between the broom having swept up the frost and its falling? The time span of "after a while" is somehow mysterious too. Having swept the frost from the road with such determination, why does he seem to leave the fallen broom where it is?

This poem is a riddle with no solution.

Shimo hakishi / hōki shibaraku / shite taoru
Frost swept / broom a little / while falls

Nomura Toshirō (1911–2001) studied haiku with Mizuhara Shūōshi and was a member of *Ashibi*. He founded and led *Oki*, which nurtured many contemporary poets. This poem is from the prizewinning *Chōshō* (1992).

Lifted by needle ice
the moss floats—
in front of his grave

Tajima Hakuyō

Hakuyō was a Buddhist priest and the head of Hōshōin, a small and very old temple in what is now Fuchū, in the suburbs of Tokyo. This poem, prefaced by the note "The grave of Ryū-u at my home," was composed at the gravestone that he erected at his temple for his revered haiku teacher, Masuda Ryū-u. Ryū-u already had a grave at Eidenji Temple in Asakusa, Tokyo, so erecting another stone for him at his own temple shows the depth of his feeling for his teacher.

The image of the needle ice lifting the moss in front of the tombstone is very precise. He must be down close to it if he can see so clearly how the ice raises the moss. He would be kneeling before the grave.

The needle ice can also be read as an image of the refinement and clarity of mind that Hakuyō admired in his teacher's poetry.

Shimobashira / *koke o ukasu ya* / *haka no mae*
Needle ice / moss makes float / tombstone in front of

Tajima Hakuyō (1900–1955) contributed to *Shundei*, the haiku magazine for which Kubota Mantarō was the selector, and edited his mentor Masuda Ryū-u's *Shimaki*. After Ryū-u's death, he became a follower of Momiyama Shigetsu, and later founded and led *Fueki*. This poem is from *Tamagawa* (1943), the only collection he published during his lifetime.

Living things sunk—
below
the wintery water

Katayama Yumiko

The poet is looking at a body of cold winter water. Things that live in the water stay beneath the surface of their own free will. Imagine a carp, say, that mostly lives "sunk" below the surface of the water, and floats up to it when it dies. The expression "living things sunk—/below" masks its opposite, "dead things float up."

This poem was composed after the Great East Japan Earthquake and nuclear disaster in 2011, and I cannot read it without thinking of those who died in the tsunami at that time. So many who had lived on the earth were dragged into the ocean by the tsunami and lost their lives. For me, that tragedy reverberates through this poem. I have the same feeling from other poems the poet wrote after the disaster, such as "The rippling waves/carry nothing—/spring nightfall" and "Swept off/by an uninvited wave—/the fiddler crab."

Inochi aru / mono wa shizumite / fuyu no mizu
Life having / things sink / winter's water

Katayama Yumiko (b. 1952) studied haiku with Takaha Shugyō. She became assistant head of Shugyō's *Kari*, and after *Kari* ceased publication, founded and now leads *Kōu*. This poem is the last poem in her prizewinning *Kōu* (2012).

Ashura, Karura,
Kinnara, Magoraga—
what a terrible fire!

Ozaki Meidō

In 734, Empress Kōmyō built the Western Golden Hall (Saikondō) of Kōfukuji Temple as a shrine to her mother. She installed statues of the Shakyamuni triad (the historical Buddha flanked by two attendants) and other Buddhist deities, including the Eight Legions (Hindu deities that were absorbed into Buddhism). These statues survived until modern times because they were made using a dry lacquer technique with a hollow core, and so were light enough to be easily evacuated during the four huge fires that occurred between 1046 and 1717 at the Western Golden Hall.

That is the history that lies behind this poem. The poem lists the names of four of the deities of the Eight Legions, and ends with a huge fire. The Ashura were demigods or titans, the Karura were giant birdmen that fed on dragons, the Kinnara were heavenly musicians, and the Magoraga (also called Sakara) were serpent deities. These are among the statues that the priests are about to bear away amid swirling flames.

The straightforward list of the deities' names, culminating in that huge fire at the end, has speed and urgency. You can almost see the forms of the priests hurrying to rescue the statues from the flames.

Ashura Karura / Kinnara Magoraga / taika kana
Ashura Karura / Kinnara Magoraga / great fire!

Ozaki Meidō (1891–1970), a Buddhist priest, studied haiku with Matsune Tōyōjō and was one of the most significant members of Tōyōjō's *Shibugaki*. He also founded and led *Egara*. This poem is from *Korin* (1941).

The propeller
comes off the boat and now come
New Year preparations

Tanayama Harō

There are only a few days left in December and today is the fisherman's last day of work. Since he won't be going out to sea again this year, he pulls the fishing boat up on land and removes the propeller from the stern. Now he can move on to preparations for the New Year celebration.

His fishing boat is a fisherman's most important possession. Grateful for how hard his boat has worked for him during the year, he removes the propeller as the old year approaches its end and lets the boat rest quietly until the new year begins. A propeller is, as its name says, what propels a boat; without it, the boat cannot move on its own, so this act of removal could also be a signal to the sea gods that the fisherman will refrain from fishing during this period.

I wonder if the setting is Noto, the poet's home region, a rural peninsula in Ishikawa Prefecture dotted with little fishing villages. The forms of the old traditional beliefs live on even for a fisherman who works with a modern propeller-equipped boat.

> *Sukuryū o / fune yori hazushi / toshi yōi*
> Propeller / boat from removing / New Year preparations

Tanayama Harō (b. 1939) was a member of *Kaze*, a founding contributor to Minagawa Bansui's* *Shunkou*, and is now *Shunkou*'s leader. This poem is from *Hōdatsu* (2008).

It's time to forget the year—
all the things around me
are now dust

Katsura Nobuko

It is the year's end and the poet is consciously trying to forget the various things that have happened this year. Doing that makes her think of everything around her as no more than dust.

At traditional "year forgetting parties" (*bōnen kai*) before New Year, people gather together to forget the past year and all its trials and tribulations by drinking and talking together. This poem references the idea of forgetting the past year, but with a very clear difference—this is an action taken alone, in solitude. The poet is creating a clean break with the sorrows of the past year, and she intends to forget them. That said, she is not running away from this world. The emphatic "all the things around me/ are now dust" makes this very clear. As someone trying to start life anew, everything in her present surroundings has ceased to have meaning for her.

This poem makes you feel the extreme strength of Nobuko's will.

> *Bōnen ya / mi hotori no mono / subete chiri*
> Year-end / body around things / all dust

Katsura Nobuko (1914–2004) was mentored by Hino Sōjō and contributed to *Kikan*. In the postwar period, she helped edit the magazine *Josei haiku* (*Women's haiku*), and later founded *Sōen*, which nurtured many young women poets. This poem is from *Juei* (1991), which won the Iida Dakotsu Prize.

Laughing so hard
I need to remove my false teeth—
the New Year's party

Ioki Hyōtei

"Laughing so hard," in Japanese the pleasantly archaic *kakataishō*, is a word any haiku poet would enjoy using for the first segment of a poem, but what makes it into a grand joke is that he laughed to the point where he had to remove his false teeth.

On the evening of December 29, 1936, thirty-four years after the death of the great poet Masaoka Shiki, a few people who had been close to Shiki gathered at his old home in the Negishi area of Tokyo to mark the year's end. Besides Hyōtei, the attendees were the painter and calligrapher Nakamura Fusetsu, the haiku poets Kawahigashi Hekigotō and Samukawa Sokotsu, and Shiki's younger sister Ritsuko. The poet's note explains that this poem is about a scroll with a comic picture by the painter Asai Chū and text by Shiki. The scroll must have had a wonderful energy that raised everyone's spirits.

Hyōtei was a notable political activist, but as a haiku poet he was an independent who did not participate in any haiku groups after his mentor Shiki died.

> *Kakataishō / ireba hazushite / toshi wasure*
> Belly laugh / false teeth removing / forgetting the year

Ioki Hyōtei (1870–1937) was a journalist and political activist. Coming from Ehime Prefecture like Masaoka Shiki, he and Shiki met in Tokyo as college students away from home, and they were close friends ever after. He became an editor of the newspaper *Nippon*, for which Shiki was the haiku and tanka editor. This poem is from *Hyōtei kunikki* (1940).

The departing year—
rain is falling on the grass
in the vacant lot

Aoki Getto

The year is about to end and the poet has gone out in the rain on some errand. The thin rain is falling steadily on a vacant lot near his house. He gazes at it for some time, forgetting how much he has to do, and regretting the passing of the year.

"The departing year" (*yuku toshi*) is a seasonal image that expresses regret for the passing year as it nears its end. "Departing spring" (*yuku haru*) and "departing autumn" (*yuku aki*) express regret for the imminent passing of a season, but regret for the entire year comes from a deeper place. The rain falling on the grass of the nearby vacant lot brings it home.

What kind of year was it for him, I wonder? It must have been quite dreary. At the year's end most of the grass would be dead but there would be some green remaining, too. The melancholy rain is soaking both the old and the new.

> *Yuku toshi ya / akichi no kusa ni / ame ga furu*
> Departing year / vacant lot's grass on / rain falls

Aoki Getto (1879–1949) was a follower of Masaoka Shiki. He played a decisive role in spreading Shiki's haiku teachings in western Japan and successively founded and led *Kurumayuri*, *Karatachi*, and *Dōjin*. This poem is included in the anthology *Shōwa bungaku zenshū: Shōwa haikushū* (1954).

New Year's Eve—
what surprised the rooster and
made it cry out in the night?

Satō Haruo

The rooster's first cock-a-doodle-doo on the morning of January 1st, known as "the first crowing," is prized, but this cry is a little early. What could have caused it?

It is the last night of the year and everything is in place to welcome the new year. The poet is looking forward to a peaceful night, when suddenly one of the chickens kept in the garden breaks the silence with a sharp cry. Perhaps a hungry predator is on the prowl—a fox or a marten. Going out to investigate, he shines his flashlight beam into the coop but there is nothing unusual there. It must have been an old rooster, slightly demented, who cried out in his dream. Along with his sense of relief, the poet realizes afresh that this is truly the end of the year. The darkness envelops everything from the garden to the hills and fields beyond.

Ōdoshi no / nani ni odoroku / yonakidori
New Year's Eve / what at surprise / night crowing chicken

Satō Haruo (1892–1964) was a free form poet and novelist. This is a so-called literati haiku, that is, a haiku by a writer well known for works in a genre other than haiku but for whom haiku was also a meaningful vehicle of self-expression. This poem is from *Nōkayajin jūshichion shishō* (1990).

Blue blue in the turning
year the turning
northern tides

Iida Ryūta

The entire poem is about the "northern tides" (*kita no ushio*) but you don't know that until you get to the last phrase, so at first reading you might interpret "blue blue" as a description of the dark blue sky on the night that the year turns from the old to the new. Then, when you read "northern tides," the skyward vista changes into an ocean view. And there it is, a northward-flowing current, blue on New Year's Eve. You may even sense the resistance the current experiences as it moves northward.

Growing up in the landlocked mountains of central Japan, Ryūta felt a romantic longing for the sea, and his longing takes shape in this poem. Among Ryūta's poems about flowing water, "January/ river in the January/ valley," composed in 1969, is better known, but this earlier poem may have been its starting point.

Aoao to / toshi kosu kita no / ushio kana
Blue blue / year turns northern / current

Iida Ryūta (1920–2007) studied haiku with his father, Iida Dakotsu, and later inherited the leadership of Dakotsu's *Unmo*. Like his father, he was a proponent of fixed form haiku and often drew his subjects from nature. This poem, composed in 1966, is from *Bōon* (1968), which won the Yomiuri Prize for Literature in poetry.

One by one the children
arrive—bringing the joy
of New Year's Eve home

Fukuda Kineo

The adult children, who are working in different places far from where they grew up, arrive at the parental home to welcome the new year in the place where they were born. The house is filled with the spirit of this special day, the last day of the year.

As each of his children arrives, greetings are exchanged and he expresses his appreciation for their hard work over the past year. He notes the development of each of his offspring with delight. The house, usually hushed and silent, comes to life. The children whose families have increased from last year make it even more lively. Children also return in the summer at Obon (Festival of the Dead), too, but not all of them can make it then, due to the pressure of work. On New Year's Eve, however, even those who could not come in the summer also return.

This description of an old-fashioned New Year's Eve at home evokes the warmth of family ties. This is how a family gathers together to greet the new year.

Tsugitsugi ni / ko ga tsuki joya no / ie to naru
One by one / children arrive New Year's Eve / house it becomes

Fukuda Kineo (1927–2005), a follower of Iida Dakotsu and Iida Ryūta, was an editor and contributor to *Unmo*. After *Unmo* ceased publication, he joined Hirose Naoto's *Hakuro* and contributed to its magazine. This poem is from *Shiranesanroku* (1982).

Waxen spaghetti
rises straight up, wound around
a fork frozen in mid-air

Seki Etsushi

This is a description of a lifelike replica of a dish of spaghetti—one of the food models seen in the windows of coffee shops and inexpensive restaurants in Japan. A forkful of "fake food" spaghetti is suspended in mid-air with strands of spaghetti dangling down. The spaghetti is made of wax, but the fork is real.

The goal of both the replica craftsman and the restaurant owner is to make the dish look appetizing so it will sell well. But for the poet its meaning is quite different. In his eyes, the food replica is reenvisioned as a strange *objet d'art*, something you would not be surprised to find in a museum or art gallery. The strands of spaghetti rise straight up, as if on their own, and the fork is frozen, floating in mid-air, as if between heaven and earth. You might even read this tower of fake spaghetti as a metaphorical link between heaven and earth, much as towers and waterfalls are sometimes perceived in Japan.

Or, moving even further afield, perhaps it is like haiku and indeed Japanese culture itself, which, the poem might be suggesting, is lightweight, undependable, and somehow unsettling in much the same way as the fake spaghetti is.

> *Rōsei no / pasuta tachinobori / fōku chū ni itsu*
> Waxen / spaghetti rises up / fork mid-air in frozen

Seki Etsushi (b. 1969) contributes to *Ani*, and cofounded and runs *Manbō* with Satō Ayaka. He is also a well-known critic of modern haiku. This poem is from his prizewinning collection *Rokujūoku-hon no kaitensuru magatta bō* (2011).

The puddle meant
to dry up—
but instead it froze

Ikazaki Kokyō

A puddle left by the rain was drying up, when there was a sudden spell of cold weather and instead it froze.

Of all seasonal landscapes, those of winter are the most desolate, and this poem confronts an especially colorless patch of bare ground. Kokyō was from Matsuyama, on the temperate island of Shikoku. Rather than lamenting the frozen puddle, he must greet it with pleased surprise and delight at its beauty.

The word used for puddle is the elegant old word *niwatazumi*, often used in haiku. Originally it was a word used in waka, from the *Man'yōshū** on. In haiku, you often find it in the background of a scene a poet describes, but it is rare for it to be front and center as it is here. I prize this poem for the way the puddle evokes an expanse of time, from the days in which it starts to dry up to the hours when it is frozen by a sudden cold snap in the weather.

Niwatazumi / kawakan to shite / itenikeru
Puddle / dry up meaning to / froze

Ikazaki Kokyō (1896–1935) was a follower of Mizuhara Shūōshi and a contributor to *Ashibi*. He was also Ishida Hakyō's teacher when Hakyō lived in Matsuyama, and is the person who suggested Hakyō's haiku nom de plume. This poem is from *Ikazaki Kokyō kushū* (1937), edited by Ishida Hakyō.

I know it's you in the snow
my sweet one—here's a snowball
for you

Sawada Hagijo

Realizing that it is you, the man I am madly in love with, walking towards me through the snow, I'll throw a snowball to surprise you.

The old-fashioned word *sonasan* is an affectionate and intimate word for "you." The dictionary quotes old puppet plays in which courtesans used it for their lovers. In real life it must also have been used among those in the performing arts. The word has a sensuous sound, like a woman's seductive whisper.

In the first two segments, *sonasan to/shitte no yuki no*, the consonant "s" sounds three times, almost like a whisper or the sound of snow quietly falling. Then suddenly everything is turned upside down by the aggression of the snowball. You feel the surprise of it suddenly hitting you. The heart of a passionate woman, charming yet somehow dangerous, is perfectly captured.

> *Sonasan to* / *shitte no yuki no* / *tsubute* kana
> You it was / I knew snow / ball!

Sawada Hagijo (1890–1982) was the first woman to have her haiku selected as the best in the miscellaneous section of *Hototogisu*, in the issue of March 1909. However, she retired from the haiku world in 1913 and would have been forgotten had not she been re-discovered by the haiku poet and scholar Ikegami Fujiko, who compiled *Sawada Hagijo kushū* (1963), the collection of Hagijo's work from which this poem is taken.

Fierce snow—
once, embraced, my breath
stopped

Hashimoto Takako

This is a love poem. It depicts the body in the act of making love, homing in on the true-to-life detail of "my breath stopped." There, at the height of passion, is the experience of near-death. The phrase candidly expresses the intensity of the lovemaking, which blends with the furiously falling snow, calling up the image of two naked bodies passionately intertwined in swirling snow.

Yet "stopped" is in the past tense and refers to something that happened before, in the past, while the snow is falling now. The man who embraced the poet is no longer here. The poem inscribes his absence.

Widowed in her late 30s, Takako wrote many moving poems in memory of her husband, and this is one of the best-known. It was written twelve years after her husband's death.

Yuki hageshi / dakarete iki no / tsumarishi koto
Snow fierce / being embraced breath / stopped

Hashimoto Takako (1899–1963) studied haiku with Sugita Hisajo and later joined Yamaguchi Seishi's group. In 1948 she became one of the founding contributors to *Tenrō* and later founded and led *Shichiyō*. She was known as one of the Four T's,* the four leading women poets of haiku in the postwar period. This poem is from *Kōshi* (1951).

Snow · bodie ·
snow · bodie · snow
I fall to my knees

Tanaka Ami

It is impossible to rephrase this poem in ordinary language, but I'll try: It has been snowing steadily for some time. Between the snowflakes a tiny human body floats. Impulsively, I kneel before it.

Needless to say, this is not the description of a real scene. Instead, it creates a new space with words as the medium. It is unclear why the poet chose to write "body" (体) using its obsolete variant kanji (躰), expressed here by the obsolete English spelling "bodie." Perhaps the usual way of writing "body" seemed too flat and unsuggestive, whereas the archaic kanji instills a sense of strangeness. I read the snow as pure white, and cold. When "snow · bodie" is repeated I have the feeling that the "bodie" is gradually turning snowy white. Or it could be the opposite, that the "bodie" is warming the snow.

The extra space between the second and third segments signifies a change of scene, at which point she suddenly falls to her knees. If you read the first two segments, with their repeated words and dots, as a kind of sacred mandala, she is here kneeling in homage or prayer. If you read them as the symbol of an erotic encounter, then it becomes a sign of surrender. Or could it be both?

> *Yuki · karada · / yuki · karada · yuki / hizamazuku*
> Snow · bodie · / snow · bodie · snow / I fall to my knees

Tanaka Ami (b. 1970), a scholar and translator of German literature, studied haiku with Kaneko Tōta and was a contributor to his magazine *Kaitei*. Since 2018, she has been a contributor to its successor, *Kaigen*. This poem is from the anthology *Shinsen 21* (2009).

Give me
an icicle filled with the stars of
Michinoku!

Takaha Shugyō

When Shugyō wrote this poem he was living in Tokyo, where the nights are neon-lit and too bright to see the stars in the night sky. Michinoku is in northern Japan, where he came from, and there the streets were dark at night, passersby were few, and the air was pristine. When you looked up at the night sky, it blazed with stars. How he longed for his home!

In haiku, longing for a starry sky on a winter's night is not enough to make a poem. He imagines stars entering the icicles that hang from the eaves on a cold night in winter and invents the expression "star-filled icicle" (*hoshi-iri-tsurara*) to describe it. The image seems a crystallization that brings the night sky close enough to touch.

In the Japanese, the last segment, *ware ni kure yo* (Give me!), is six syllables instead of the usual five. It makes me think of a spoiled child bursting out with a demand for what he wants.

> *Michinoku no / hoshi-iri-tsurara / ware ni kure yo*
> Michinoku / star-containing-icicle / me to give

Takaha Shugyō (b. 1930) studied with Yamaguchi Seishi and Akimoto Fujio. After being a contributor to *Tenrō* and *Hyōkai*, he founded and now leads *Kari*. This poem is from his prizewinning collection *Tanjō* (1965).

Through the icicle
that just fell
you can see the ocean

Hashimoto Keiji

The icicle that just fell is floating on the surface of the ocean and you can see the color of the water through it.

Ordinary icicles hang from places like the eaves of a house, but not in this poem. This is why the words "you can see the ocean" come as a surprise. You are left dangling until you realize that this icicle must have formed on a seaside cliff or the like. Not specifying where the icicle fell from works well. And being able to see the water through the icicle creates another surprise. When an icicle falls to the ground from the eaves of a building it splinters, but when it falls into water it remains in one piece and floats. And since it is transparent, you can see the color of the water through it.

By observing as closely as possible, the poet discovered an icicle in an unexpected place. Through thoroughgoing realism, he succeeds in approaching the strangeness of the world.

> *Ima ochishi / tsurara ga umi ni / sukete ori*
> Now fell / icicle sea into / transparent

Hashimoto Keiji (1907–1990) was a follower of Takahama Kyoshi and a friend of Hasegawa Sosei. He founded and led *Nenrin*. This poem is from *Taka no mune* (1981).

Freezing cold and
not a particle of dust—
sheer rock face

Iida Dakotsu

The note for this poem is: "Boat ride on Fuji River." In the fierce cold the sheer rock face on both banks rises straight up; not a particle of dust clings there.

Two inland rivers meet to create the Fuji River, which flows into the Pacific. It was once used as a canal that linked the inland areas and coastal towns, taking three to four hours to go down, but four to five days to return, in sailboats pulled upstream by men on a towpath. This poem was composed in 1926, so the train line was already in operation and river transport had declined. By then, the river had become part of a tourist route to see the famous Fuji Five Lakes at the base of Mount Fuji. According to Kobayashi Fujio,* Dakotsu and his friends took this route, returning upstream by boat on the Fuji River, all along the way walled in on both sides by the towering cliffs.

The pure, untouched rock face without a particle of dust rebuffs the human. The cliffs seem to embody the verticality that is a distinctive feature of Dakotsu's haiku, suggesting that his poetry too may last as long as them.

> *Gokkan no / chiri mo todomezu / iwafusuma*
> Extreme cold / dust not a particle / rock face

Iida Dakotsu (1885–1962) was mentored by Takahama Kyoshi. After becoming the editor in chief of the haiku magazine *Kirara* he changed its name to *Unmo*, and under his leadership it gained a national following and nurtured many poets. He spent his life in Kōfu at the foot of Mount Fuji. This poem is from his first collection, *Sanroshū* (1932).

I don't have wings and
I don't have fins but still
I look forward to spring

Fujii Akari

A bird can fly and a fish can swim so they can go to a different world, but all I can do is stay here and wait until the cold gives way to spring.

"I don't have wings and/ I don't have fins" describes her own body, but it is more than a simple description. It makes you feel that she used to dream of becoming a bird or a fish. However, now she realizes that she can never exist as a creature other than herself or travel to a different dimension. She has come to accept herself as she is, limited to her present reality.

And yet, when spring comes, the present winter reality itself will undergo a change. She knows that everything will be totally transformed—plants will come into bud, flowers will bloom, the birds will return. She understands that the change from winter to spring is much more significant than whether or not she herself can fly like a bird or swim as easily as a fish.

> *Hane mo naku / hire mo naku / haru matte ori*
> Wings without / fins without / spring awaiting

Fujii Akari (b. 1980) is a follower of Ishida Kyōko and a contributor to *Muku*. This poem is from her prizewinning collection *Fūkan* (2015).

無季

Seasonless

Again and again
I ask myself—is that sound
my wife's footsteps?

Hino Sōjō

Sōjō became bedridden from chronic tuberculosis after the war, and relied on the devoted care of his wife. In this poem, he is lying in bed anxiously awaiting her return from some errand. Every time he hears a noise, he thinks that she might have come home. The poem captures the pain of the moment when he realizes that his imagination has betrayed him yet again.

The poem has no seasonal image. This lack throws into sharp focus the absence of his wife, and feels like a necessity rather than a choice or an effort to be original. There is no room for anything material in this poem, which is totally permeated with his longing for his wife. In a way, it creates its own season, the season of longing.

> *Matashite mo / tsuma no ashioto / ka to omou*
> Yet again / wife's footsteps / I think

Hino Sōjō (1901–1956), once a young and promising protégé of Takahama Kyoshi, was expelled from *Hototogisu* for his unorthodox poems. He went on to found *Kikan*, a hub of the New Rising Haiku movement,* and continued to advocate haiku without seasonal images. After the war he founded and led *Seigen*. This poem is from *Jinsei no gogo* (1953).

They laugh because it's funny!
Foot soldiers walking
into the wind

Suzuki Murio

As a soldier in World War II, Murio fought in continental China and the Philippines and wrote haiku about his experiences. When he says "they laugh because it's funny," you feel reason claiming its place at the table. They are not laughing because they have gone mad. Even on the battlefield where death is an everyday event, there are funny things, and things that make you smile. The need to insist on this, holding on to your sanity in the face of death, is part of what makes war so brutal.

You can imagine you are seeing the soldiers through the wind's transparent veil, half within the kingdom of death.

This is a seasonless haiku. But as a poem about war, in which death is an everyday event, that seems natural. This suggests that the seasons are in fact strongly related to life itself.

> *Okashii kara / warau yo kaze no / hoheitachi*
> Funny and so / they laugh wind's / foot soldiers

Suzuki Murio (1919–2004) was a follower of Saitō Sanki and participated in the New Rising Haiku movement.* After the war he was an advocate of so-called socially relevant haiku (haiku composed on social and political issues and themes). In 1971 he founded and became the leader of *Kayō*, and he continued to write seasonless haiku and poems based on his war experiences. This poem comes from his first collection, *Kōten* (1949).

Chaos rules the land of Wa—
even huge wolves
and pit vipers
rush everywhere

Takayanagi Jūshin

This multi-line haiku, typical of Jūshin, is written in four separate lines. It is included in a group of poems set in the "Land of Wa," a country described in the third-century Chinese chronicle *The History of the Kingdom of Wei*. There, "Wa," the ancient Chinese name for Japan, was depicted as having been a chaotic, unruly country until the Empress Himiko came to power and unified it.

The word used for "wolves" is the archaic *magami*, close in sound to *mamushi* (pit viper). *Mamushi* itself is usually written with the single character 蝮 but the poet writes it in the old way, as 真虫, so creating a visual and auditory head rhyme. The literal meaning of the word *magami*, "true gods," is thought to be rooted in ancient wolf-worship, a detail that adds to the ancient aura. The image of animals as well as humans rushing about has the humor of a fable. Are these wolves and snakes fleeing from a battlefield? Or are they coming to offer aid?

"Pit viper" and "wolf" (in its modern form, *ōkami*) are season words for summer and winter respectively, but neither image is central in this poem. I consider it seasonless.

> *Wakoku jūran / magami / mamushi mo / isogu nari*
> Wa country disorder / wolf / viper too / are rushing

Takayanagi Jūshin (1923–1983), a leading figure of the New Rising Haiku movement,* contributed to Tomizawa Kakio's *Taiyōkei*. After the war he founded *Haiku kenkyū* and as editor in chief nurtured many emerging poets. An advocate of multi-line haiku, he was also a forerunner of avant-garde haiku. This poem is from *Sankaishū* (1976).

Twenty Haiku by Ozawa Minoru
From *Kinuta* (1986)

The stack of books
    collapses—shark in
        a distant ocean

Hon no yama kuzurete tōki umi ni same

Eating cured whale meat—
    in the twilight days
        of the human race

Sarashi kujira jinrui sude ni tasogarete

One asari clam's tongue
    touching another
        asari clam's tongue

Asari no shita betsu no asari no shita ni sawari

The shellfish in the
    Nirvana painting—
        how did it come all that way?

Nehanzu no kai ika ni shite kitarikemu

Fluffy little owlet
    blowing fluffily
        in the wind

Fuwafuwa no fukurō no ko no fukareori

From *Ryūzō* (1997)

The baby sparrows about
to spill out of the nest
somehow don't spill

Kosuzume no koboremu bakari koborezaru

I opened a window and
the house itself rejoiced—
autumn clouds

Mado akeba ie yorokobinu aki no kumo

School excursion—
kids tumbling endlessly
out of the bus

Ensoku basu itsu made mo ko no ide kitaru

A life of poverty
has its own smell—
hollyhocks in bloom

Binbō ni nioi arikeri tachiaoi

I must go home to the mountain
misted over now—
off I go!

Kaerubeki yama kasumi ori kaeramu ka

From *Shunkan* (2005)

Here in the forest
    my clear stream runs free—
        the year's first flush of dawn

Rinchū ni waga izumi ari hatsuakane

Toads have toads and
    people have people
        to love in the night

Hiki wa hiki hito wa hito kou yo narikeri

With every cell
    of my body I greet
        the season of Greater Heat

Waga saibō zenko taisho to narinikeri

It's 767 AD
    and a sutra copyist
        takes five

Jingo-keiun gannen shakyōshō hirune

It's here, the last day
    of summer break—
        with its special light

Natsuyasumi saigo no hi naru hikari kana

358

From *Sawa* (forthcoming)

The whole island turns to
    the Empire of Cicadas
        from dawn on

Shima subete kumazemi ryō ya ashita yori

A ray of light seen by
    the birds as they fly south—
        Mogami River

Hitosuji no hikari wa Mogami tori wataru

Ripples and then
    ripples again—
        the cherry blossoms are awaited

Sazanami ni sazanami arata hana materu

How deeply I slept
    with autumn flowers arranged
        by my bed

Fukaku nemurinu akikusa no ike areba

Almost sliding into the sea
    the winter sun
        lights the horizon

Umi ni iru chokuzen fuyubi hirogareru

Afterword

This book began as a decade long series I wrote for *Haiku arufa* (nos. 95–163, 2008–2018) highlighting approximately three hundred modern and contemporary haiku. I wanted to introduce the poets whose works shaped modern and contemporary haiku, so each installment took up a single haiku from sometime between the mid-nineteenth century to our own day. Although I have revised and expanded, this book has the same basic structure. The arrangement is not chronological, but rather in the order of the seasons. This is the traditional way of arranging haiku, but here I think it has the added benefit of helping readers hear the subtle and varied echoes between the poems of different periods.

When I first began to write the series, I worried that it might be impossible to write enough about one poem to fill most of a page, as I had promised, but when I sat down with each poem and pondered its world the words came easily, and as I wrote I felt anew a sense of the plenitude of poetry. I began by examining the words of the poem, sound patterns, and the use of seasonal images and cutting words. At the same time, I allowed myself to express personal responses that I thought might make the poem more approachable for readers.

Many poems in the book are by living poets, along with quite a few by the younger generation of poets whose place in the history of haiku is still to be determined. But I have included only poems for which I have great admiration, and which I believe will stand the test of time.

When these explanations began to be published, I soon learned that quite a few Japanese readers found haiku's old-fashioned literary grammar and cutting words to be barriers to appreciation. I did not want haiku's conventions to become an insuperable obstacle to enjoyment, so I made up my mind to provide each poem with a paraphrase into everyday language. In the translation, some of the paraphrases have been retained, but others have been rendered redundant by the poem's translation itself, which is of course in contemporary English.

The history of modern haiku contains two great early figures, Masa-oka Shiki and his disciple Takahama Kyoshi. Then come the movements born from opposition to Kyoshi: the poets of New Tendency Haiku, Free Form Haiku, and New Rising Haiku, and, during the postwar period, other styles as well. However, histories of modern haiku often ignore the so-called literati haiku, poems by novelists and others for whom haiku was an avocation. I have included Kubota Mantarō, who was the most influential of these poets, as well as a number of poets connected to him.

There are many more haiku and haiku poets that I could have included. In fact, I have begun to think that I would like to expand the poems in this book into a larger anthology. While putting the book together, I have become aware that the work of a haiku poet consists of not only composing poems, choosing those of others for publication in newspapers and magazines, and writing essays about haiku, but also choosing and collecting the very best poems. I consider these tasks to be a central part of my activity from now on.

I offer my deepest thanks to those who advised me in the making of the original Japanese edition of this book, and to the authors of the poems themselves, living and dead, without whom the book would not exist.

Ozawa Minoru
Tokyo
August 2018

Supplementary Notes

p. 6 *1 Matsuo Bashō (1644–1694) is considered the greatest of all poets of the form we now call haiku. He first studied *haikai* linked-verse, and also composed many *hokku* (see p. 23 note 1). At a time when word puns were prevalent in *haikai*, Bashō wrote poems that expressed his personal view of the world. By 1680, he had a large following, and he is credited with establishing the 5-7-5 syllable as an independent poetic genre. Many of Bashō's most famous poems first appeared within the travelogues he composed starting in 1684. His most famous work is the travelogue *The Narrow Road to the Deep North* (*Oku no hosomichi*), a classic of Japanese literature.

*2 Free form haiku (*jiyūritsu haiku*) does not follow the traditional 5-7-5 syllable scheme of traditional haiku, contains no cutting word (see p. 47 note 1) or classical grammar, and is written in colloquial Japanese. A poem with one or two syllables more or less than 17, but clearly intended to have the traditional three-segment structure, is not considered to be free form haiku.

p. 19 *1 Ishizuka Tomoji (1906–1986) was a founding member of Ishida Hakyō's *Tsuru*. He edited its magazine and took over leadership of the group after Hakyō's death.

*2 Hoshino Bakukyūjin (1925–2013) studied haiku with Ishida Hakyō and Ishizuka Tomoji (above). He succeeded Ishikawa Keirō as an editor of *Tsuru* in 1953 and later became the publisher of the magazine, and in 1986 became the third leader of the group.

p. 22 *1 *Man'yōshū*, literally "Collection of Ten Thousand Leaves" is the oldest extant anthology of waka poems. Compiled between the late seventh century and the late eighth century, its 20 volumes contain more than 4,500 waka composed by people from all walks of life.

*2 *Kokin wakashū* is an anthology of waka poems complied in the early tenth century. Its 20 volumes contain more than 1,000 poems. It was the first of the 21 waka anthologies that were commissioned by the Imperial court.

p. 23 *1 *Haikai* linked verse (*haikai no renga*) is a genre of collaborative poetry that became popular in the seventeenth century. It is a chain of verses composed by two or more poets gathered together, made up of alternating verses of 5-7-5 and 7-7 syllables. It usually goes on for 36 to 100 verses. The modern haiku originated from the *hokku*, the first poem of a haikai linked verse chain.

*2 Setchūan was the name generationally assumed by the poets of the haiku school established by Hattori Ransetsu (1654–1707), one of the most distinguished disciples of Matsuo Bashō (see p. 6 note 1). Masuda Ryū'u was Setchūan the Twelfth, the last of the lineage.

p. 26 *1 Ushiro Boseki (1899–1995) studied haiku with Matsuse Seisei, and founded and led *Unga*.

*2 Ōmine Akira (1929–2018) was a philosopher and a Buddhist monk. As a haiku poet, he first studied with Takahama Kyoshi and later with Hatano Sōha, and co-founded *Shin* in 1984.

p. 28 * Ōmine Akira (see p. 26 note 2)

p. 29 *1 Sketch from life (see note to p. 246)

*2 The Four S's were the four leading poets of the *Hototogisu* group in the 1920s, whose poetic sobriquets all begin with "S": Mizuhara Shūōshi, Yamaguchi Seishi, Awano Seiho, and Takano Sujū.

p. 31 *1 *Ogura hyakunin isshu*, compiled by Fujiwara no Teika (1162–1241), contains 100 poems by 100 poets and is one of the best-known waka anthologies of Japan. In the early seventeenth century it was made into a card game, which was initially played by ladies-in-waiting of the shogun's court then spread to the ordinary people, and has become a traditional New Year's game.

*2 Ozaki Kōyō (1868–1903) was a novelist with a passion for haiku, and was a forerunner of modern Japanese literature. He believed that haiku needed to be modernized while keeping its classical aesthetics, and later founded a haiku society called Shūseikai with Kakuta Chikurei and others.

*3 The Shūseikai group was founded in 1895 by Kakuta Chikurei, Ozaki Kōyō, Iwaya Sazanami, and others. It was formed to bring together different groups and poets who were in favor of haiku reform but against the direction in which Masaoka Shiki and his followers were taking haiku. The group published several magazines and haiku collections between 1896 and 1903 but died out by 1909.

p. 32 *1 In the Edo period (1603–1867) all daimyo were obliged to leave their home domains and serve the shogun in Edo (now Tokyo) every other year.

*2 Hasegawa Reiyoshi (1886–1928) studied haiku with Naitō Meisetsu, and became an editor of *Hototogisu*. He later founded and led *Kareno*. His wife Hasegawa Kanajo was also a haiku poet.

p. 47 *1 A cutting word (*kireji*) is a brief word or part of a word that has no semantic meaning but serves to mark a pause in the haiku or to emphasize its end. They can be thought of as verbal punctuation marks, and include verbal endings such as the negative -*zu*, as well as such exclamatory words as "*kana*," "*ya*," and "*keri*."

*2 Nakahara Michio (b. 1951) studied haiku with Nomura Toshirō and contributed to *Oki*. He founded and leads *Ginka*.

p. 50 * The New Rising Haiku (*Shinkō haiku*) movement opposed the traditionalism of the powerful haiku group *Hototogisu* and its leader Takahama Kyoshi. It started when one *of Hototogisu*'s leading members, Mizu-

hara Shūōshi, left the group in 1931, followed by Yamaguchi Seishi and Hino Sōjō. Other poets, including non-*Hototogisu* members, joined the movement and its agenda espoused ideals such as seasonless haiku, fictional haiku, modernist haiku, and socially relevant haiku. In 1940, on the eve of World War II, in a government move to suppress the voice of "radicals," poets associated with the movement were arrested for violating the Maintenance of Public Order Law. The crackdown continued until 1943 and resulted in the prosecution and imprisonment of dozens of haiku poets. After the war, the ideals originated by the movement developed into various forms of avant-garde haiku.

p. 52 *1 *Man'yōshū* (see p. 22 note 1)

*2 Sketch from life (see note to p. 246)

p. 54 * Sketch from life (see note to p. 246)

p. 55 *1 *Man'yōshū* (see p. 22 note 1)

*2 Yamada Mizue (1926–2013) was a follower of Ishida Hakyō and a contributor to *Tsuru*, and later founded *Mokugo*.

p. 56 * Ayabe Jinki (1929–2015) was a follower of Ishida Hakyō and later Ishizuka Tomoji (see p. 19 note 1). He joined *Izumi* and contributed to its magazine, eventually becoming its editor and leader of the group.

p. 57 * Inagaki Taruho (1900–1977) is known as the father of the short short story in Japanese because of his maiden work, *Issen ichibyō monogatari* (One Thousand and One-Second Stories, tr. Tricia Vita). The work consisted of brief surrealistic sketches in a childlike vein about the moon and stars, and was published in various editions and with varying content from 1923 to 1936.

p. 58 * Kaneko Tōta, *Jisen jikai 99 ku* [99 haiku by Kaneko Tōta, selected and explained by the poet], (Kadokawa Gakugei Shuppan, 2012).

p. 59 * The Four T's were four of the most significant female haiku poets of the modern period between the 1930s and 1960s, whose poetic sobriquets all begin with "T": Nakamura Teijo, Hoshino Tatsuko, Hashimoto Takako, and Mitsuhashi Takajo.

p. 63 ＊Ishihara Yatsuka (1919–1998) was influenced by his haiku poet father and became a follower of Iida Dakotsu. He edited and contributed to *Unmo* and later founded *Aki*.

p. 64 ＊New Tendency Haiku (*Shinkeikō haiku*) was a movement named after Ōsuga Otsuji's essay "New Tendency in the Haiku Scene" (*Haikukai no shinkeikō*, 1908), advocated by Kawahigashi Hekigotō and others. The movement advocated breaking away from the conventional fixed form and the use of seasonal images, and focused instead on scenes from daily life and the poet's inner world. It initially won a strong following, but later came to be criticized as extreme, and lost momentum by 1915, but aided the advancement of free form haiku (see p. 6 note 2).

p. 66 ＊1 Bashō (see p. 6 note 1)

＊2 Takahama Toshio (1900–1979) was the oldest son of Takahama Kyoshi. He studied haiku with his father, contributed to *Hototogisu*, and helped with administrative tasks for the magazine's publication. In 1959, after his father's death, he succeeded to leadership of the group.

p. 72 ＊1 "Contentless tanka" is a term invented by Orikuchi Shinobu (1887–1953) to describe what he considered the essence of tanka as residing in its very lack of message or idea.

＊2 Yamaguchi Sōdō (1898–1985) studied haiku with Mizuhara Shūōshi and contributed to Shūōshi's *Ashibi*, and later founded and led *Nanpū*.

p. 77 ＊Bashō (see p. 6 note 1)

p. 78 ＊One fathom is 1.8 meters, and one *hiro* is 1.5 meters (*hyakuhiro* is 100 *hiro*). Both were originally used as measures of length and depth but are now mainly used as measures of depth.

p. 79 ＊1 Yamamoto Kenkichi (1907–1988) was a literary critic and scholar known for his extensive study of haiku and haiku poets. He

published several acclaimed compendiums of seasonal images (*saijiki*).

＊2 Izumi Kyōka (1873–1939) was a novelist mentored by Ozaki Kōyō (see p. 31 note 2). Influenced by seventeenth-century Japanese literature, he established a unique style characterized as a mix of romanticism, mysticism, and archaism.

＊3 Tsukamoto Kunio (1920–2005) wrote tanka, haiku, novels, and literary criticism. He was regarded as one of the most talented avant-garde poets and influenced many artists in a variety of genres.

p. 82 ＊1 Sakura mochi is a confection made of pink, sticky rice filled with sweet red bean paste and wrapped in a pickled cherry leaf.

＊2 Abe Midorijo (1886–1980) studied haiku with Takahama Kyoshi and later founded and led *Komakusa*.

p. 84 ＊Takahama Toshio (see p. 66 note 2)

p. 85 ＊New Tendency Haiku (see note to p. 64)

p. 86 ＊1 Translation by Meredith McKinney in *The Pillow Book of Sei Shōnagon*, (London: Penguin Classics, 2007), section 1.

＊2 Ōmaki Hiroshi (1931–2019) studied haiku with Nomura Toshirō and contributed to *Oki*, and later founded and led *Minato*.

＊3 Nakahara Michio (see p. 47 note 2)

p. 87 ＊Tsubouchi Nenten (b. 1944) began composing haiku in high school. He founded and leads the haiku group *Sendan*, and through it has nurtured many talented poets. As a haiku scholar, he has written extensively about Masaoka Shiki.

p. 89 ＊The "humanist" poets (Ningen Tankyū-ha) were known for writing poems that are more personal, subjective, and expressive of their emotions than the poems from nature that appeared in *Hototogisu* and were advocated by Takahama Kyoshi. The group included Nakamura Kusatao, Katō Shūson, Shinohara Bon, and Ishida Hakyō, and its name was derived from an article in the magazine *Haiku kenkyū* published in August 1939.

p. 96 * New Rising Haiku (see note to p. 50)

p. 99 * Four S's (see p. 29 note 2)

p. 100 * Tsuji Momoko (b. 1945) studied haiku with Fujita Shōshi (see note to p. 298) and Hatano Sōha, and later founded *Dōji*.

p. 101 * Bashō (see p. 6 note 1)

p. 105 * Translation by Meredith McKinney in *Essays in Idleness and Hojoki*, (Penguin Classics, 2014), section 137.

p. 107 * Sketch from life (see note to p. 246)

p. 111 * Motoi Ei (b. 1945) first studied haiku with Kiyosaki Toshio and later with Hoshino Tatsuko. She founded *Natsushio* in 2007 and leads the group.

p. 112 * Nishino Fumiyo (1923–2019) studied haiku with Hatano Shōha and Abe Midorijo, and later founded *Fumi* and led the group through 2007.

p. 113 *1 Shūseikai (see p. 31 note 3)

*2 Ozaki Kōyō (see p. 31 note 2)

p. 119 * This anecdote by the early Daoist thinker Zhuangzi (ca. 369–ca. 286 BCE), is from Chapter 2 ("On the Equality of Things") of the eponymous *Zhuangzi*.

p. 120 * Bashō (see p. 6 note 1)

p. 123 * Four S's (see p. 29 note 2)

p. 124 * New Rising Haiku (see note to p. 50)

p. 125 *1 Bashō (see p. 6 note 1)

*2 "Humanist" poets (see note to p. 89)

p. 131 * Yokomitsu Ri'ichi (1898–1947), a novelist and essayist, was one of the most influential literary figures in the 1920s and 30s. He was also friends with many haiku poets, including Takahama Kyoshi and Mizuhara Shūōshi, and wrote haiku throughout his adult life.

p. 151 * New Tendency Haiku (see note to p. 64)

p. 156 * *Goshūi wakashū* is an imperial anthology of waka poems compiled between 1075 and 1086. Its 20 volumes contain 1,218 poems, a relatively large number of which (roughly 30%) were written by women such as Izumi Shikibu (ca. 976–ca. 1036).

p. 157 *1 Bashō (see p. 6 note 1) wrote this poem based on personal experience after seeing cormorant fishing from a boat.

*2 The Ashura sculpture of Kōfukuji Temple has a somewhat feminine face and a slender body, and gives the impression of androgyny, especially in comparison to the other statues of the Buddhist Eight Legions (which are clearly represented as male) that are housed together in the temple's Western Golden Hall (Saikondō). The figure dates from 734, has three-faces and six-arms, and is 153.4 centimeters tall.

p. 160 * Sketch from life (see note to p. 246)

p. 161 * *Nozarashi kikō* is Matsuo Bashō's (see p. 6 note 1) first poetic travelogue. He composed it during his travel to western Japan begun in 1684, and it was included in his collection *Hakusenshū* (1698).

p. 164 * Kumano encompasses three major shrines connected by an ancient pilgrimage route (the Kumano Kodō) that dates to prehistoric times in the deeply wooded mountains of the Kii Peninsula of southwestern Japan. Religious practices in the area reflect an old form of Shinto with a strong emphasis on nature worship.

p. 166 *1 Sketch from life (see note to p. 246)

*2 Cutting word (see p. 47 note 1)

*3 New Rising Haiku (see note to p. 50)

p. 167 * Nippon Shimbunsha newspaper company published the daily newspaper *Nippon* between 1889 and 1914. Masaoka Shiki was the editor of its haiku column, which eventually became the home ground of Shiki's haiku reform.

P. 168 * Four T's (see note to p. 59)

p. 169 *¹ *Konjaku monogatari* (translated as *Tales of Times Now Past* by Marian Ury) is a collection of tales believed to have been compiled in the early twelfth century. It contains more than 1,000 tales from India, China, and Japan, mostly drawn from Buddhist narratives and folklore.

*² Four S's (see p. 29 note 2)

p. 170 * Tsukamoto Kunio (see p. 79 note 3)

p. 173 * Ishizuka Tomoji (see p. 19 note 1)

p. 175 *¹ Taneda Santōka (1882–1940) studied haiku with Ogiwara Seisensui (see note to p. 322) and was known for his free form poems (see p. 6 note 2). He later became a monk and adopted an itinerant lifestyle.

*² Morioka Shōsaku (b. 1949) studied haiku with Nomura Toshirō and contributed to *Oki*, and also founded *Shukkō*.

*³ Bashō's *Oku no hosomichi* (see p. 6 note 1)

p. 177 * New Rising Haiku (see note to p. 50)

p. 178 * Minagawa Bansui (1918-2010) studied haiku with his older brother and uncle, both of whom were haiku poets. He was a member of *Kaze*, a group that was active in the 1950s and nurtured many haiku poets. He founded *Shunkou* in 1966 and led it until 2008.

p. 188 * Kishimoto Naoki, *Jisen jikai besuto 100* (Furansudo, 2011).

p. 189 *¹ Ozaki Kōyō (see p. 31 note 2)

*² Shūseikai (see p. 31 note 3)

p. 193 *¹ The moon, snow, and flowers have traditionally been thought to link friends together. The notion originated in this poem by the Chinese poet Bai Juyi (Po Chü-i, 772–846): "I think of you most when admiring the snow, the moon, and the flowers," which nostalgically recalls time pleasantly spent enjoying the beauty of the seasons with a friend who now lives far away. Snow-flower-moon (*setsu-getsu-ka*) is now recognized as the ultimate symbol of the beauty of Japanese landscapes.

*² New Rising Haiku (see note to p. 50)

p. 194 * New Rising Haiku (see note to p. 50)

p. 199 * New Rising Haiku (see note to p. 50)

p. 201 * Bai Juyi on friendship (see p. 193 note 1)

p. 217 * New Rising Haiku (see note to p. 50)

p. 219 * Ishizuka Tomoji (see p. 19 note 1)

p. 220 * Yorimitsu Masaki (b. 1962) studied haiku with Saitō Kafū and contributed to his *Yane*, then founded *Kuntsuaito* in 1992.

p. 223 * A "humanist" poet (see note to p. 89)

p. 224 *¹ Matsuo Bashō (see p. 6 note 1)

*² *Renshi* is a collaborative poetic form whose roots are in the haikai linked verse tradition (see p. 23 note 1). It was developed in the 1970s primarily by Ōoka Makoto (1931–2017), a poet of modern verse and an influential literary critic. While traditional linked verse has rules about length and form, renshi is free in style and can be composed by poets of various backgrounds and languages working together.

p. 225 * New Tendency Haiku (see note to p. 64)

p. 226 * Four T's (see note to p. 59)

p. 229 * Kaneko Isekikō (1889–1977), the father of Kaneko Tōta, was a contributor to Mizuhara Shūōshi's magazine *Ashibi*.

p. 233 * Rinpa is one of the major schools of Japanese art, established by Hon'ami Kōetsu (1558–1637) and Tawaraya Sōtatsu (active in the early seventeenth century). Works by Rinpa artists are often highly stylized depictions of nature against a gold or silver background.

p. 235 *¹ In the "Mountains and Waters Sutra" (*Sansuikyō*) in *Treasury of the True Dharma-Eye* (*Shōbōgenzō*).

*² In *Kanshō gendai haiku zenshū*, vol 7 (Rippū Shobō, 1980).

p. 236 * Namekata Katsumi (b. 1944) studied haiku with Kiyosaki Toshio and Tomiyasu Fūsei, and contributed to Fūsei's *Wakaba*.

p. 237 *1 Four S's (see p. 29 note 2)

*2 New Rising Haiku (see note to p. 50)

p. 239 * Poem by Bai Juyi (see note to p. 193)

p. 240 * Shida Sokin (1876–1946), a haiku poet and scholar, served as a judge for several haiku magazines including *Kakeaoi*, and later cofounded *Tōen*.

p. 244 * Shūseikai (see p. 31 note 3)

* Ozaki Kōyō (see p. 31 note 2)

p. 245 * Cutting word (*kireji*, see p. 47 note 1)

p. 246 * Masaoka Shiki was the most influential promoter of haiku reform among the several like-minded poets active during the end of the nineteenth century. He sought to modernize haiku and tanka poetry with the concept of the sketch from life (*shasei*), a practice in Western art that he applied to haiku. Shiki learned the concept of "sketching" from his friend, the painter Nakamura Fusetsu (1866–1943). With this new concept, Shiki went outdoors with a notebook and pencil almost every day to compose haiku in a "*shasei*" style, reaching the conclusion that sketching was also effective in literature. In his essay "The Haiku Scene in Meiji 29" (*Meiji 29 nen no haikukai*, 1897) Shiki purposefully mentioned the word "*shasei*" as "sketch from life" and spread this concept among his haiku followers.

p. 247 *1 Sketch from life (see note to p. 246)

*2 Yokomitsu Ri'ichi (see note to p. 131)

*3 Yamamoto Kenkichi (see note to p. 79)

p. 248 * Takahashi Etsuo (b. 1934) studied haiku with Nozawa Setsuko and contributed to Setsuko's *Ran*, and is the founder and leader of *Umi*.

p. 249 * Shimada Gajō (b. 1957) is a haiku poet and leads the group *Sato*. He also runs the publishing company YOU Shorin, which specializes in haiku and tanka related books and collections.

p. 258 * In "Hi to mizu no hito Kubo Yorie" in *Kanshō josei haiku no sekai*, vol.1, (Kadokawa Gakugei Shuppan, 2008), pp. 173–186.

p. 259 * Hasegawa Reiyoshi (see p. 32 note 2)

p. 261 * Kajishima Issō (1883–1947) studied with Matsuse Seisei and was active in the haiku community of his hometown of Kuwana in Mie Prefecture.

p. 263 * Bashō (see p. 6 note 1)

p. 264 * Kishi Fūsanrō (1910–1982) studied haiku with Yamaguchi Seishi, later became a follower of Tomiyasu Fūsei, contributed to and edited Fūsei's *Wakaba*, and founded and led *Shunrei*.

p. 265 *1 Yamamoto Kenkichi (see note to p. 79)

*2 Ishihara Yatsuka (see note to p. 63)

p. 266 * Translation by Meredith McKinney in *Essays in Idleness and Hojoki*, (Penguin Classics, 2013) section 155.

p. 267 * Tsubouchi Nenten (see note to p. 87)

p. 268 *1 The three poems were composed by three different poets, Jakuren (ca. 1139–1202), Saigyō (1118–1190), and Fujiwara no Teika (1162–1241). All end with the same phrase, *aki no yūgure* ("autumn evening"), and are conventionally grouped together as the "Three Evening Poems."

*2 New Rising Haiku (see note to p. 50)

p. 272 *1 Ozaki Kōyō (see p. 31 note 2)

*2 Shūseikai (see p. 31 note 3)

p. 273 * Takemura Shūchiku (1875–1915) founded the haiku group Hokuseikai for the followers of Masaoka Shiki in Kanazawa, where he attended high school. After moving to Tokyo, Shūchiku frequented Shiki's residence and arranged for Shiki to meet Nakagawa Tomijo whom he knew from Kanazawa.

p. 276 * Imahashi Mariko, "Kachō fūei o tsura-nuite" in *Kanshō josei haiku no sekai*, vol. 2, (Kadokawa Gakugei Shuppan, 2008), p. 97.

p. 278 * New Tendency Haiku (see note to p. 64)

p. 284 *1 Bashō (see p. 6 note 1)

    *2 Taneda Santōka (see note to p. 175)

p. 288 * New Tendency Haiku (see note to p. 64)

p. 298 * Fujita Shōshi (1926–2005) studied haiku with Mizuhara Shūōshi, and founded and led *Taka*.

p. 299 * Tanaka Umajirō (1907–1973) studied haiku with Mizuhara Shūōshi and contributed to Shūōshi's *Ashibi* before he joined *Tsuru*, and later founded and led *Shigi*.

p. 301 * Nakagami Kenji (1946–1992), a novelist, essayist, and one of the most influential literary figures of postwar Japan, died of cancer at the height of his literary career at age 46.

p. 305 * Shimomura Hibun (1902–1987) studied haiku with Matsumoto Takashi and contributed to *Hototogisu*. In 1964, he took over the leadership of the group *Sazanka* after its founder's death.

p. 306 *1 Bashō (see p. 6 note 1)

    *2 New Rising Haiku (see note to p. 50)

p. 310 *1 New Rising Haiku (see note to p. 50)

    *2 Yoshioka Zenjidō (1889–1961) first studied with Takahama Kyoshi. He contributed to *Hototogisu* and founded *Amanogawa* in his home town of Fukuoka, but later became distanced from the fixed-form haiku with seasonal images and became involved with the New Rising Haiku movement (see note to p. 50).

p. 312 * Ōba Hakusuirō (1890–1962) began writing haiku on the recommendation of Kubota Mantarō, and in 1980 founded *Shunran*.

p. 315 * New Rising Haiku (see note to p. 50)

p. 316 * Kobayashi Kōji (1912–1992) studied haiku

with Ishida Hakyō and contributed to Hakyō's *Tsuru*, and was the leader of *Izumi* and *Hayashi*.

p. 317 * Naruse Ōtōshi (1925–2004) was the third generation leader of *Shuntō*, the group founded by Kubota Mantarō.

p. 318 * Takahama Toshio (see note to p. 66)

p. 320 * Fujita Shōshi (see note to p. 298)

p. 321 * New Rising Haiku (see note to p. 50)

p. 322 * Ogiwara Seisensui (1884–1976) was active in the New Tendency Haiku movement (see note to p. 64) and was one of the most vocal proponents of free form haiku (see p. 6 note 2). He was known for mentoring two of the most significant free form haiku poets, Taneda Santōka (see p. 175 note 1) and Ozaki Hōsai.

p. 324 * Yamaguchi Sōdō (see p. 72 note 2)

p. 326 * Ono Bushi (1888–1943) studied haiku with Hara Sekitei and led the group *Keitōjin*.

p. 327 * Ishihara Yatsuka (see note to p. 63)

p. 335 * Minagawa Bansui (see note to p. 178)

p. 343 * *Man'yōshū* (see p. 22 note 1)

p. 345 * Four T's (see note to p. 59)

p. 349 * In *Dakotsu hyakkei* (Dakotsu, a hundred views), (Mokujisha, 1979), pp. 82–85.

p. 352 * New Rising Haiku (see note to p. 50)

p. 353 * New Rising Haiku (see note to p. 50)

p. 354 * New Rising Haiku (see note to p. 50)

Index of Seasonal Images

A

ageha························ 165

aki···························· 216

akikaze ···· 254–257, 259–262, 264

akikusa ··············· 233, 358

aki no hiru ················ 218

aki no kaze ··········· 258, 263

aki no koe ················· 265

aki no kumo················ 356

aki no kure ··········· 266–268

aki no matsuri ············· 276

aki no niji ················· 253

aki no oni·················· 217

aki no yo·················· 230

amagoya··················· 111

aoba······················ 163

aobayami·················· 164

aodaishō·················· 170

asane····················· 123

asari····················· 355

ase······················· 184

ase no hito················ 185

atataka···················· 70

atatakashi················· 69

atsusa···················· 172

B

bai······················· 278

bai uchi··················· 279

bōnen····················· 336

boshun···················· 132

C

chō ······················ 119

chūrippu·················· 115

D

daiko hosu················ 300

daisekkei················· 179

dojō nabe················· 190

E

ensoku···················· 356

F

fukinotō··················· 57

fukurō no ko·············· 355

furuhiina·················· 61

fuyubi····················· 358

fuyugi····················· 326

fuyugomori················ 319

fuyuhibari················· 307

fuyuki·············· 310, 311

fuyu no hoshi············· 298

fuyu no mizu·············· 333

fuyu no nami·············· 315

fuyu nukushi·············· 304

fuyuta···················· 308

fuyuzare·················· 313

G

gaganbo··················· 162

gogatsu··················· 144

gokkan···················· 349

gōsho····················· 193

H

hadashi··················· 198

hae umaru················· 124

haka arau················· 221

hakuren···················· 85

hakusho··················· 147

Hakyō ki·················· 299

hana ······················ 95

hanabi···················· 222

hanabie···················· 96

hanadanemaku·············· 75

hana endo················· 118

hanafubuki················· 99

hanamatsu················· 358

hanano··················· 232

hana no ame················ 98

hana no hiru··············· 97

hane······················ 30

haru ·················· 44, 86

harukaze·················· 121

harumatsu················· 350

haru no ie················· 71

haru no kaze·············· 120

haru no kure··············· 88

haru no mizu··············· 64

haru no yo················· 90

harusame··················· 72

harutatsu··················· 46

harutomoshi················ 91

haruyūbe··················· 89

hatahata·················· 316

hatsuakane················ 357

hatsuakari·············· 23, 24

hatsugeshiki··············· 26

hatsumisora··············· 25

hatsumoroko··············· 65

hatsusanga················· 27

hatsushōrai················ 28

hazakura ············· 145, 146
hebi ··················· 169
hechima ················ 246
hehirimushi ·············· 238
higurashi ············ 223, 224
hiki ··················· 357
himawari ················ 206
hina ···················60
hinaosame ···············62
hirugao ················ 168
hirune ················· 357
hiyashinsu ··············· 116
hiyayaka ················ 249
hōbō ··················· 317
hoko ··················· 191
hōrensō ·················56
hotaru ············· 155,156

I
ichihatsu ················ 150
ikimitama ················ 219
imo arashi ··············· 240
inazuma ················· 226
itsu ················ 342, 343
iwayaku ················· 194

J
jinchōge ·················83
joya ··················· 341

K
kabi ·············· 152,153
kagamimochi ···············29
kagerō ··················79
kagirou ··················80
kaki ··················· 318
kame naku ···············93
kame no ko ··············· 154
kamikiri ················· 178
karasu-uri ··············· 275
kare ··················· 312

kareno ·················· 314
kasumi ·················· 356
katakage ················ 192
katakago ·················55
kawazu ·················· 128
kayano ·················· 280
keito ··················· 328
kiku ··················· 277
kinbyōbu ················ 320
kitakaze ················ 329
koineko ·············· 51, 52
komorigaki ··············· 274
koneko ·················· 125
konomi ·················· 272
konomi otsu ········· 282, 283
konomi u-u ···············54
koorogi ················· 237
kosuzume ················ 356
kotori wataru ············· 271
kozokotoshi ·········· 18, 19
kumazemi ················ 358
kumo ··················· 159
kumo no ito ·············· 160
kumo no mine ············· 175
kuri ··············· 284, 286
kuri no mushi ············· 285

M
mategai ················· 112
mijikayo ················· 151
mitsumata no hana ········84
mizubana ················ 325
mizugi ·············· 202, 203
mizu sumu ··········· 250, 251
mokusei ················· 247
morogaeri ················ 301
mugiwara bōshi ··········· 173
mugiyu ·················· 189
mushi ··················· 236

N
nasuyaki ················· 205
natsu ··············· 142,143
natsukusa ················ 167
natsumikan ··············· 188
natsuno ················· 166
natsu no kure ············· 186
natsu no umi ············· 199
natsuyase ················ 204
natsuyasumi ··············· 357
nehanzu ·············· 68, 355
neshaka ··················67
niji ··················· 177
nowaki ·················· 229
nuriaze ·············· 126, 127

O
ōashita ··················22
oborozuki ················92
ōdoshi ·················· 339
okaizome ·················32
oniyanma ················ 241
otamajakushi ··············94

R
ragā ··················· 305
rakka hika ················ 100
ringo ··················· 273
risshun ··················45

S
sabagumo ················ 245
Saigyō ki ·················66
saki-iwashi ··············· 244
sakura ············· 101–108
sakuragai ············ 113, 114
sakuramochi ···············82
same ··················· 355
samui ··················· 309
sanshōkui ················ 129
sarashi kujira ············· 355

sawara ⋯⋯⋯⋯⋯⋯ 76
sawayaka ⋯⋯⋯⋯⋯ 248
seki ⋯⋯⋯⋯⋯⋯ 322–324
semi ⋯⋯⋯⋯⋯ 195, 242
semigara ⋯⋯⋯⋯⋯ 196
shabondama ⋯⋯⋯⋯ 122
shiguru ⋯⋯⋯⋯⋯⋯ 306
shimizu ⋯⋯⋯⋯⋯ 182
shimo ⋯⋯⋯⋯⋯⋯ 331
shimobashira ⋯⋯⋯⋯ 332
shinnen ⋯⋯⋯⋯⋯ 21
shinryō ⋯⋯⋯⋯⋯ 225
shirauo ⋯⋯⋯⋯⋯ 53
shitamoe ⋯⋯⋯⋯⋯ 59
shōgatsu ⋯⋯⋯⋯⋯ 34
shōji ⋯⋯⋯⋯⋯⋯ 321
shōji haru ⋯⋯⋯⋯⋯ 287
shūchō ⋯⋯⋯⋯⋯ 243
shunchū ⋯⋯⋯⋯⋯ 87
shundei ⋯⋯⋯⋯⋯ 73
shunkan ⋯⋯⋯⋯⋯ 50
shuro no hana ⋯⋯⋯⋯ 149
sora sumu ⋯⋯⋯⋯⋯ 252
suashi ⋯⋯⋯⋯⋯⋯ 197
suika ⋯⋯⋯⋯⋯⋯ 227
suiren ⋯⋯⋯⋯⋯ 200
sukimakaze ⋯⋯⋯⋯⋯ 330
sumire ⋯⋯⋯⋯⋯⋯ 81
sun-ika ⋯⋯⋯⋯⋯ 158
susuki ⋯⋯⋯⋯⋯ 234
suzushi ⋯⋯⋯⋯⋯ 183

T
tachiaoi ⋯⋯⋯⋯⋯ 356
tachioyogi ⋯⋯⋯⋯⋯ 201
taifū ⋯⋯⋯⋯⋯⋯ 228
taika ⋯⋯⋯⋯⋯⋯ 334
taisho ⋯⋯⋯⋯⋯ 357
taka ⋯⋯⋯⋯⋯⋯ 302
takarabune ⋯⋯⋯⋯⋯ 33
taki ⋯⋯⋯⋯⋯ 180, 181

tamamatsuri ⋯⋯⋯⋯ 220
tebukuro ⋯⋯⋯⋯⋯ 327
tokage ⋯⋯⋯⋯⋯ 171
tonbo ⋯⋯⋯⋯⋯⋯ 242
tōrei ⋯⋯⋯⋯⋯⋯ 303
tori sakaru ⋯⋯⋯⋯ 117
tori wataru ⋯⋯⋯ 269, 270, 358
toshi arata ⋯⋯⋯⋯⋯ 20
toshi kosu ⋯⋯⋯⋯⋯ 340
toshi wasure ⋯⋯⋯⋯ 337
toshi yōi ⋯⋯⋯⋯⋯ 335
tsubaki ⋯⋯⋯⋯⋯⋯ 77
tsukimisō ⋯⋯⋯⋯⋯ 174
tsuki o matsu ⋯⋯⋯⋯ 239
tsuki suzushi ⋯⋯⋯⋯ 187
tsurara ⋯⋯⋯⋯ 347, 348
tsuyu ⋯⋯⋯⋯⋯ 235

U
u ⋯⋯⋯⋯⋯⋯ 157
udo ⋯⋯⋯⋯⋯⋯ 78
uji ⋯⋯⋯⋯⋯⋯ 161
ume ⋯⋯⋯⋯⋯⋯ 58
usurai ⋯⋯⋯⋯⋯ 48, 49
usuzumizakura ⋯⋯⋯⋯ 110
utagaruta ⋯⋯⋯⋯⋯ 31
utsuta ⋯⋯⋯⋯⋯⋯ 74

Y
yama warau ⋯⋯⋯⋯⋯ 63
yarehasu ⋯⋯⋯⋯⋯ 281
yōkihizakura ⋯⋯⋯⋯ 109
yomato ⋯⋯⋯⋯⋯ 148
yonaga ⋯⋯⋯⋯⋯ 231
yūdachi ⋯⋯⋯⋯⋯ 176
yuki ⋯⋯⋯⋯⋯ 345, 346
yukigegawa ⋯⋯⋯⋯⋯ 47
yuki tsubute ⋯⋯⋯⋯ 344
yuku aki ⋯⋯⋯⋯⋯ 288
yuku haru ⋯⋯⋯⋯ 130, 131
yuku toshi ⋯⋯⋯⋯⋯ 338

Index of Poets

A

Abe Seiai ··················· 177
Aijima Kyokō ··············· 238
Aioigaki Kajin ·············· 330
Akao Tōshi ················· 159
Akezumi Reiko ·············· 25
Akimoto Fujio ·············· 124
Akutagawa Ryūnosuke ···· 172
Ameyama Minoru ·········· 314
Ando Tsuguo ··············· 224
Aoki Getto ················· 338
Arima Akito ················ 24
Awano Seiho ··············· 169
Aza Yōko ··················· 87
Azukizawa Yūko ············ 249
Azumi Atsushi ············· 306

B

Baba Ikuko ················· 229
Bōjō Toshiki ··············· 318

C

Chiba Kōshi ················ 56

D

Doi Akiko ·················· 69

E

Enomoto Yoshihiro ········· 78
Enomoto Yumi ············· 112

F

Fubasami Fusae ············ 265
Fujii Akari ················· 350
Fujimatsu Yūshi ············ 49

Fujimoto Miwako ·········· 198
Fukami Kenji ··············· 48
Fukuda Haritsu ············· 167
Fukuda Kineo ·············· 341

G

Gotō Hinao ················· 33
Gotō Yahan ················· 68

H

Hara Gesshū ··············· 30
Hara Sekitei ················ 255
Hasegawa Kai ··············· 60
Hasegawa Kanajo ·········· 259
Hasegawa Shunsō ·········· 131
Hasegawa Sosei ············ 321
Hashi Kanseki ············· 147
Hashimoto Keiji ··········· 348
Hashimoto Takako ········· 345
Hashizume Sajin ··········· 329
Hatano Sōha ··············· 115
Hatta Kogarashi ··········· 325
Hayashi Kei ··············· 242
Hayashi Shō ··············· 187
Higano Yuki ··············· 248
Hino Sōjō ·················· 352
Hirose Naoto ·············· 34
Horimoto Yūki ············· 164
Hoshino Bakujin ··········· 189
Hoshino Takashi ··········· 98
Hoshino Tatsuko ··········· 59
Hoshino Tsubaki ··········· 239
Hosokawa Kaga ············ 219
Hosoya Ryōryō ············· 144

I

Ibaraki Kazuo ·············· 26
Igarashi Bansui ············· 29
Igusa Keiko ················ 75
Iida Dakotsu ··············· 349
Iida Ryūta ················· 340
Iijima Haruko ·············· 320
Ikazaki Kokyō ············· 343
Ikeda Sumiko ············· 205
Ikenouchi Takeshi ········· 80
Imai Chizuko ·············· 243
Imai Kyōtarō ·············· 173
Imai Sei ··················· 174
Imai Tsurujo ··············· 276
Imase Gōichi ··············· 101
Inagaki Kikuno ············ 312
Inahata Kōtarō ············ 192
Inahata Teiko ·············· 84
Inoue Katsuko ············· 51
Inoue Seigetsu ············· 284
Ioki Hyōtei ················ 337
Ishibashi Hideno ·········· 247
Ishibashi Tatsunosuke ····· 194
Ishida Akiko ·············· 129
Ishida Hakyō ·············· 89
Ishida Katsuhiko ·········· 316
Ishida Kyōko ·············· 55
Ishii Rogetsu ·············· 286
Ishikawa Keirō ············ 93
Itō Hakuchō ··············· 299
Itō Inao ··················· 178
Iwata Yumi ················ 251
Iwaya Sazanami ············ 272

K

Kabata Yoshio · · · · · · · · · · · · 117
Kagiwada Yūko · · · · · · · · · · · · · 62
Kai Michiko · · · · · · · · · · · · · · · 86
Kakuta Chikurei · · · · · · · · · · · 113
Kamikawai Riyō · · · · · · · · · · · 148
Kaneko Senjo · · · · · · · · · · · · · · 32
Kaneko Tōta · · · · · · · · · · · · · · · 58
Katayama Tōshi · · · · · · · · · · · 193
Katayama Yumiko · · · · · · · · 333
Katō Chiyoko · · · · · · · · · · · · · 204
Katō Ikuya · · · · · · · · · · · · · · · 315
Katō Shūson · · · · · · · · · · · · · · 125
Katsura Nobuko · · · · · · · · · · · 336
Kawabata Bōsha · · · · · · · · · · · 235
Kawahigashi Hekigotō · · · · 278
Kawakita Handeishi · · · · · · 261
Kawasaki Tenkō · · · · · · · · · · · 81
Kinbara Tomonori · · · · · · · · 241
Kinoshita Yūji · · · · · · · · · · · · 233
Kishimoto Naoki · · · · · · · · · · 188
Kitahara Shimako · · · · · · · · · · 45
Kiyohara Kaidō · · · · · · · · · · · 127
Kiyosaki Toshio · · · · · · · · · · · 126
Koide Shūkō · · · · · · · · · · · · · · 327
Komakine Junko · · · · · · · · · · 102
Kōno Saki · · · · · · · · · · · · · · · · 163
Kosugi Yoshi · · · · · · · · · · · · · 128
Kōzai Teruo · · · · · · · · · · · · · · 287
Kubo Yorie · · · · · · · · · · · · · · · 258
Kubota Mantarō · · · · · · · · · · · 90
Kume Masao (Santei) · · · · · 225
Kurata Kōbun · · · · · · · · · · · · 308
Kuroda Momoko · · · · · · · · · · 183
Kusama Tokihiko · · · · · · · · · 266
Kyōgoku Kiyō · · · · · · · · · · · · 185
Kyūgyū Nami · · · · · · · · · · · · · 175

M

Maeda Fura · · · · · · · · · · · · · · 156
Mamura Shun'ichi · · · · · · · · · 79

Manabe Kureo · · · · · · · · · · · · 96
Masaki Kōichi · · · · · · · · · · · · 311
Masaki Yūko · · · · · · · · · · · · · 275
Masaoka Shiki · · · · · · · · · · · · 246
Masuda Ryū-u · · · · · · · · · · · · · 23
Matsumoto Takashi · · · · · · · · 61
Matsumoto Tefuko · · · · · · · · 100
Matsune Tōyōjō · · · · · · · · · · · 182
Matsuo Shizuko · · · · · · · · · · · 191
Matsuse Seisei · · · · · · · · · · · · 222
Mimura Jun'ya · · · · · · · · · · · · 305
Mitsuhashi Takajo · · · · · · · · 168
Miyairi Hijiri · · · · · · · · · · · · 170
Mizuhara Shūōshi · · · · · · · · 123
Momiyama Shigetsu · · · · · · · 279
Mori Sumio · · · · · · · · · · · · · · · 65
Moriga Mari · · · · · · · · · · · · · · 202
Morikawa Gyōsui · · · · · · · · · 152
Murakami Kijō · · · · · · · · · · · 106
Murakami Seigetsu · · · · · · · · 150
Murakami Tomohiko · · · · · 132
Murayama Kokyō · · · · · · · · · 240
Murayama Takajo · · · · · · · · · 149
Murō Saisei · · · · · · · · · · · · · · · 21
Mutō Noriko · · · · · · · · · · · · · 263

N

Nagai Kafū · · · · · · · · · · · · · · · 145
Nagashima Yū · · · · · · · · · · · · 245
Nagata Kōi · · · · · · · · · · · · · · · 326
Naitō Meisetsu · · · · · · · · · · · · 52
Nakagawa Tomijo · · · · · · · · 273
Nakamura Kusatao · · · · · · · · 223
Nakamura Rakuten · · · · · · · · 83
Nakamura Teijo · · · · · · · · · · · 226
Nakamura Yasunobu · · · · · 304
Nakao Sumiko · · · · · · · · · · · · 201
Nakata Yoshiko · · · · · · · · · · · 228
Nakatsuka Ippekirō · · · · · · · 130
Nara Fumio · · · · · · · · · · · · · · 309
Narita Senkū · · · · · · · · · · · · · 120

Natsui Itsuki · · · · · · · · · · · · · 116
Natsuishi Banya · · · · · · · · · · 181
Natsume Sōseki · · · · · · · · · · · 277
Nawa Sankanchiku · · · · · · · · 97
Nishijima Bakunan · · · · · · · 256
Nishimura Kazuko · · · · · · · · 236
Nishimura Kirin · · · · · · · · · · · 76
Nishiyama Haku-un · · · · · · · · 54
Nomiyama Asuka · · · · · · · · · 161
Nomura Kenzō · · · · · · · · · · · · 88
Nomura Toshirō · · · · · · · · · · 331
Nozawa Setsuko · · · · · · · · · · 105

O

Ōgushi Akira · · · · · · · · · · · · · 230
Oikawa Tei · · · · · · · · · · · · · · · · 67
Ōishi Etsuko · · · · · · · · · · · · · · 19
Okada Nichio · · · · · · · · · · · · · 179
Okada Teihō · · · · · · · · · · · · · · 270
Okamoto Hekisansui · · · · · · 231
Okamoto Hitomi · · · · · · · · · 264
Okamoto Shōhin · · · · · · · · · 162
Ōki Amari · · · · · · · · · · · · · · · · 196
Ono Emiko · · · · · · · · · · · · · · · · 20
Ōno Rinka · · · · · · · · · · · · · · · · 95
Ōoka Kōji · · · · · · · · · · · · · · · · 158
Ōsuga Otsuji · · · · · · · · · · · · · 151
Ōtake Seiji · · · · · · · · · · · · · · · 317
Ōtani Hiroshi · · · · · · · · · · · · · 22
Ōtani Jōseki · · · · · · · · · · · · · · 108
Ozaki Hōsai · · · · · · · · · · · · · · 322
Ozaki Meidō · · · · · · · · · · · · · 334
Ozawa Hekidō · · · · · · · · · · · · 288
Ozawa Minoru · · · · · · 355–358

R

Ra Sosanjin · · · · · · · · · · · · · · · 31

S

Saitō Gen · · · · · · · · · · · · · · · · · 53
Saitō Kafū · · · · · · · · · · · · · · · 300

Saitō Miki ⋯⋯ 18
Saitō Sanki ⋯⋯ 268
Sakamoto Shihōda ⋯⋯ 107
Sakurai Do'on ⋯⋯ 74
Satō Ayaka ⋯⋯ 203
Satō Haruo ⋯⋯ 339
Satō Kōroku ⋯⋯ 319
Satō Onifusa ⋯⋯ 104
Sawa Kōma ⋯⋯ 143
Sawada Hagijo ⋯⋯ 344
Seki Etsushi ⋯⋯ 342
Senda Yōko ⋯⋯ 63
Settsu Yoshiko ⋯⋯ 73
Settsu Yukihiko ⋯⋯ 216
Shiba Fukio ⋯⋯ 206
Shibata Shōkyoku ⋯⋯ 46
Shibuya Michi ⋯⋯ 280
Shiga Yasushi ⋯⋯ 274
Shimamura Hajime ⋯⋯ 94
Shimizu Keiko ⋯⋯ 221
Shimomura Kaita ⋯⋯ 323
Shimosaka Sumiho ⋯⋯ 220
Shinoda Teijirō ⋯⋯ 195
Shinohara Bon ⋯⋯ 146
Shinohara Hōsaku ⋯⋯ 310
Shinohara Ontei ⋯⋯ 257
Shinozaki Hisako ⋯⋯ 227
Sōda Yasumasa ⋯⋯ 119
Sōma Senshi ⋯⋯ 303
Sudō Gojō ⋯⋯ 271
Sugihara Yūshi ⋯⋯ 111
Sugita Hisajo ⋯⋯ 109
Sugiyama Hisako ⋯⋯ 165
Suhara Kazuo ⋯⋯ 27
Suzuki Hanamino ⋯⋯ 160
Suzuki Masajo ⋯⋯ 155
Suzuki Murio ⋯⋯ 353
Suzuki Shigeo ⋯⋯ 197
Suzuki Takao ⋯⋯ 283
Suzuki Uson ⋯⋯ 200

T
Tabata Michijo ⋯⋯ 70
Tabata Mihojo ⋯⋯ 110
Tagawa Hiryoshi ⋯⋯ 171
Tajima Hakuyō ⋯⋯ 332
Takada Chōi ⋯⋯ 103
Takada Masako ⋯⋯ 154
Takaha Shugyō ⋯⋯ 347
Takahama Kyoshi ⋯⋯ 254
Takahashi Awajijo ⋯⋯ 313
Takahashi Masō ⋯⋯ 260
Takahashi Mutsuo ⋯⋯ 44
Takano Mutsuo ⋯⋯ 307
Takano Sujū ⋯⋯ 99
Takaya Sōshū ⋯⋯ 166
Takayanagi Jūshin ⋯⋯ 354
Takayanagi Katsuhiro ⋯⋯ 298
Takehisa Yumeji ⋯⋯ 92
Takenaka Hiroshi ⋯⋯ 180
Takeshita Shizunojo ⋯⋯ 184
Takigawa Gubutsu ⋯⋯ 244
Tamaki Aiko ⋯⋯ 82
Tanaka Ami ⋯⋯ 346
Tanaka Hiroaki ⋯⋯ 142
Tanayama Harō ⋯⋯ 335
Terada Kyōko ⋯⋯ 302
Terashima Tadashi ⋯⋯ 281
Terayama Shūji ⋯⋯ 262
Tomiyasu Fūsei ⋯⋯ 282
Tomizawa Kakio ⋯⋯ 217
Tomooka Shikyō ⋯⋯ 118
Tsugawa Eriko ⋯⋯ 122
Tsujita Katsumi ⋯⋯ 285

U
Uchida Misa ⋯⋯ 267
Uda Kiyoko ⋯⋯ 301
Ueda Gosengoku ⋯⋯ 250
Ueda Hizashi ⋯⋯ 114
Uemura Sengyo ⋯⋯ 153
Uesaki Bochō ⋯⋯ 66

Usami Gyomoku ⋯⋯ 218
Usuda Arō ⋯⋯ 85

W
Wada Gorō ⋯⋯ 71
Wada Kōzaburō ⋯⋯ 252
Washisu Shigeo ⋯⋯ 50
Washitani Nanako ⋯⋯ 72
Watanabe Chieko ⋯⋯ 57
Watanabe Hakusen ⋯⋯ 199
Watanabe Keiko ⋯⋯ 157
Watanabe Suiha ⋯⋯ 232

Y
Yajima Nagisao ⋯⋯ 269
Yamada Hiroko ⋯⋯ 253
Yamagami Kimio ⋯⋯ 324
Yamaguchi Seishi ⋯⋯ 237
Yamaguchi Seison ⋯⋯ 176
Yamaguchi Yūmu ⋯⋯ 47
Yamamoto Shikō ⋯⋯ 64
Yamamoto Yōko ⋯⋯ 28
Yamanishi Masako ⋯⋯ 186
Yamashita Chizuko ⋯⋯ 328
Yanagihara Kyokudō ⋯⋯ 121
Yasui Kōji ⋯⋯ 234
Yoshida Tōyō ⋯⋯ 77
Yoshimura Akira ⋯⋯ 190
Yoshiya Nobuko ⋯⋯ 91

Photo Credits

pages	Title	Location	Date	Photographer
New Year				
10	Sunrise over a Frozen Sea	Ōmu, Hokkaido	2005	Maeda Akira
11	Running Shadows	Biei, Hokkaido	2015	Maeda Akira
12–13	Dawn, -30°C	Ōmu, Hokkaido	2005	Maeda Akira
14	Butterbur in Light Snowfall	Biei, Hokkaido	2007	Maeda Akira
15	Snowy River	Biei, Hokkaido	2010	Maeda Akira
16–17	Mount Fuji in the Deepening Dusk	Kōfu, Yamanashi	2009	Maeda Akira
Spring				
36–37	Spring Song	Biei, Hokkaido	2019	Maeda Akira
38	Island in Bloom	Nagasaki	1981	Maeda Shinzō
39	Dogtooth Violet (*Erythronium japonicum*)	Biei, Hokkaido	2018	Maeda Akira
40	Horsetails	Nara, Nara	2018	Maeda Akira
41	Peach Orchard	Fuefuki, Yamanashi	1992	Maeda Shinzō
42–43	Shower of Cherry Blossoms	Hachiōji, Tokyo	1983	Maeda Shinzō
Summer				
134–135	Terraced Paddy Fields in Oku-Shinano	Iiyama, Nagano	1976	Maeda Shinzō
136	Shining Sunflowers	Takahagi, Ibaraki	2012	Maeda Akira
137	Mountain Road	Shitara, Aichi	1986	Maeda Shinzō
138	Cliff and Ocean	Onna-son, Okinawa	1980	Maeda Shinzō
139	Mount Hotaka	The Northern Alps, Nagano	2010	Maeda Akira
140–141	Hillside of Glowing Wheat	Kamifurano, Hokkaido	1981	Maeda Shinzō
Autumn				
208–209	Fireworks at a Village Festival	Shitara, Aichi	1984	Maeda Shinzō
210–211	Cosmos Flowers behind a Rice Field	Takatori, Nara	2017	Maeda Akira
212–213	Mount Hakkōda, Autumn Morning Light	Towada, Aomori	1984	Maeda Shinzō
214	Japanese Silver Grass Field, Autumn Light	Minakami, Gunma	1981	Maeda Shinzō
215	Mysterious Moonglow	Biei, Hokkaido	1984	Maeda Shinzō
Winter				
290	Oriental Staff Vine (*Celastrus orbiculatus*)	Biei, Hokkaido	2017	Maeda Akira
291	The Residence of Mr. Kumagai Covered with Snow	Toyone, Aichi	1984	Maeda Shinzō
292–293	Deep Silence on Taisho Pond	Kamikōchi, Nagano	1982	Maeda Shinzō
294–295	Bohemian Waxwing (*Bombycilla garrulus*)	Biei, Hokkaido	2020	Maeda Akira
296–297	Moon at Dawn	Biei, Hokkaido	1987	Maeda Shinzō
Seasonless				
351	Water Lily (*Nymphaea tetragona*)	Yanohara Marshland, Shōwa-mura, Fukushima	2018	Maeda Akira

About the Author

Ozawa Minoru (b. 1956) is a prominent Japanese haiku poet and critic. He began writing haiku while a student at Shinshu University and went on to graduate studies in literature at Seijo University. In 2000, after fifteen years as editor in chief of the prominent haiku magazine *Taka*, he founded *Sawa*, which he continues to direct. His first haiku collection was *Kinuta* (1986), followed by *Ryūzō* (1997), which won the Association of Haiku Poets Emerging Poet Prize. *Shunkan* (2006), his third haiku collection, won the Yomiuri Literature Prize for Poetry. For *Haiku no hajimaru basho* (2007) he won the Association of Haiku Poets 22nd Prize for Criticism. He is a member of the board of directors of the Association of Haiku Poets, and serves as judge for haiku columns in the *Yomiuri Shimbun*, the *Tokyo Shimbun*, and other publications.

About the Translator

Janine Beichman (PhD, Columbia University, Professor Emerita of Daito Bunka University) is author of the literary biographies *Masaoka Shiki: His Life and Works* (2002) and *Embracing the Firebird: Yosano Akiko and the Birth of the Female Voice in Modern Japanese Poetry* (2002), as well as the original Noh play *Drifting Fires* (first performed in 1985). She is also the translator of Ōoka Makoto's anthology *Oriori no Uta: Poems for All Seasons* (2002). Her most recent book is *Beneath the Sleepless Tossing of the Planets: Selected Poems 1972-1989* by Ōoka Makoto (2019), which won the 2019-2020 Japan-U.S. Friendship Commission Prize for the Translation of Japanese Literature. She is a judge for the JLPP Translation Competition of the Agency for Cultural Affairs of Japan.

〈英文版〉名句の所以　近現代俳句をじっくり読む
Well-Versed: Exploring Modern Japanese Haiku

2021年3月27日　第1刷発行

著　者　小澤　實
訳　者　ジャニーン・バイチマン
発行所　一般財団法人 出版文化産業振興財団
　　　　〒101-0051 東京都千代田区神田神保町2-2-30
　　　　電話　03-5211-7283
　　　　ホームページ　https://www.jpic.or.jp/

印刷・製本所　大日本印刷株式会社